Gender, Identity, and Self-Esteem

Deborah Anderson, PhD, is the Associate Director of Research at the National Center for Women and Retirement Research at Long Island University's Southampton College. She has a doctorate in Developmental Psychology and Gender Studies and is Assistant Director of the Long Island University's Master's Program in Gerontology. In addition, Dr. Anderson has co-authored a book entitled *Our Turn: Women Who Triumph in the Face of Divorce* (1993), and co-published an article based on the NCWRR National Divorce Study in the *Journal of Women and Aging.* Dr. Anderson also designed a course for a community college based on the National Divorce Study entitled: Women and Divorce, A Developmental Perspective. She has also been a member of the NCWRR research team that designed and implemented two national surveys for corporate financial institutions on gender and financial knowledge, and personality and gender attitudes. She has also served as the National Center for Women and Retirement Research's newsletter editor and feature writer.

Christopher L. Hayes, PhD, is a Professor of Psychology and founding Chairman of the Master's Program in Gerontology at Southampton College of Long Island University, Southampton, NY. In 1988, he established the National Center for Women and Retirement Research (NCWRR), the first academic unit in the country to focus on the pre-retirement planning needs of mid-life women. Under the leadership of Dr. Hayes, NCWRR has received over $2 million in governmental and corporate support for national research studies addressing mid-life developmental issues. Dr. Hayes has been the principal investigator of four Administration on Aging demonstration projects including PREP (Pre-Retirement Education Planning for Women), which has continued since 1986. His innovative work on behalf of women and adult development concerns has been showcased on a vast array of television, radio, newspaper, and magazine stories. The author of many articles and books in aging, his most recent work was entitled *Our Turn: Women Who Triumph in the Face of Divorce* (1993).

Gender, Identity, and Self-Esteem

A New Look at Adult Development

Deborah Y. Anderson
Christopher L. Hayes

Springer Publishing Company

Springer Publishing Company, Inc.
536 Broadway
New York, NY 10012–3955

Cover design by Margaret Dunin
Production Editor: Pamela Lankas

96 97 98 99 00 / 5 4 3 2 1

Library of Congress Cataloging-in-Publication Data

Anderson, Deborah Y., 1946–
    Gender, identity, and self-esteem: a new look at adult
development / Deborah Y. Anderson, Christopher L. Hayes.
        p.   cm.
    Includes bibliographical references and index.
    ISBN 0-8261-9410-9
    1. Sex role.   2. Self-esteem.   3. Adulthood.   4. Life cycle,
Human.   I. Hayes, Christopher L.   II. Title.
HQ1075.A53   1996
    305.3—dc20   96-18388
                                                            CIP

Printed in the United States of America

Contents

Acknowledgments

Dr. Hayes and Dr. Anderson would like to thank the following people for their support during the research phase of this project on gender, identity, and self-esteem as well as for their assistance in helping us complete this book. Thanks to Emily Weiss, a gerontology graduate student, who helped out during the initial phase of the survey design and implementation and to the staff of the National Center for Women and Retirement Research. We are grateful for the support given to us by Long Island University at Southampton, New York.

Special thanks to Wendy Morris of Williams College for her hard work and the very professional research work she did on behalf of this project while she was our research assistant during the summer of 1994.

Dr. Anderson would especially like to thank her husband Miles for the support and very tangible contributions he made through reading, editing, and critiquing the manuscript material. She would also like to thank her son Jeffrey and her daughter Samantha for their support and encouragement during this process.

Dr. Hayes would especially like to thank his wife Diane for all her support and nurturing of his work. In addition, he would especially like to show his enormous gratitude to his father, Maurice L. Hayes, MD, for editing and critiquing this work.

Prologue

The odyssey through life is like a navigator steering a boat to a known destination—the overall course is constant when measured from beginning to end, but over shorter periods of time the line is jagged. The navigator sometimes sets the course to the North of the track to avoid collision with another vessel. At other times the navigator steers to South of the track, in response to a wave or gust of wind. Sometimes the vessel runs before the wind dead on course; at other times to make progress into the face of the wind it is necessary to tack or jibe to one side or the other. When the vessel is on a tack, far off the base line of the course, it is impossible to tell what the intended destination is. When all of the course changes are put together over time, however, the vessel will be seen to move on a direct course.

Introduction

The study of adult development is mainly the study of change. Americans are getting married later, staying married for shorter periods, having fewer children, redefining the work and educational environment, and reformulating the definitions of what it means to be middle-aged and old. At the same time, gender roles and behavior are undergoing radical transformations resulting in new caregiving experiences for men and greater career options for women. Both laypersons and scholars are obliged to reflect anew upon what it means to be a male or a female. Adult life in the 1990s, without question, is an evolving, ever-changing, unpredictable experience—a human odyssey.

Within the last decade politicians, actors, and other respected public figures in their 80's, 90's, and beyond have radically expanded our understanding of what can be accomplished during the middle and later years. Thus, it comes as no surprise that scholarly research into what comprises the adult years is rapidly growing (U.S. Department of Health and Social Services, 1991).

The authors of this text thought it was time to reexamine how we have perceived the adult years and to reevaluate both our own

views and previous theoretical notions to these altered circumstances. As societal contexts change, so must the theories and ideas
that reflect them. In this text we offer an alternative perspective
that can enrich our understandings within life-span developmental
thinking.

The focus of this book will be a combination of information
based on survey data and qualitative first-person stories. The chapters will focus on specific developmental life-ties. *Life-ties* are a set of
related experiences and the perceptions these experiences evoke
within the lives of the women and men who participated in this study.

The study will explore how people shape, form and integrate
their identities and self-worth within this framework of influential
life-ties. The National Center for Women and Retirement Research
(NCWRR) study found that, for its respondents, self-esteem and
identity development were in large part determined by how the
respondents connected and interacted at many different and
unpredictable times during their adult years with the life-ties of
family, education, work, intimate relationships, children, friends,
and mentors. The study revealed that all of these events make
growth and development an ongoing process.

Life-ties do not always affect both genders at predictable life
points; but rather, the elasticity of the life-ties implies that people
will connect again and again throughout their lives with these ties
that will continue to reshape and alter perceptions of personal
identity, regardless of age or gender. By choosing to look at human
development in the context of these meaningful ties, rather than
by age or gender, we begin to understand and accept the com-
monalities and differences that exist between the sexes, regardless
of age.

LIFE-TIE THEME

First, it is necessary to explain the life-tie theme and describe how
a sense of self may develop within this context as well as how self-
esteem may play into this theme. The following definition and
explanation of the life-tie theme represents the findings and work
of the NCWRR study.

What is the life-tie theme? The Life-Tie theme is *idiographic* in nature,
in order to allow for understanding and studying people individually.

Life-ties are a set of related experiences and the perceptions these experiences evoke within the lives of adults. The life-tie theme provides an individual framework for interpreting one's life and its larger context beyond gender and age/stage evaluations.

The life-tie theme is inclusive as opposed to being exclusive. It embodies and embraces similarities as well as differences. Men and women are both affected by similar thematic life-ties. The life-tie theme accommodates and includes gender-based differences. Differences among individuals experiencing the life-tie occur due to context, timing, gender, and personal meaning.

The life-tie theme addresses an individuation process, by not organizing developmental concepts around gender, age-stage, or group behaviors. Theories built around gender, age, or particular stage tend to be theories of exclusion. The life-tie theme is not based on restrictions or dichotomies, nor does it allow for value-laden judgments as to individuals' social or moral stature.

The life-tie theme is a fluid model of adult development. Personal development and continued growth in adulthood depends on a process of contraction and expansion within the life-tie framework. Contraction and expansion may occur at any time or within any context during the life course, independent of gender, age, or stage.

How does a sense of self or identity develop within this context? A person draws meaning from the life-tie through the interpretation and evaluation that she or he attaches to each experience. In other words, the self becomes the interpreter of the experience by making connections, drawing conclusions and formulating various life-tie themes. Identity is shaped and reshaped by the unique patterns created by those personal interpretations, evaluations, and symbolic meanings of the life-tie experiences. The important threads of this pattern continue to be woven in such a way as to create a personal composition that is capable of change all through adulthood.

Just as everyone has her or his own fingerprint, or can be identified by a personal DNA thread, a person's identity is composed from a uniquely personal and symbolic interpretation of a life-tie event. For example, two people can experience the loss of a child, but the symbolic interpretation and meaning is uniquely each one's own. The meaning derived from this event will be woven into an ongoing pattern that contains other symbolic meanings from other life-tie experiences that contribute to a sense of self and identity. Each person's pattern, though unique, may be derived from the same life-tie source.

How does self-esteem enter into all this? Self-esteem is based on the evaluative component of a person's interpretation of a particular experience. In this case it would be their life-tie experience that is evaluated. The study, backed up by interviews of both women and men, found that people who have a positive self-concept usually have interpreted their life-tie experience with clarity and certainty. Clarity means that study participants were able to interpret their life-tie experience without ambiguity or confusion, and, combined with insight enabled the individual to use that experience as a resource.

Other study participants who have been less certain, less clear about their life-tie experience—and whose self-knowledge structures may be less clearly defined and flexible—may often have negative or low self-esteem. Perceiving themselves as having little control within a life-tie situation, they may suffer a loss of self-esteem through a life-tie experience.

Positive self-esteem and identity development occur in an individual when the life-tie ceases to be a control and begins to become a resource for that individual.

Identity and self-esteem are affected by the bidirectional movement of the *individual/life-tie relationship.* A person interacts with the life-tie and the life-tie interacts with the individual. Thus, components of adult identity may be shaped and go through change as a result of psychological, physical, and social/emotional interactions.

The contraction-expansion process depends on the elasticity of the life-tie/individual relationship. For example, consider the family of origin. Growing up we have a large physical, emotional bond with this life-tie. The relationship is an "expanded" one. At other times of life, such as early adulthood, an individual can "contract" from the family of origin, only to expand within this relationship again at some later time (e.g., from a family member's death, illness, crisis, or joyful event) binding the family together again with all the psychological, physical, and emotional dimensions of past and present interactions.

THE GENDER, IDENTITY AND
SELF-ESTEEM STUDY

The National Center for Women and Retirement Research (NCWRR) began the Gender, Identity and Self-Esteem Study in 1990. Utilizing a life-span perspective, our study focused on the following pragmatic questions:

1. What life events (leaving home, finding work, marriage, motherhood, disability, etc.) trigger fluctuations in self-esteem? Do women, as compared to men, have high or low self-esteem at particular developmental periods? Are gender differences in self-concept more pronounced in one developmental period than another?

2. How has society and social stereotypes influenced and maintained sexual differences? If psychological differences do exist, how do they limit the potential of the individual? What cultural factors impact on definitions of sex-role identification?

3. Do women, compared to men, differ in their emotional reactions to people and events? Do the sexes differ in how they perceive life's problems and how they solve them? Do they have equal potential for acquiring knowledge and skills to create a positive and rewarding life?

4. Does self-esteem remain stable and linear over time as past research has suggested; or is it more fluid, depending on the developmental period, sociocultural context, external and chance events as well as gender? What are the gender differences and/or similarities in positive identity development? Is self-esteem necessarily enhanced in people who have achieved a strong and positive role identity through, for example, business success, academic achievement, a stable marriage or successful parenting?

5. What myths do women and men labor under that prevent them from understanding each other and that incite conflict and mistrust?

Limitations of the Study

This study was primarily composed of white females and males, who were predominantly college-educated, and were products of a middle-class backgrounds. Although the subject group is not representative of the United States population, the findings can be widely applied to a growing segment of the population who are better educated than their counterparts fifty years ago. Although the authors of this text do not want to imply that the experiences and transitions of the subjects in this study can be considered "mainstream," yet, we do believe that their stories chronicle a new viewpoint of what constitutes adulthood. It is our belief that the majority of midlife adults who participated in this study provide the reader with a compelling rationale for carefully reviewing the importance of understanding the totality of human development (see Table I.1 and Appendix B)

People are lifelong "meaning makers." A person is not a stage of development, but is part of a long and meaningful process. In order to understand the way a person creates his or her world, it is necessary first to understand how the world creates the person. By focusing on life-ties, the study and chapters that follow have tried to look at the process of human growth, and to avoid associating human potential, identity, and self-worth solely with a particular age stage or gender determination.

The developmental life-ties and the important stories that people have told in our study will change again and again. These life-ties hold us, let us go for a while and then bring us back. They can be viewed as natural connections, controlling influences, and crucial supports, as well as resources for self-worth. Life-ties provide that very human and very essential common ground for both women and men over a lifetime.

Table I.1 Demographic Background of Survey Population

Age:	Close to 60% of women and men were between the ages of 31 and 55
Education:	34% postgraduate school 29% some college 22% college graduates
Racial/ethnic background:	93% Caucasian 3% African-American 1% Native American 1% Hispanic 1% Asian
Sexual preference:	91% Heterosexual 4% Homosexual/lesbian 2% Bisexual 3% Celibate
Marital status:	40% were married 26% separated/divorced 30% never married
Household Income:	62% of women and men were in the $25,000–$75,000 range
Number of respondents:	
Female:	215
Male:	160
Total:	375

CHAPTER 1

Reexamination of Adult Development

Due to radical demographic changes now underway, we are quickly becoming a society dominated by two specific age groups of adults. During the past decade, the number of Americans between the ages of 35 and 44 has increased by 42%. This population boom of midlife adults was generated soon after the Korean War, 50 years ago and, coupled with the "graying of America," is testing our understandings of what constitutes adulthood. As Hudson (1991) notes, we are moving away from the world of our parents—which was typified by stability, predictable life transitions, and fixed roles within uniform cultural expectations—and moving toward a terrain marked by volatile change and an overwhelming array of lifestyle options.

What does it mean to be an adult today? The adulthood experience in the 1990s can be characterized by the following realities:

1. Life transitions such as marriage, divorce and childrearing, are experienced throughout the entire adult life-cycle.
2. Increased longevity and health have extended the boundaries

of physical activities that were once dominated by youth.

3. Due to changes in the work environment, adults have multiple choices in career paths and options that have extended educational training.
4. Shifts in family role responsibilities have radically re-shaped gender role expectations.
5. An erosion of faith in our social institutions has threatened our belief in continuity and stability throughout the adult years.

Thus, adults of today are assured a life typified by change. However, most existing models of adult development do not reflect the realities of change in our personal lives. Most psychological literature treats identity development and self-esteem as stable components of human personality. Once developed in adolescence and early adulthood, an individual's self-evaluation has been thought to remain static through adult life. The NCWRR study on gender and self-esteem found that, to the contrary, a person's sense of self, whether male or female, constantly adjusts to the changing context of life as mediated by situations, time, and internal and external shifts. During adulthood, women and men often face transitions, changes and crises in their lives. For many individuals, maturation is a slow, ongoing, lifelong process. The intent of the following section is to succinctly review theoretical positions that have had an overwhelming impact on our notions of what constitutes the adulthood experience. Our position is not to "throw the baby out with the bath water," but, on the contrary, to examine traditional thinking and encourage a scholarly dialogue on the development of a new framework for understanding adult experience.

TRADITIONAL ADULT DEVELOPMENT RESEARCH

> True, my theory is no longer accepted,
> but it was good enough to get us to the next one!
>
> —*Donald Hebb*
> (whose theory of intelligence was popular in the 1940s)

Early developmental psychology focused primarily on the first two decades of life. Childhood, the main area of research, was the period when an individual underwent large and numerous physiological and psychological changes. Adults were thought to remain rigid and static; they were perceived as an end product rather than as continuously developing persons. Human longevity was relatively short, so adulthood was thought to be unworthy of close scrutiny (Freud, 1935, Piaget, 1926).

In recent years the focus has altered, and studies have begun to explore the changes experienced by individuals throughout their lives (Baltes, 1968; Baumrind, 1989; Bloom, 1980). Although there is less biological change in adulthood than in childhood, the diversity of experience and interaction with others make the patterns of growth worthy of study. At the same time, these patterns of growth are hard to identify and explain in a universal, cohesive manner. Each person experiences adulthood as a unique blend of meaningful events and as a constant process of adaptation to changing circumstances and perceptions of the world at large. Childhood, which is bound by predictable and changing physiology predicated on gender, mandatory education, and family structure, makes an easy fit for developmental theories to be based on chronological age and gender, and to be patterned into sequential stages.

Many of the early pioneers of adult development such as Erikson (1978) and Levinson, Darrow, Klein, Levinson, and McGill (1978) were venturing onto new ground. Adult life was partially mapped, but there were vast unexplored territories, replete with odd shapes, sizes and uncharted terrain. It is natural when exploring the unfamiliar to take along reliable tools and equipment. Early adult developmental psychologists brought along the familiar tools and equipment of childhood development to help in their understanding of adulthood. To help acclimate themselves to this unmapped territory of adulthood, these developmental pioneers framed their ideas through the use of gender categories and sequential stages based on age. This framework might be fine for the analysis of childhood, but is too restricting and limiting for the full understanding of an adult man's or woman's life. With increased longevity and new knowledge based on the lives of women, the developmental framework based on the confines of gender and age/stage constructs is about to collapse.

The familiar territory that many adult developmentalist psychologists were using was based on the work done by Piaget (1926).

Piaget, as described in his book, *The Language and Thought of the Child,* structured childhood into a sequential and linear pattern. He felt that growth and development followed stages in consecutive order, neither skipping nor regressing. Sequence is ensured only when the elements of one stage form a logically necessary base for later stages.

Erik Erikson (1968, 1978) pioneered this exploration during the 1950s by examining development in adulthood. Erikson's theory was based on eight stages that he believed to be universal and which occurred in a sequence of predictable environments. This principle determined a chronological time frame in which certain developmental tasks gain ascendance in the person's life span. This ascendant period presents a series of optimal moments for resolving the developmental crisis of each stage. Erikson believed that age grading reflected the interaction between a person's internal drive for change and the social structure. For instance, marriage would be a reflection of the stage of intimacy, and the optimal time for this to occur would be during a person's twenties.

Erikson reflected the culture of the 1950s with its adherence to specific age and gender behaviors. Erikson's theory reflects the male-dominated culture of his time with its emphasis on sequential linear growth, separation, differentiation and increasing autonomy. The social changes of the last 30 years, specifically the evolving of gender roles, should lead us to a reexamination of how psychologists evaluate and study adult development.

Erikson believed that developmental lines were clearly drawn between men and women. Although his theory was based only on the study of males, he did propose that a woman's "inner space" (her female organs and hormones) predispose her to activities marked by union and care. According to Erikson, a man is inclined toward "outer space," marked by assertiveness and independence, whereas a woman defines herself through the selective nature of her search for a mate.

Erikson's perspective does not fully address the notion that development is also about *attachment, integration and inclusion.* Differentiation (the stereotype of male development) is favored for the argument leading to a strong identity and positive self-esteem. Attachment and inclusion (the stereotype of female development) has been associated with dependence and immaturity, leading to a weak identity and low feelings of self-esteem.

Frameworks constructed around the sequential forms of development continued under other theorists. For example, Bernice Neugarten (1968) felt that cultural events were especially significant in that they provide a rhythm or timing for adult development. She defined the *social clock* as the timing of a set of norms for movement through the phases of adulthood. Neugarten proposed age-graded expectations for the marriage, childraising, and achieving work goals, thus providing a tight, linear plan for assessing adult development.

Vaillant (1977) studied college-aged men through their fifties and reported on the maturation of adaptive styles of men as they progress developmentally in a linear march. He believed that some remained immature in adulthood, while others developed adult maturity only through what Erikson called *generativity*.

Baltes (1968, 1977) became an enthusiast for the multicausal approach, arguing that developmental patterns may be shaped by internal and external forces acting in isolation or in concert. He believed that people change their environment and are in turn changed by it, proposing a strong interaction between the two. He focused on change, but adopted a strategy that analysed development through structured sequences and causal relationships.

Gould (1978) built upon Erikson's work using the sequential stages of adulthood as a framework to show how adult males resolve "false assumptions" about their personal experience. He described adulthood as a time to demythologize the false views that were carried over from childhood.

Daniel Levinson (1978) examined adulthood by studying forty males using four age-related linear sequences, separated by transition periods. He broke development into childhood/adolescence, early adulthood, middle adulthood, and late adulthood. He emphasized development in relation to biological changes, generational changes and, especially, around career roles. In his view, life structures are built and revised and then periodically abandoned as a person changes over time.

Gisela Labouvie-Vief (1982a, 1982b) and cognitive theorist Michael Basseches (1984) expanded on the work done by Piaget to analyze adulthood. They proposed an extended stage—beyond Piaget's stage of formal operations. Basseches described a stage called *dialectical thinking,* which builds upon an analysis of competing relationships. A dialectical thinker is aware that interactions between ideas and facts, as well as interactions between people and information, create truth within a particular system of thought or historical period. Labouvie-Vief believed that some adults progress beyond formal operations and also beyond dialectical thinking to the stage of *autonomous thought.*

Life-Span Development Theory

Existing adult development literature has been shaped by at least three opposing views as to how individuals progress during the middle and later years. The first is the widespread notion that the midlife period signals the onset of decline. As Hesse and Camion (1984) found, that attitude toward aging tended to view the process as inevitable deterioration and devaluation. The second view, which originates from the psychoanalytic camp and followers of Freud (1935), indicates that midlife and older adults are no different from the young. Finally, there is the view, pioneered by Baltes (1968), that the adult years are characterized by change and growth.

To address these conflicting views, some psychologists have adopted what can be characterized as the *life-span developmental approach,* which attempts to embrace all three of the above perspectives (Baltes, 1968; Brim, 1980; Havighurst, 1982). Although this perspective is not a defined theory or assumption, it is a prescription to be open-minded and pluralistic in explaining psychological functioning throughout adulthood. Life-span developmentalists perceive the adult years as multidirectional. Different aspects of behavior change in diverse ways. In addition, as individuals differ greatly from one another, so, too, do their patterns of addressing the various transitions that encompass the adult years.

Life-span developmentalists are groping with a variety of basic issues that are germane to this text. First, the debate as to whether developmental changes appear abruptly or as a result of a slow but steady progression (Rutter, 1989) is particularly relevant to any examination of adulthood because lifestyle transitions and changes can be the result of an immediate crisis or a well-conceived out plan. For example, many midlife adults today are having to formulate a "new" work identity because of a sudden employment layoff, while others have worked for years to develop a secondary career. Although the above example illustrates dissimilarities in terms of motive in formulating a new work identity, is the process identical?

Another major issue is whether the adult years can be characterized as a period of continuity or of change. In general, there are two distinct theoretical camps related to adult personality. On one side, there are those who believe that adults remain basically the same—adult personality undergoes little change (McCrae & Costa, 1984). Others propose that adult personality is a constant process of adaptation and change (Erikson, 1963, 1975; Gould, 1978; Levinson, 1978; Vaillant, 1977).

The issue of continuity versus change becomes increasingly problematic when exploring whether adults can rebound from early life traumas. For example, if an adult experienced sexual abuse at a young age, will he or she be "scarred" for life? Some developmental literature indicates that adults are able to recover from physical and psychological trauma (Robins & Rutter, 1990), while others indicate that flexibility has its limits.

A third major area that is being widely explored and debated is the significance of the timing of experiences and individual reactions to them. Many life-span psychologists adhere to the notion that there are certain times in the life-span when a particular experience has a greater and more lasting impact than at other times (Rutter, 1989). This notion of *sensitive periods* raises a variety of critical concerns when applied to transitions and experiences during adulthood. For example, can an adult experience the value of establishing a mentor in later life, even though he or she "missed out" on finding one during earlier years?

Critique of the Age-Stage Approach

If, as these past developmental views suggest, changes are influenced by a multitude of events, then the search for a particular cause or crisis in confined, linear, age-linked categories is insufficient to account for the changes in adult human behavior. This is especially true as it relates to an ever-changing social and historical context, gender considerations, and expanding longevity. A developmental view that organizes adulthood and the changes that accompany self-definition around contexts, or, using the present terminology, Life-Ties, may have far greater utility.

Due to the complexity of men's and women's adult lives in the 1990s, we need to reexamine the utility of an age-stage-based approach and views that don't consider the reciprocal nature of influence of a person with his or her environment. Changing contexts and events will alter the nature of adult self-concepts. Our study on adult development and gender found that continued growth and change may occur as new talents are discovered, as new motives and roles emerge to direct behavior, as relationships begin, end, or are redefined; and through many other situations. Contexts do not totally shape and modify people: There remain areas of choice, direction and preference that people impose on their settings which result in an interdependence.

Although previous developmental models that focused on chronological age and linear stages have made a significant contribution to understanding certain aspects of life transitions, we need a new paradigm to explain adulthood. Adult change and growth suggests movement and fluidity, a back-and-forth motion that may be best observed in general as opposed to trying to capture change in age-specific categories. Although the social age clock as suggested by Neugarten (1968) still has some applicability, the concept needs to be revised to incorporate our society's movement away from age boundaries. Other factors such as socioeconomic background and vocation may be more important than age in understanding what constitutes the adult years. For example, members of the blue-collar class and people living in poverty often seem to reach both middle and old age much sooner than do white-collar workers. One whose life depends on intense physical labor such as a coal miner may be perceived as being old by age thirty. A professional person who is hired and paid well to think may appear to be relatively still youthful at age 65 due to his financial ability to maintain health and leisure pursuits.

Family arrangements, marriage, having children, work roles, educational pursuits, and retirement can no longer be tied to predetermined time periods. Adult women and men within our society are reformulating what can be accomplished within a select period of development or time. They continuously have to adapt their lives to change that unfolds within themselves and as a result of interactions with their environment. Through our study we have observed adults rearrange, sometimes repeat, and often reinvent their life themes and self-views within the context of family, work, education, intimate relationships, children, friends and mentors. These lifeties, persist, evolve, and are renewed from childhood through adulthood, often with no particular pattern or sequence. Research conducted by Dorothy Eichorn and her associates at Berkeley (Eichorn, Clousen, Naan, Honzik, & Mussen, 1981; see also Sears & Sears, 1982) also seem to support our contention that adulthood is a time of reformulating traits and behaviors that are anything but stable.

The major adult developmental theory work began and came of age during the 1950s and late 1960s. Many of these theories aligned well with the dominant culture of that time, especially the 1950s. The world was a fairly stable place: Governments provided and maintained order and security, people prospered and knew what to expect from their world. Linear patterns of marriage, work, children, and retirement coexisted with governments and social institutions that were based on predictability and constancy. Transitions and crisis were viewed as beyond the norm: It was thought if one could not stop a transition or crises, at least one should be able to predict it and plan for it.

Beginning with the social upheavals of the 1960s, the world we inhabit has become unpredictable, chaotic and ever-changing. A search for meaning and self-definition cannot be provided by governments or benign social institutions. People are responsible for their own searches and use whatever tools they have at their disposal. Ambiguity and chaos is challenged and met with personal flexibility and personal resilience. The study of adult development must be just as flexible and resilient as the people it wishes to observe. Fortunately, more and more literature is appearing that demonstrates the potential of finding personal growth and identity development during the adult years. For example, in the book written by Bob Woodward (1991) entitled *The Commanders,* the author examines Colin Powell's development of character and self-identity during the Gulf War. Another provocative book that discusses human potential and growth during adulthood is Maslow's (1987) *Motivation and Personality.*

THE NEW FEMALE PSYCHOLOGY

The unbalanced male-dominated view of adult development held by those past traditionalists gave rise to a new developmental view in the 1970s and 1980s, of what female psychologists call the "relational" view of development. Characteristic of this view is the centrality of gender and gender difference. Chodorow (1974), Miller (1976), Josselson (1987) Gilligan (1982), and Belenky, Clinchy, Goldberger, and Tarule (1986) are a few of the pioneers of female developmental theory who believed that women develop and gain a sense of identity within a context of connections with others. That is, a woman's sense of self becomes organized around building and maintaining relationships—not through differentiation and separation. The female models of development discuss changes and continuities of the internal self, but focus less on discussing how external events influence self-esteem, identity, and life choices.

Common Ground

Female psychology and developmental psychology share an interest in the political, social and historical context of human behaviors. Context may have been more central to female psychology to than traditional developmentalists because attention to context—especially social context—is a skill women are encouraged to develop early in life. Attentiveness to the needs and feelings of others has been a survival skill not only for women but also for all oppressed people who survive by keeping those who have power over them happy.

In developmental psychology, the context issue has been explored in terms of different cognitive styles associated with men and women and also in terms of different ways of looking at human development. The kind of thinking that looks at interconnections and sees the whole has often been associated with women, while thinking that isolates specific behaviors from their contexts and analyzes them as if they occurred in a vacuum has been associated with men (see the study conducted by Farrell & Rosenberg, 1981). Isolating variables and analytical thinking is part of the scientific method, and women have been historically and traditionally excluded from the community that practices it.

However, developmental psychologists have been questioning reductionist views of human behavior and have begun to explore the impact of changing social and cultural contexts on the course of human development (Bronfenbrenner, 1979; Riegel, 1979; Rogoff, 1991). Research examining the gender-related aspects of the two different cognitive styles has also increased in recent years (e.g., Belenky et al., 1986).

The picture of human development painted by traditional psychology is no more objective than research from a feminist perspective; in fact it may be less so, because many of its assumptions are so deeply ingrained that most people are not conscious of them. Combining ideas from both perspectives can shed new light on gender issues in development.

Psychological Models of Female Development: An Overview

Psychological models of normal identity development of women were not available in the literature until the late 1980s, as noted by Belenky et al. (1986) and Josselson (1987). Most of the available psychological literature describing the normal development of women was extrapolated from clinical cases and samples of distressed women. Research supports the contention that women perceive, organize, and respond to their internal cues and external environments differently from men. It has also been stated that this pattern of differences represents a different phenomenological reality, or world view (Belenky et al., 1986; Chodorow, 1974, 1978; Gilligan, 1982; Miller, 1976; Rosaldo & Lamphere, 1974; Sassen, 1980). However, research has also shown that within one cultural group, there are more similarities than differences between men and women in terms of their beliefs, values, assumptions, and worldviews (Furn & Ibrahim, 1987).

Miller (1976) noted that the development of a person's sense of identity is linked very early with her or his sense of being a female or male. Her central premise was that women's sense of self develops in a context of social connections with others; that is, a woman's sense of self becomes organized around building and maintaining relationships.

Building on this early thesis of Miller, other psychologists have developed female relational models of female development. Carol Gilligan's study of the development of female identity revealed that women define themselves in relational terms that imply maturity and extent of their intimate relationships. Men define themselves in nonrelationship terms, meaning they do not define themselves by their relationships, and use criteria that focus on separation from dependency and on individual achievement. Women also perceive more danger than in competitive achievement; men are more likely to be threatened by issues involving intimacy. Gilligan herself believes that individuals can be empowered by participating in the development of others. The main goal is developing an effective balance of self-nurturance and care for others.

A second model regarding the resolution of the status of women's identity was developed by Ruth Josselson (1987). This model was built on an earlier theory of Marcia (1976). Josselson postulated four potential outcomes of Erikson's identity stage: *foreclosure, achievement, moratorium,* and *diffusion.* Josselson then used Marcia's method to examine how women proceed through Erikson's identity stage. Her goal was to determine in what ways the identity status of women in early adulthood might influence later life choices. Josselson concluded that the formation of women's identity could be represented by what she termed a *separation/individuation continuum.* The foreclosure group attached the greatest importance to relationships, whereas women in the moratorium and diffusion groups attached the least importance to relationships. Women classified in the achievement group showed a balance of needs for relatedness and separateness.

A third model proposed by Belenky et al. (1986) described five positions or stages women adopt as they approach knowledge:

1. *Silence.*Women do not perceive themselves able to learn.
2. *Received knowledge.*Women acquire knowledge only from authoritative sources.
3. *Subjective knowledge.*Women engage in a quest for self-understanding.
4. *Procedural knowledge.*Women use objective thought to learn procedures that give them the power to compete.

5. *Constructed knowledge.*Women integrate intuitive, subjective knowledge with objective, external reason.

Belenky et al., (1984, p. 101) found that "connected knowers" experience personality growth as they receive validation and confirmation. In the absence of validation, women may feel crippled and incompetent. She also discovered that women who prefer communal learning may experience lower self-esteem when they are required to interact with people or institutions who demand that they present clear objective procedures. Magolda (1989) also observed gender differences in how women and men acquire knowledge. Women preferred collecting others' ideas to debating opinions and they relied on more personal interpretation than men.

Finally the *self in relation model* proposed by Jordan and Surrey (1986) proposes that healthy development is a result of "relationship-differentiation" rather than "separation-individuation." This particular theory underscores four positive aspects of the mother / daughter relationship that molds the self: (a) the early emotional attentiveness between mother and daughter, (b) the experience of mutual empathy between them, (c) the expectation that relationships are a mutual source of growth, and (d) the relationship develops mutual empowerment and maturation.

The self-in-relation theory also states that the social connections of women validate their capacity as relational beings, and provide a foundation for autonomy, competence and self-esteem. Developmental problems don't necessarily occur because of a failure to separate, but rather because of a conflict between remaining connected while asserting one's differentiation. However, because women spend time enhancing their relationship-building skills, they are likely to blame themselves for a failure in a relationship and this damages their self-esteem.

The Fallacies of the Relational Models

The reevaluation of relatedness is central to creating all-inclusive models of personhood. There is a problem in defining women strictly in terms of their affiliative capacities and men in terms of their instrumental capacities (see Reinke, Ellicatt, Hanis, & Haucock, 1985) because the capacity to be independent and nurturing is available to all people. Luria (1986) and Kerber (1986) expressed concern that the theories focusing on the superior nurturing qualities of women might prompt a return to the oversimplification of womanhood and their maintenance in a subordinate status. Lerner (1989) stated that the behaviors and strengths associated with relationship theories have been associated with the subordinate group.

Under current circumstances, skills for autonomy or relatedness may result more from one's location in the social structure than from an individual's efforts. Economic dependence for one or more children may rule against the realization of autonomy for many women. Societies that pressure men to be a good provider seem to rule out affiliative roles for them. Unless tendencies to generalize about women and men are tempered by research that identifies the effects of circumstances and individual differences in behavior, old stereotypes that attribute gender differences to inborn traits rather than to social and cultural influences may be revived.

It is important to note that many samples studied by Gilligan (1982), Josselson (1987), and Belenky et al. (1986) included only women, making direct comparisons with men statistically inappropriate. However, Luria et al. (1989), found that when studies control for education, social class, work history and gender, differences disappear. Donnbery and Hoffman (1988) finding that women and men use the same justice and care when deciding moral issues, concluded that empathy is a human, rather than a feminine, trait.

The relational models suggest that women's sense of self and identity are more strongly tied to other people, than to work-related themes or environmental factors. In contrast, a study of women's lives by Barnett and Baruch (1987) noted that themes of achievement and work dominated women's discussions, and nearly half of those surveyed reported that the most rewarding aspect of their life was related to achievement in work or education. Roles not connected to work are high-strain roles and related to stress problems. Coleman and Antonucci (1983) found that middle-aged working women have higher self-esteem and less psychological anxiety than homemakers. Working women in their study also reported better physical health than did homemakers. Therefore, work may function as a stabilizing force for women during critical periods throughout the life cycle. These findings caution against romanticizing women's caregiving roles and encourage the view that achievement tasks as central to personal gratification.

Reassessing Gender Dichotomies

One of the big problems that traditional developmental models share with the feminist models is the ease with which they fall back on the predictable, linear, and age-stage frameworks to explain human development. For example, Ruth Josselson expanded on Erikson's identity stage by proceeding to examine the identity formation of women. Belenky, as noted above, based her understanding of the way females gain knowledge by advancing through sequential stages. But, some authors have addressed the problem. "So for women, the 'age and stage' theories are not the answer to understanding the pattern of life. Theories of women's lives that are now evolving take into account the fact that the times do change, and as environments change, people change with them" (Baruch, Barnett, & Rivers, 1983, p. 242).

The feminist models of development fail to consider how the context of an individual's life promotes or sometimes deters growth in adulthood. Many times it is the unexpected event or a reinterpretation of an old event that will produce a turning point, rather than growth through predictable relational events. Both traditionalists and feminists must paint with a wider, more tolerant and encompassing brush stroke to describe the adult journey through life. The picture must take into consideration the emotional impact and personal meaning that both women and men attach to life's events and experiences.

The authors of both traditional and female-oriented developmental theories tend to create artificial dichotomies comparing the identities of women and men. Generalizations such as women's orientation to nurturing and caretaking versus men's orientation toward development through differentiation and autonomy only encourage polarized caricatures of maleness and femaleness. Reevaluating relatedness is central to creating inclusive models of adult development.

According to Wolfson (1989), "Men are taught to avoid, at all costs, showing any signs of vulnerability, weakness, or helplessness, while women are taught to cultivate these qualities." Psychologist Jean Baker Miller writes that a "necessary part of all experience is a recognition of one's weaknesses and limitations. The process of growth involves admitting feelings, and experiencing them so one can develop new strengths" (1976, p. 31).

Various researchers have perceived the midlife period as focusing on a continual and deep examination of inner experiences, feelings, fantasies, conflicts, values, and attitudes (Schroeder, 1992). Gutmann and his colleagues (1975, 1980) indicate that a massive turnover of sex roles takes place in middle age. Men have the opportunity to adopt outward passivity, sensuality, and tenderness— attributes that he indicates were previously repressed. Women are free to become domineering, independent, and unsentimental. Without the responsibility of growing children, wives and mothers no longer need to admire male assertion and are now free to recognize and enjoy such energies in themselves. In other words, the sharp distinctions of earlier adulthood break down and each sex becomes, to some degree, what the other used to be.

Existing developmental literature indicates that emerging midlife opposite-gender components can precipitate pathological symptoms and significant role confusion for both men and women. According to Schroeder (1992), "The emerging passive-dependent needs of men may not be gratified by their new, more autonomous, independent, and assertive wives or female partners. Men may then develop alcoholic or psychosomatic symptoms. The midlife husband who leaves his wife for a younger, more dependent woman may do it not to prove sexual potency, but to help him deny his emerging passivity" (p. 432). Research conducted by Crouter, Perry-Jenkins, Houston, and McHale (1987), found that men who are forced to participate in child care responsibilities (and to develop their nurturing side) often experienced significantly more marital stress. According to Cytrynbaum (1980), this marital discord is a result of a common dilemma faced by many dual-career families—emerging passive-dependent needs in the husband to be cared for, to be loved, and to love comes at a time when a wife is moving toward autonomy, independence, and assertiveness that are necessary in continuing a career.

Before his death, Levinson (1994) turned his attention toward understanding how women proceed toward maturity. Levinson concludes that females, like males go through an alternating series of structure-building and structure-changing stages. He found, for example, that men in their late thirties want to "become their own man." He also found that at just this time, women desire to "become their own woman"; that is, they want greater connection both from the people in their world and from themselves. An important point Levinson makes is that although male and female growth toward maturity may be similar, there are major differences between the genders in terms of needs within each respective stage.

Based on these observations, there is a greater need to understand the capacity of women and men to be both independent and nurturing, to support the developmental needs of the significant other. The present research paints an overwhelmingly confused image of the capacity of the opposite sex to adapt and change to new role-based trends. For example, while some research suggests that men are doing more housework than ever before (Pleck, 1985), others conclude that men do about the same amount of household work as they did in the 19th century (Cowan, 1987). For an excellent overview of this issue, read *The Second Shift* by Arlie Hochschild (1992). An obvious conclusion that many psychologists still make is that men derive their self-image, self-esteem, and identity from work-based roles, and are increasingly threatened by the entrance of women into the workplace.

According to Dacey and Travers (1994), we are at a cultural crossroads in terms of understanding gender development. Both authors see the old division of male and female roles and their accompanying behaviors breaking down, but no clear new direction has yet appeared. The study that prompted this book has been an attempt to address this issue by observing and asking women and men the same questions about their life experiences. Both traditionalists and feminists must paint with a wider, more tolerant, and more encompassing brushstroke to describe the adult journey through life that takes in the experiences and personal meaning attached to those experiences of both women and men.

PRIOR RESEARCH ON SELF-ESTEEM

The field of developmental psychology and research done in the areas of self-esteem have been value-laden with the idea that

healthy identity, mature adulthood, and high self-esteem are associated with the so-called male norms of achievement, independence,
and mastery (Spence, 1985). Self-esteem, for the most part, was
based on characteristics and behaviors that were typically masculine in nature. Being female, with its emphasis on nurturance and
maintaining relationships, encouraged feelings of collective, low
self-esteem based solely on their gender (also see Fagot, Leinbach,
& O'Boyle, 1992).

Self-esteem is usually considered a stable component of the personality. Once developed in adolescence and early adulthood, an
individual's self-evaluation has been thought to remain static
through maturity. This position dovetails with Erikson's stage theory (see Harter, 1993; Santrock & Yussen, 1992), but the statement
that identity and self-worth are crystallized in late adolescence/
early adulthood, may be too simplistic. The developmental theme
refers mainly to male forms of development with their emphasis on
acquiring career and achievement goals within that particular time,
hence assuring identity and self-worth. Females are completely out
of the developmental loop as to when they are supposed to gain a
sense of self-esteem and develop a strong identity. This fast-track
approach is not emotionally healthy for males, either.

Theorists have been engaged in debates over the idea that males
and females develop along different pathways, hence affecting
their feelings of self-worth differently. (Block [1983] has done an
excellent job of summarizing how males and females develop in different learning environments, which impacts, on their psychological development.) Freud's Drive Theory (1905/1961) covering the
Oedipal period was descriptive of the male child's development of
self. Freud (1935) admitted he did not understand women, but
proceeded to postulate female development as an aberration from
the normative male model. He noted the more socially embedded
nature of women's identities. He felt their lives were dominated by
emotions of affection and hostility, along with themes of female
passivity, masochism, and narcissism. Freud's negative portrayal of
women did much to legitimize beliefs of female inferiority, hence
reinforcing low self-esteem and low status among women.
Loevinger and Wessler (1970) found that change in ego development and self-esteem was common during adolescence, but change
in personality either slowed down or stopped for most adults. Later,

in 1976, Loevinger implied that the average adult is unlikely to advance in ego development and in perceptions of self after high school or college.

Blos (1962) based his theory of the development of self on the theme of individuation/separation as the hallmark of self-esteem. He professed that separating from parental internal objects would result in a lasting sense of oneself as a unique person, resulting, in turn, in high self-esteem.

According to Levinson et al. (1978), the young adult male was viewed as pursuing the dream—active, striving and competent. His relationships were seen as a means to an end; career achievement was that end. Maslow (1956) acknowledged the importance of relationships, but stated that a self-actualized person, one with high self-esteem, can be independent of the opinion of others.

When Contratto (1984) reviewed the work of the turn of the century American psychologists, he found that their beliefs reflected the idea that women were of mediocre intellectual capacity and that any rigorous, mental activity on their part would diminish their reproductive capabilities. These early ideas further promoted the inferior status of women, hence creating collective low self-esteem among women based on having been born female.

Feminist psychologists have studied self-esteem, and many have found that self-worth is derived in large part from social experience. Chodorow (1989) found that cultural and social pressures exert an influence on the pathways of development for males and females and on their feelings of self-worth. Chodorow and Gilligan (1982) have described how females follow a pathway that allows for the development of self as an empathetic being in relationship to others. Males, they found, were concerned more with occupation and one's status in the world of work for resources of self-esteem.

Belenky et al. (1986) found that female connected knowers experience growth and high self-esteem when they receive external validation and confirmation. In the absence of validation, they feel crippled and incompetent. Those who prefer communal learning may feel a loss of self-esteem when they encounter people and institutions who want detached objectives.

Research published in 1992 by Josephs, Markus, and Tafarodi examined the processes of self-esteem in both women and men. Their findings suggest that self-esteem for women is linked mainly to a process in which social connections and attachments to important others are emphasized. In contrast, they found that the self-esteem of men was linked to an individuation process in which one's personal achievements are emphasized.

Generally, feminist psychology avers that women's social connections validate their capacities as relational beings and provide the foundation for self-esteem. As discussed previously in the section on development, women may run into difficulties in remaining socially connected while at the same time asserting a differentiated self-concept. When this happens, they are much more likely than men to blame themselves for relationship failures, thus creating self-esteem problems.

Critique

A significant number of the studies done in the area of self-esteem model themselves after the major theories of adult development. For the most part, the researchers of self-esteem have determined that the attainment of high self-esteem occurs in late adolescence/early adulthood. Their conclusions coincide with those of psychologists (such as Erikson) who believe that identity is established and stabilized at this phase of personality development. However, the theory that a positive sense of self-worth is acheived mainly in early adulthood is biased against women. The theory of identity development, which promotes establishing early and often unchanging career goals for women, is being seriously questioned by new findings. For example, Serakan (1989) found that women experience increased self-esteem and feelings of self-worth in developing and revising career goals and ambitions.

Donald Super has been one of the foremost recognized experts in developing theories of career choice, development, and self-esteem during the last three decades. Super (1957, 1983, 1990) developed a life-stage theory of career development to address how career identity develops over time and to determine a person's readiness to make a career transition. Super describes five career stages, which he originally associated with different developmental periods. In a revision of his earlier thinking (Super & Thompson, 1981), Super suggests that individuals recycle through each stage several times during their lives. This new viewpoint speaks to the heart of the thesis of this book, that development is characterized by the fluid re-evaluation of goals and ambitions.

Female psychologists have tried to correct the inadequacies that exist within traditional frameworks, but unfortunately they seem to be as guilty as the traditionalists when stating that, for the most part, women's sense of self and self-worth is more or less reflected in their inborn proclivity to establish, maintain and nurture relationships. They have not examined other areas of social experience and personal meaning that might change across the life course, hence influencing a changing self-concept.

The NCWRR study found that components of self-esteem are derived in large part from social experience; that individuals fit these social impressions together to form a gestalt, an integrated whole; and that these components are unstable and vary over the course of the life of a woman or a man. The transitions of self-esteem is an ongoing life process and is both flexible and elastic depending on all personal, social experiences. We have found that over a span of years very few women and men have a static sense of self or consistent feelings of self-esteem. Self-esteem is shaped by the manner in which people frame a unique judgment of themselves and shaped by the changing meaning they may attach to events relating to themselves from time to time.

We can now take another approach to the new female psychology that supports the view that the self-worth of women is based on relationships alone. We found that women's positive feelings of self-worth are established and maintained from achievements and meaningful work, whereas relationships are of lesser importance. Conversely, we found that men also value achievement for a sense of positive self-worth, but that personal relationships are significantly more important than previously believed. Self-esteem can too easily become genderized with too much importance given to particular stereotypes about women and men.

Caution has to be taken when assuming that there is a particular time frame for gaining a substantially strong sense of self, or that self-esteem, once established, is inflexible or remains rigid throughout adult life. A major study by Reinke and others (1985) found that there were, indeed, important transitions in the lives of women, but not exclusively clustered around one particular developmental period. Each transition throughout the life span modified and changed one's perception of self-worth and self-esteem.

A NEW CONCEPTUAL VIEW OF
ADULT DEVELOPMENT

A person who passes from infancy through childhood, adolescence, adulthood and on to old age necessarily acquires, builds upon, enhances, refines and reflects upon an intrinsic sense of self. "Who am I?" "How do I fit into the world around me?" "How do I measure up?" "What pleases me?" "What can I point to with pride?" "What have I accomplished?" Society has conditioned us to believe that the process and often the answers to these questions are somehow different for women than for men.

The goal of this national study by the National Center for Women and Retirement Research has been to engage women and men in a serious dialogue about how they view themselves and view their development of self-worth. Understanding the sources of self-worth can help make sense of why people adopt particular identities and how these identities in turn become salient. People try to commit to identities that foster self-esteem. Reflection about such issues enable women and men to recognize that there are critical choices to be made about how they define themselves.

The object of the study was to look at a sample of both women and men, to identify those accomplishments and life experiences that made them feel good about themselves, to allow them to reflect on their lives as an integrated whole, and to compare the results.

Before undertaking the study, the NCWRR expected to uncover large differences in the life experiences and expectations of women and men regarding their formation of a positive identity and self-worth. The NCWRR also expected to find support for the traditional theories that have men drawing their sense of identity and feelings of self-worth from achievement pathways only, and women drawing their primary sense of self from nurturing relationships with spouses and intimate partners, parents, children, and friends. The findings of the study, however, contradicted expectations. Contrary to previous notions and theories, men and women derive a large part of their identity and self-worth from the same sources.

This book, based on the NCWRR study findings, open-ended

questions and personal interviews, will describe the following critical themes concerning the development of self-identity and self-esteem in women's and men's lives:

- The full expression of "self" in adulthood is based on an ongoing reappraisal of life events from earlier periods of development. Identity development does not crystallize in early adulthood for most women and men. Identity development for both women and men is evolving and ongoing throughout adulthood.
- The shaping of an identity must be viewed in terms of movement that consists of a process of contraction and expansion of the self not as the stop-and-start process so often characterized by stage theory.
- Prior studies have clearly documented the shift between the sexes (men become more relational which women become more achievement/mastery-oriented) during midlife. Instead of focusing on this phenomena as a shift of opposites or occurring only in midlife, we take the view that earlier processes of development prepare both women and men to slowly begin to exercise and crystallize qualities that are paramount in forging self-identity. The mistake has been to view this shift as a "switch" in gender identity instead of viewing it as a natural and integrating process of a growing, expanding self.
- The evolutionary development of self-identity during the adult years has radically changed due to societal and cultural mandates. A major contribution of this work is to offer an understanding of why sources of self-esteem reflect the challenges and transitions that make up adult development from a 1990s' perspective.
- A major concern in adult development research is to learn what fuels the desire on the part of men and women to become more integrated and interdependent during their adult years. New sources of self-esteem are found through a reappraisal process that highlights areas of one's life that have yet to be fulfilled or have changed in personal meaning.
- There are more similarities between the sexes regarding their perceptions about the context of their life experiences than was previously thought. It is the manner in which men and women

relate those experiences that is different. When men tell about their life experiences the narrative tends to be a structured and ordered description of events, even though the events may be random or unstructured. When women relate the same events, the narrative is often unstructured, almost a stream of consciousness propelled by emotional considerations.

- Adult development, as it relates to identity and self-esteem, does not occur at predictable times, through particular stages or necessarily through separation. The process is neither a totally male-oriented separation process nor is it a totally female process of embeddedness (connection). Rather it is a process that suggests a back-and-forth movement between the two extremes. It is similar to what H. D. Winnicott (1965, pp 74–75) described as a "holding and letting-go" process between the person and his/her environment .

This process of holding and relinquishing, similar in nature to Winnicott's (1965) theme of movement between the individual and the environment, will serve as the framework for this book. The framework is based on the social experience and personal meaning from which women and men develop, reappraise, change, and gain a sense of self. The holding environment we describe will be called life-ties, and consists of (a) the family of origin; (b) education; (c) work; (d) intimate relationships; (e) children, friends, and mentors. Life-ties can be considered a holding environment that at times nourish and at other times deter personal growth and development. When they deter, there is a letting-go or separating of that particular holding environment or life-tie. To understand adult development in another way it may be informative to look into the meaning and content of the life-tie relationship that will evolve and change in many different ways over time.

The essence of this developmental framework does not rely on a sequencing of age-related events, stages, or gender polarization, but rather in its capacity to enlighten a process of finding personal meaning through these life-ties that provide the context for personal identity and self-esteem. It is emotionally costly to separate from old meanings and, often, from the actual events and people who have come to represent those personal meanings.

This present study observed women and men developing new relationships within the life-tie framework; it also noted changes in self-representation. The gender differences that were observed were not totally a matter of what women and men do differently, but how they perceive themselves or experience themselves in relation to their life-tie experience. The struggle for women and men to understand each other may benefit from their recognition that adult development does not depend solely on separation/differentiation from the life-tie relationship or totally on connection/ embeddedness with that life-tie. Rather, it is the movement and balance between separating and connecting with the life-tie experience as well as the evolving and ever-changing meaning of that experience across the life-course that shapes identity and self-worth in both women and men.

CHAPTER 2

Family of Origin

The family only represents one aspect, however important
an aspect, of a human being's functions and activities. . . .
A life is beautiful and ideal, or the reverse, only when we
have taken into our consideration the social as well as
the family relationship.

—Havelock Ellis

$\mathbf{B}$y the year 2000 the family tree will certainly be firmly
rooted in the American soil, but it will be growing new branches
and sprouting a varied assortment of blossoms. The earliest social
influence on every individual's development comes by way of his or
her *family of origin*. At the most basic level, this means the influence
of a parent or parents—their nurturance, teaching, and presence
as role models. But the common notion of family, as well as its very
real impact, is far broader than this. Family, in this sense, denotes
something more than just a collection of individuals joined together
by kinship and shared living arrangements. It is a social context, one
that reflects, not only the people who comprise the family unit, but
also the more general effects of historical, economic, community,
and religious forces prevailing in the society as a whole.

Family is not a place of residence, but rather a place that houses
relationships and personal meaning. The sociological meaning of
family is changing (Hess & Sussman, 1984). The powerful impact

26

of those changes on both women and men can last an emotional lifetime. Contemporary family is diverse, fluid, and always in a state of ongoing resolution. No longer is there a single, culturally dominant family pattern to which the majority of Americans conform. Today, Americans have created a multiplicity of family and household arrangements that we inhabit uneasily and reconstitute frequently in response to changing personal and employment circumstance.

The 1990s family is not a new model of family life, nor the next stage in an orderly progression of family history, but exists in an era in which the belief in a logical progression of life stages breaks down. Rupturing evolutionary models of family history and incorporating both experimental and nostalgic elements, the 1990s family lurches forward and sideways into an uncertain future. Family is not necessarily a nucleus that includes an intact pair of parents, with a full-time mother, male breadwinner, regular means of income, planned family vacations and a life together with the kids until they go off to work or college (Sidel, 1990). This very predictable and often mythical linear family model has been held up as a standard that few families can or could ever attain.

The purpose of this chapter is to illustrate a variety of changes that are reconstituting our understanding of the typical family structure. Although it is impossible to accurately portray a representative, all-encompassing picture of adult family life today, our goal is to discuss and highlight specific changes that will have an increased impact on the nature of familial relations in the decades to come.

A DEVELOPMENTAL VIEW OF FAMILY

Rodgers (1973) defined the family as a semi-closed system of actors occupying positions defined by the society they live in. Previous developmental research has put great emphasis on the timing of events when tracking growth, change, and their consequences within the family. Supposedly, the timing of events is strongly affected by normative expectations concerning the appropriate age for certain family tasks. The length of an engagement; the right time for marriage, timing of the first baby, length of time between births, the age of parents when last child should leave home, and marriage for life are some of the family events that have had a societal timetable attached to them. Hareven (1987) described the historically specific nature of the timing of life events and the social awareness of various age periods when studying the family.

Certain developmentalists who study the family assume that there are normative patterns of family life (Erikson, 1978). It is assumed that marriage will occur before a child is born; couples will not dissolve marriage until the death of one spouse; couples are supposed to have children in their twenties; the last child will leave home for good by age 21. Constantly changing events that reshape the family as we know it, however, must be considered. Children conceived out of wedlock, single parents, older couples having children, grandparents taking on the role of parent, aged parents being taken care of by midlife children, divorce, economic hardships, abuse, incest, neglect, alcohol and drugs—all are events that shatter developmental timetables and forestall or prevent completion of so-called developmental tasks. These types of events and the context in which they occur are gender-neutral, affecting both women and men over the course of their lives.

The changes that are taking place within the American family must be compared to the tasks that accurately reflect the changing values within society today. Many of these family changes do not correspond to developmental task theory nor to the social values of a past time (Tavris, 1986). Duvall (1971) described the developmental tasks that families must successfully meet in order to grow to maturity as (a) physical maintenance, (b) allocation of resources, (c) division of labor, (d) socialization of family members, (e) reproduction, (f) maintenance of order, (g) placing members in a larger society, and (h) morale and motivation. For a growing number of families, these eight developmental tasks are being modified and transformed.

The timing, age-relatedness and even the nature of a particular developmental task as they relate to family development are no longer realistic for many families (Sussman, 1984). For example, divorce often fractures the task of allocating resources and physical maintenance (Weitzman, 1985). Division of labor is no longer a reality or expectation. Most families now have both spouses working because of economic need and the desire for personal fulfillment (Hochschild, 1989). There is no division of labor in single-parent-headed households, for the head of the house does it all, from child care and maintenance of the home to working outside that home. Some couples are choosing not to have children or put the question off indefinitely (Moore, Spain & Bianchi, 1984). Physical, sexual, and emotional abuse, as well as substance abuse, will often cripple any attempt to maintain family order (Johnson & Ferguson, 1990). Economic hardships often delay or postpone attempts to place family members in a larger society. Sometimes adult children leave the nest only to fly home again because of economic or emotional necessity, and their return can affect the collective morale and self-esteem of the family.

Many families today must examine built-in expectations for the success of tasks which influence self-worth. We may ask ourselves: Did we succeed or fail? What is a measure of success in a changing society and family? Who is now setting the standards? Should there be standards and expectations when society changes so quickly? If a couple divorces, if a child is gay, if an individual does not want to go to college, if a couple decide not to have children—are these family failures? With wide-ranging abilities, circumstances, resources, and variations within and among families, socially prescribed normative expectations and tasks are no longer appropriate to describe the lives of families.

The NCWRR study found that adults continue to develop and to gain a sense of personal worth over the course of their adult lives, due in part to their personal integration with family history, events, and experience. Personal meaning and sense of self within the context of the family of origin depend on the interactions among family members at the time they occurred, plus the perceived change and integration in personal meaning regarding those interactions over time (Sanford & Donovan, 1985). Adults employ the family past as a resource for creating and reshaping meaning and self-worth in the present.

AN HISTORICAL LOOK AT THE
MARRIAGE OF FAMILY

People often say that they wish they could return to the "good old days" of family life. The myth of the stable, predictable and "all-loving family" always may have represented the exception rather the common standard of family life. Many people feel, and have always felt, that their families are emotionally and physically deficient. They compare their family life and upbringing to storybook tales that have been told for centuries about "happily-ever-after" families.

The mother-at-home, father-at-work model, with plenty of physical and emotional nourishment and stability, was a description of family life in the 1950s (Hess & Sussman, 1984). It was actually an aberration. At best it lasted for a short time coincident with nationwide prosperity and full employment, and was unrepresentative of many families. In order to put the family in a clear perspective, it is necessary to take a brief look back at the historical meanings of family life.

Historian Judith Stacey described different types of family units from the past. The "Godly" family was an element of colonial times. The family's leading patriarch wielded unlimited authority. The family served the social, religious and economic purposes of larger kin groups. The purpose of the family groups was decided by the patriarchs, who controlled property ownership and allocated labor and economic resources. Modern-day families often look to these earlier family units with envy and nostalgia. Yet what is rarely understood is how often death obliterated whole families. Calamities and diseases inflicted early and serial widowhood and gave rise to a large number of second marriages. These early families were very similar to modern-day families with single parents, blended households, and stepchildren.

The dogma of innate sin demanded that a determined parent break the will and save the souls of their potentially doomed children. This severe method of childrearing relied heavily on paternal involvement. The father was an ever-present, forceful, and often brutal influence on his family. This father did not disappear behind newspapers, and he was not a vague presence in family life. There were few boundaries between family and work. Both mother and father worked in close proximity. Contrary to modern notions that fathers were emotionally and physically absent, we find historically that the paternal influence, and the father's physical presence, were very much an active reality in 19th century family life.

According to Stacey, there were four main events that changed life in this *pre-modern family* in the direction of the modern-day version: First, with the industrial revolution, family work and economic work became separate. As a result, women, and their work, became socially invisible; and both women and children were economically dependent on husbands and fathers. Second, "love" became the main purpose of marriage, rather than an arrangement based on parental, economic, or social constraints, third, privacy became an entitlement of every person. This idea withdrew families from the public eye altogether and reinforced the invisibility of the contributions of women. Both women and children were economically dependent on husbands and fathers. Fourth, there began the emergence of the *child-centered family*. Home-bound women began having fewer children, but at the same time began increasing their attentions to child-rearing and expending their full-time energy on it. This led to motherhood being placed on a sacred and exalted, but limiting, pedestal.

What we so easily ignore in passing is that, over the course of history, the family has been anything but a static concept (Walters, Carter, Papp, & Silverstein, 1988). Families grow and shrink in size; they prosper and fail economically; they alternately cohere and disperse. A childhood is but a snapshot in a lifetime. It is set against a backdrop of people and events, shaped, changed and reshaped by the flow and flux of a changing social milieu. Probably the greatest single external force bearing upon the family is economics (Sidel, 1987). Every era has had its rich and its poor. Where a family stands in the continuum between wealth and poverty shapes nearly every aspect of its daily life.

Among the very wealthy, money substantially alters the relationship between men and women and between parents and children. The presence of wealth and the likelihood of its persistence has brought men of every age at least the opportunity for more leisure time to be spent in familial pursuits. Financially fortunate women have found liberation from household tasks and, in many instances, freedom from the daily chores of childrearing. If and when marriage dissolve by divorce, or collapses into widowhood, however, it is usually the women who bear the financial brunt of consequent hardship (Sidel, 1987). This is because so many of them have been too preoccupied otherwise to prepare for and deal with the realistic possibility that they may suddenly have to earn a living and sustain a life independent of a breadwinner. Family

wealth has brought children the benefits of costly higher education, superior nutrition, and monitored health care. With the
alliances and social connections of their wealthy family, they can
enjoy work opportunities and a certain measure of self-assurance
in embarking on the journey to adulthood.

The alteration of family relationships also holds for those
exposed to the opposite polarity of grinding and unrelenting
poverty. The inevitable lot of both adult partners—and more so in
the case of single-parent households—is a lifetime of heavy labor in
a series of marginally fruitful endeavors, and sometimes includes
the necessity of holding a second or third job in times of extra
financial need or crisis (Edelman, 1987). Leisure time becomes a
luxury. Young children, aged and infirm relatives—in short, anyone
who cannot contribute economically to the family's welfare—
become liabilities that affect everyone's standard of living.
Concomitantly, older children, able to take their place as wage
earners, become a tangible asset to the family economic unit. If
work is unavailable to these families, the welfare net may be their
only means of survival. They are often encouraged to abandon educational aspirations, perhaps even to postpone marriage, for the
monetary betterment of their parents and siblings. Self-worth is
nonexistent; futility is the main legacy that is passed down to the
next generation.

Between these two extremes lies the vast middle class. On the
economic ladder, they remain rooted with one foot on the rung
above and the other on the rung below. There is always the grim
realization of the chasm yawning beneath—the potentially cata-
clysmic effects of a plant closing, or an expensive injury or illness. The
middle class is a fertile ground for both hope and fear, ambition
and apprehension, risk taking in the promise of something better,
and conservatism rooted in the terror of something worse. But middle class doesn't necessarily exemplify the statistical norm of family
life. Dysfunction, breakups, abandonment, crisis, and joy sometimes coexist within the American middle-class family.

Economics is only one of the extrinsic factors that help to mold
the family and to shape the life experiences of its members. There
has also been a series of societal changes, many of them impacting
most directly upon women, and leaving men and their families to
address staggering issues. Chronologically, these changes include:

1. *The rise of public entertainment* and its potential for creating nationally shared values and attitudes, starting with motion pictures in the decade between 1910 and 1920, followed by radio in the late 1920s, and then television after the late 1940s. Public entertainment and the media gave rise to portrayals of the unattainable "perfect" family that everyone would like to emulate, but can't. It made people feel that their families couldn't quite measure up to this mythical type of family pattern.

2. *The women's suffrage movement* of the early 1920s, and the acceptance of women into the labor force. Women were no longer personal slaves; they had the vote, and they were able to earn their own incomes.

3. *The Jazz Age* of the 1920s with its rejection of conservative religious beliefs, a growing emphasis on individual freedom, and general nose-thumbing at the traditional pieties of American small town life. For women, this meant physical freedom of dress, more exposure to public life, and the ability to say what they felt. Alcohol, and the inhibitions that were released with it, had an impact on men, women and their families.

4. *The first sexual revolution* of the 1920s and 1930s, began when effective contraceptives became widely available. Women got the first glimpse of what their lives would be like if it were not tied to their reproductive organs. Family planning became a possibility, and an increase in extramarital sex became a fact.

5. *World War II* not only brought a rare degree of national unity, but for the first time exposed literally millions of American men and women who would, in the ordinary course of events, have lived and died within 50 miles of their birthplace, to sights and cultures half a world away. Children witnessed their mothers marching off to work to contribute to the war effort. Fathers came back from war with tales of horror and a need for security, peace and stability for themselves and their families.

6. *The explosive growth of higher education and the immediate prospect of home ownership* were the twin legacies of the postwar GI Bill. The GI Bill made it possible for many returning servicemen to enter or finish college with little or no personal expense. The government footed the bill for their education and also

made it financially realistic for these returning servicemen to purchase homes with the help of government loans.

By the end of the 1950s virtually all economic work had left the home. Talcott Parsons described how the nuclear family structure was in harmony with the division of roles into female "communal" and male "instrumental" domains. The rise of the nuclear family also coincided with the way developmental theorists (such as Erikson) described adult development. This family was the model upon which developmentalists based their linear and age-specific stages of growth. The nuclear family during this period followed socially-sanctioned time-frames: When to go to school; when to marry; when to have children; when to work; and when to retire.

Society experienced increased longevity, available alternative lifestyles and greater automotive mobility that stretched families out across the country to unprecedented distances. But the post-World War II and Cold War years would prove to be the last gasp for nuclear family cohesion. The profound influence of industrialization on the family also led to its transition. The post-industrialization era, especially after the 1970s, shifted work from unionized heavy industries to smaller, non-union, and less skilled clerical and service industries. Employers were attracted to cheap, non-union female workers (Bergmann, 1986) usually married women with children. Because of their domestic situations, they were willing to settle for part-time jobs at low wages. Massive consumer demands, the rise in coeducational colleges, and escalating divorce rates gave women opportunities to make a sizable portion of their identity and self-worth associated with the instrumental spheres of paid labor. Middle-class women joined ranks with working class women in the male domain of paid work. The old structure of cultural rules that had bound families to traditional roles began to loosen and crumble.

The aberrations of the 1950s also gave way to the family revolution of the sixties and seventies. The clash of past family ideology with new family behaviors promulgated many challenges to the established concept of a traditional family. Women's liberation, gay liberation, legalized abortion, the contraceptive pill, a growing divorce rate and increased longevity would all transform our understanding of family development.

THE AWESOME FAMILY

One of the major findings of the NCWRR study was that the influences of one's family of origin, parents, siblings and extended family members continue to impact on the identity and self-esteem
(both positive and negative) of women and men throughout all of
adult life. Men and women integrate the experiences of their early
years into their ongoing adult pattern of living. Sometimes a particularly impressive family incident or event that will trigger integration and reorganization of something personal, such as when an
adult son sees his once overpowering and larger-than-life farther
become frail and dependent in his older years. There may be a
reorganization of the son's own self-image based on the reality and
current context of his father's image. Sometimes change doesn't
happen suddenly, but rather through a series of intermittent
unpredictable family life reviews, the subtle influence of a memory,
or a meeting of thoughts that will give something new meaning.
From this develops a revised sense of self—good or bad—and an
altered image of who a person is or may still want to become.

Adult Daughters and Mothers

Every woman may not be a mother, but every woman is a daughter.
A woman's identity, self-worth and personality growth are partially
dependent on the nature of her life-tie with her mother. From their
mothers, daughters derive their first feeling of security, courage, a
sense of being of value and having value, a personal vision of competence, the ability to love and be loved, and their first glimmer of
selfhood.

Mothering is a very complicated task. It is a tense business of
holding on and letting go. Too little or too much of either can be
damaging to a growing daughter. Coming to terms with Mother,
renegotiating and transforming the relationship from time to time
will affect the perception a daughter has of her own adult life. This
important "settling" of the mother/daughter bond does not always
occur in late adolescence when we usually put on the superficial trappings of adulthood (Bassoff, 1988). We found that women and men
have a lifelong task of reworking and reweaving their "mother-tie."

Transforming this tie, whether it happens as early as late adolescence or in late adulthood, means dissociating from the little-girl's mother-tie and making a better-fitting tie with Mother based on adult things in common, mutual respect, and empathy. This is very difficult for many women to accomplish, for historically the mother/daughter bond has been a very strong and close attachment. Because they are both female, there is a natural identification between mother and daughter. A problem may develop (Johnson & Ferguson, 1990), when this influencing tie is with a less-powerful and less-valued parent. The daughter's devaluation of the mother's role in this case can damage a mother/daughter relationship. The daughter can see herself as deficient; or she may try defensively to deny that any part of her is like her mother, thereby disavowing all identification. As Nancy Friday stated in her book, *My Mother, My Self* (1977):

> First impressions of life cut the deepest and last the longest. They form the grooves of character through which experience comes to us, and if this groove becomes distorted, this or that emotion becomes blocked or twisted. Certain patterns that come heavily laden with ambivalence, rejection, and humiliation from the past have us and tend to keep us in their grip. (p. 45)

A troubled relationship with a mother can produce behavior patterns that may prevent a woman from achieving her full potential. She may become over anxious and inhibited and may recoil from experimenting and taking healthy risks in life. Her neurotic self-image of inadequacy can negatively influence her choice of friends and intimate partners and can hinder the pace of her personal growth. Even if she reaches her goal, she may not be gratified or may be filled with self-doubt, and may feel that the achievement was not deserved. H. D. Winnicott (1965, p. 277) stated that if we have "a good enough mother," we will stockpile and build upon the loving, worthy and nurturing feelings we received from her.

The findings of our study show that over 50% of all women surveyed still felt the profound influence of their mother on their life as an adult. The influence didn't end when they left home, went to some distant school, found work in another state or when they married and became preoccupied with husband and children of their own.

The mother-daughter life-tie therefore persists, influencing and continuing to shape an adult daughter's sense of self. Sometimes the influence is good and sometimes not so good. As Dr. Robertiello (1975) emphasized in *My Mother, My Self:* "I've never met anyone yet, for whom it had ended, man or woman" (Robertiello, cited in Friday, 1977, p.68). The following personal accounts describe some of the ways the mother/daughter life-tie continues to revise an adult daughter's development and growth.

The Cold Blue Ties: Three Generations of Women

Sixty-seven-year-old Rita had just moved from Florida to a resort town on Cape Cod to be close to Peg, one of her two daughters. Peg had suggested to her mother in an offhand way that it might be nice if she lived closer, so she could be near her two grandchildren. Much to Peg's surprise, Rita made the move. Now both are having great difficulty renegotiating the emotionally weakened mother/ daughter tie that time, distance, and events had diluted. Nevertheless, Rita's old life-tie still had its roots entwined in the close relationship she had had with her own mother. She presented the following story:

> My mother was a shut-out person, a cold blue woman, but she was also a hard worker and a survivor. You see, I was born in Vienna, an only child, and when I turned thirteen, my parents and I were forced to leave. Hitler had invaded Austria. We came to America in July. . . . The war started in September. We lived in New York City for a time, but eventually settled in Connecticut. It's strange, but even before this uprooting from Austria, I had very few memories of my mother. What I do remember is a woman with a severe limp. She had two dislocated hips when she was born, yet she worked long hours in my grandfather's business. She was always in pain, always poor, always frowning, always working. . . . But she was always strong.
>
> I am the daughter of this frowning, suffering survivor. It seems like she was never home. I guess I was an early version of what everybody now calls a "latch-key kid." I had a family, but not a real mother. Back then, I was alone most of the time. I remember walking to see my uncle at his place. He would feed me lunch before I went home.
>
> I had occasional glimpses of what mothering was all about when

my grandmother sometimes took me with her to her afternoon card game. I would sit off to one side eating cakes and watching the ladies play cards. That's a warm memory. I grew up around adults, grew up quickly and grew up a serious person, like my mother. I had a hard time watching other people act differently and trying to act like them.

After Rita married in the 1950s, she wanted to start her own family. She had one daughter and was determined that Peg wouldn't be an only child as she was. Twenty-one months later she gave birth to a second daughter. Her husband worked long hours. She felt restless at times, but at the same time, "strong" enough to handle both job and family. Although her children were still quite young, she went back to work in the educational system as a labor relations negotiator.

Rita was the disciplinarian and authority figure in the family. This was a serious, no-nonsense household. Education was stressed. Her daughters were bright, and both excelled in high school and later in college. Rita's relationship with her daughters never was close. She is perplexed by their attitude toward her:

The younger one was a rebel, always shouting and testing me; the older one was more serious, but she kept everything inside. Both have always been respectful enough, but distant from me. I've tried to get closer to them, but it doesn't work. Sometimes this isolation makes me feel that I wasn't a good mother to them. That makes me feel real bad about myself.

The younger one, Marie . . . . We took a vacation trip to Europe together a few years ago. My God, that trip was a disaster! We ended up squabbling over there. I didn't want to go where she wanted to go, and she didn't want to see the same things I did. So we went through Europe traveling separately.

Marie lives on the West Coast on a farm that she runs single-handedly. She never married nor wanted to have any kids. She's surrounded by her animals, and I guess she's happy that way.

"I've been trying to change the relationship I have with Peg, my other daughter. I'm going to move close to her family soon. It's important to me, and I think about her a lot. We're both trying to work at it. She's a doctor, and she's working hard and even on call at night. . . . We've tried to find more time together, and when we can, we seem to be able to meet halfway emotionally now. I'm glad! I find myself loosening up. . . . I laugh with my grandchildren over silly things. . . . They're good kids. . . . Silly things make me feel good about myself.

Three themes have run through Rita's life that also ran through her mother's life: emotional distance, emotional strength, and hard work. Rita has tried to renegotiate her current daughter/ mother tie by balancing the "cold blue side" of both their personalities with the emotional strength and hard work that both women have used to overcome crises and move forward with their lives. Rita said,

> When my dear husband died in a Florida car crash ten years ago, we had just retired. People were amazed that I was in the hospital alone with no family or friends to comfort me. I told them I was okay, that I'd survived before. . . . You know, as I said that, it came to me that they are the exact same words my mother used when someone asked her about a crisis in her life.

Rita's identity and self-worth changed over time. Being castigated by her daughters as a cold, uncaring mother while they were growing up made her dislike herself the way she disliked the negative image of her now-dead mother. When Rita looked in the mirror she seemed to resemble her mother. Her self-esteem always took a fall whenever she compared herself to her emotionally unresponsive mother. She felt trapped in a cycle of repeating with her daughters what her mother had done to her—of withdrawing from them.

It was only in later life that she began to feel comfortable with herself by accepting and weaving into her self-image a woman who was not all cold and blue. Spending time with her grandchildren, being a little silly, a little affectionate, and listening to these little people made her realize that she was not the cold and uncaring woman her daughters believed her to be. Through the positive memories of her mother, the mother's strength and ability to provide and protect her family during times of hardship, Rita started to identify with her mother's strengths and ability to provide and protect her family. The good memories of her mother automatically became incorporated into her own identity. When she did this, she unconsciously circled back to reweave her self-image by incorporating into herself these same positive features, the strengths, the giving, protecting and sturdy instincts for survival.

Rita is an example of a woman whose important elements of identity, development, and self-worth evolved over a long time period. Striving for growth and self-worth was an ongoing struggle into her mid-adult years. The significance of her story is that it shows a woman whose adult years were characterized by a process in which she surmounted depressing events and regressions. Her revelations about achieving personal growth, a measure of maturity, self-esteem, and happiness by thinking about her mother's positive traits came to her deep into adult life.

Late-Life Ties Trigger Old Behaviors

Fifty-two-year-old Celia looked years younger than her age. She was healthy-looking, tan, shapely and dressed in a floral print sun dress. She wore a wide-brim sun hat from which escaped a long, finely woven, black braid down her back. When I first met her and complimented her, she confided that the year before, she was anything but healthy and had little to smile about. Last year, she said, she felt bewildered and scared by the recurrence of some self-destructive behaviors that threatened to overwhelm her life once again.

The relapse had started while she was taking care of her elderly mother who had been diagnosed with Alzheimer's disease. Her mother's mind was slowly being devoured by this hideous condition, and the strain of worrying and nursing her day and night began to take its toll on Celia. When not involved with her mother's care, she slipped into episodes of bingeing on food. Eventually the extra pounds on Celia's body began to show. She panicked and started an extremely strict, rigid diet and exercise routine. She lost weight, but then couldn't stop the dieting and fanatical exercising. Her weight plummeted to a dangerously low level, but her compulsion continued. She still perceived herself as ugly and fat. At last she realized that she had done battle with similar behavior as a young woman many years before.

Celia grew up in a suburban neighborhood of Chicago with her parents and two older brothers. Her father had his own insurance company. As an absentee father, he traveled extensively but always provided Celia's family with many extra comforts and niceties. Her mother necessarily acted as both parents for about 15 days each month. Celia related how her mother's life revolved completely around her and her brothers. They were all talented in some way, good looking and smart. Her two brothers were athletes and did well in school.

> It seemed so easy for them. . . . I was tested out as smart, too, but I just didn't have the drive that they had. My mother was always on my case, yelling at me to get better grades, dress better and look better. I couldn't understand why I could never quite make the grade with her. A couple of times she even humiliated me in front of other people, telling them that I could do better in school, but that I was just lazy.
>
> All of this stuff my mother was doing to me eventually began to affect me. I did improve! I lost weight, dressed better and started wearing lots of makeup. My mother conceded approval of these efforts, but I didn't find it rewarding. I just became known as "the skinny one." I had something over my brothers, though, for they tended to be too big and beefy. Me, I was like a speeding car out of control. I couldn't and didn't stop losing weight. If I didn't lose it fast enough to satisfy me, I'd start taking diet pills. Then all of a sudden my seventeen-year-old body came to a halt. I ended up in a hospital with an ulcer and intestinal problems.

Counseling helped young Celia. It was suggested that she put some geographical distance between herself and her mother. After entering an out-of-state college, she was able to gain back good eating habits. She fell in love and got married. Over the years that followed, she spent little time with her family of origin, especially with her mother. The usual holidays were spent together, but Celia was always glad to hop on a plane with her husband and son and go back home. After awhile she got a job working part-time as a reporter for her local, small town newspaper. She found friends, and life was good.

After her father passed away, her mother lived alone, although one of Celia's brothers lived within 30 miles of her and looked after her.

Problems for Celia began when her mother was diagnosed in the early stages of Alzheimer's. She recalls getting telephone calls at work from her mother; yelling and screaming at Celia to be a good daughter and take her home—even though she was still living safely in her own home. The phone calls soon began to trigger the old eating disorder. At work, Celia would reach into her desk drawer, pull out a bag of potato chips and devour them all in twenty minutes.

Her brother and his wife helped out occasionally those first few years, but then his company transferred him to California. Celia's mother had a fall, fracturing her arm and an ankle bone. Celia found it necessary to stay with her mother until she was sufficiently healed to fend for herself. Because her daughter was away at college and work was very slow, she was able to take a leave of absence.

> Taking care of my mother, even though she was frail and losing ground mentally, brought me full circle back to the time when I was at a very low point in my life. I knew my mother was in pain and that she was saying atrocious things that were symptomatic of her illness. I didn't like it, yet I started internalizing all the crazy, verbal assaults she would hurl at me. Sometimes in delirium, she was back in her old house making dinner for us. She would yell at me for not helping to make dinner, saying that I was a lazy, selfish girl. I knew this was all mental rambling, but I felt it anyway. I started to nibble at things, then overeat—anytime, anything. When I wasn't taking care of her needs, I was stuffing my face. The first six weeks I put on ten pounds. Then I went into a panic and plunged into my crash diet. On top of that, I tried to run about five miles every day with very little food, if any, in my stomach. The longer I stayed with her, the more I became obsessed and compulsive with dieting and exercise. I literally got sick and tired out at the same time. There I was, wallowing all over again in that hell.

Celia and her mother never worked through their relationship problems, and then it was too late. Her unschooled mother ignored the significance of Celia's symptoms and chalked them off to selfish rebellion. She probably assured herself that the girl would outgrow it. Celia eventually put a lot of miles between herself and her abusive mother, but there remained very unhealthy emotions that miles couldn't erase. Suddenly being thrust into the role of her mother's caregiver reactivated all those old, latent feelings.

I knew in my mind that my mother should no longer be in control of my life, but somewhere inside me she was still able to push all those miserable buttons. She made me angry all over again, and I felt lousy about myself, like I was an imperfect little brat. I felt stupid reverting back to my neurotic lust for food, starving and stuffing my body over and over, but I simply couldn't help myself.

Her mother's doctor was perceptive and could see the problem. He suggested that it might be beneficial if Celia came in for a checkup herself, that taking care of her mother could be harmful for both of them. With the encouragement of her husband, Celia found a live-in health care worker. After awhile it became necessary for her mother to enter a residential home that specialized in caring for Alzheimer's patients. "I make sure all my mother's needs are met and monitor the care she is being given," Celia reported. "I'm doing the best I can for her, and by trying to do the best for myself too, I've regained my health and happiness."

Celia is still struggling with an eating disorder and she sees this as an issue she will have to keep on addressing. She may not be able to renegotiate her mother/daughter life-tie and help with her mother's illness, but Celia is getting her master's degree in gerontology and plans to work with elderly patients. Celia feels that by helping others with conditions similar to her mother's, she is also working through many of her mother/daughter issues. With brief counseling, Celia's full expression of selfhood and recovery was based on her reappraisal of the events of her whole life—including insight into the significance of her mother's limitations. Forgiveness followed.

The 1990s and beyond will see people living much longer lives. Many adult children, especially women, will be thrust into a caregiving role for a parent, usually an elderly mother. (For a neglected parent's perspective on this issue, see *As We Are Now* by May Sarton [1973], a novel in the form of a diary of a retired female schoolteacher who is put in a nursing home by her daughter.) Daughters and their mothers will probably find themselves renegotiating their relationships, especially when the daughter adopts a mothering role. Old feelings will reappear, some warm and nurturing, others perhaps wounding and hurtful. Some adult daughters, like Celia, may be in a position to renegotiate the relationship through counseling in order to rebuild and fortify the sense of self and clarify their real identities without the presence of their mothers. The close mother/daughter tie, once severed by time, distance and events, will present itself again and again to be reshaped. This process usually enhances the personal maturity of each.

The Guilt-Laden Tie

Guilt is a powerful emotional control that levels any human playing field with a force that immobilizes and is sometimes impossible to shake over time. Guilt can transform powerlessness into a form of misguided power. Guilt delivers the message that someone else is responsible for another's sadness and misery. Thus, it is highly significant that the study findings show that 62% of women surveyed felt that their mothers made them feel guilty. Because females are so emotionally entwined with their mothers it is hard for both to put distance on this relationship, especially in their later years.

Annette says that she was brought up on "mother's milk"—with a large portion of it soured by mother-induced guilt. It was easy enough to be weaned from mother's milk, but it took decades before she could be weaned from mother's guilt. Forty-six-year-old Annette sat in the chair nervously twisting her long, naturally curly hair. The more she talked about her mother, the more she twisted her hair.

> I've made an uneasy peace with memories of my mother . . . or maybe I should say I've made a tentative peace with myself. It's taken me years to shed most of that old guilt-tie. It's taken years to really know "me" and what I'm all about. I' m okay now; I like the fit of the new me, and I hope to keep it.
>
> After difficulty attempting to conceive, with two miscarriages, my mother finally produced her "perfect" little girl, complete with a curl in the middle of her forehead—me. My early years were spent trying desperately to please myself while trying to please my mother. I was happiest sitting on my rocking horse in front of the TV watching Annie Oakley, the Cisco Kid and the Lone Ranger. I would put on my cowgirl outfit, complete with holster and guns and enter the make believe world of good guys and bad guys. When I was older, my mother was happiest when I was twirling around a dance floor in white tulle and satin ballet slippers or parading around a stage as the next 'Little Miss Something' hopeful. I was her pretty little doll.

"Voyez, mais ne touchez pas!" You can look, but don't touch! I used to get a lot of compliments from people. Mother just sort of shrugged them off, saying, "Well, she is just as nice as she looks!"

My mother was able to believe in this too-good-to-be-true image of me until my teen years. It was then that the pretty little doll came out of the glass case, and boys weren't paying a bit of attention to a look-but-don't-touch girl. Mama's doll had a loud mouth, though. In rebellion, and making a bid for independence, she started to smoke, and her pretty, white tulle was turned in for tight skirts that were five inches above her knees. Mama went simply berserk. She rocketed into orbit over this socialized, teen image. She was losing control fast, and every time she saw me, she became absolutely hysterical.

This mother's fears of losing control (stemming from her own anxious dependency) were so great that she stifled all Annette's attempts to explore the shadowy areas of her persona.

Mom eventually regained her control of me with large displays of self-pity and big doses of heavy guilt. She would promptly become pathetically sick every time I did something that she didn't like. It worked for a very long time—way past my adolescence—and spread into many areas of my later life. I had such a hard time trying to turn off those messages that she had drummed into my head. The worst part about it was that she believed the things she would say. They made me feel like I was an ugly, miserable human being, and that I not only brought pain and suffering to her, but to everyone else.

The mother/daughter tie was in a stranglehold knot, until Annette physically broke the tie by getting married right after high school and joined her husband in Oregon while he waited to be shipped out to Vietnam. The physical distance between mother and daughter relieved immediate tensions, but Annette carried this baggage of guilt into other areas of her life.

Annette's image of herself was completely identified with her mother's image of her. Annette never had a "me"; it was always an integral "we" image. Annette's identity was never separate or independent from her mother's reflection. Her mother mirrored back to Annette feelings of unworthiness and selfishness. When Annette looked into her psychological mirror, she did not see her own reflection, rather she saw her mother's imperfect portrayal of her image. This distortion in her mind was shattered by the pressures of adapting to her peers in high school. Her mutual interest in boys naturally prompted her to explore her own sexuality, and to strive for individuality. She pulled away from her mother's domination. But her mother reacted as if these changes represented extreme rejection. As if fighting for self-preservation, she fired back with the best ammunition she had—large doses of guilt. Being immature, the mother's loss of control over her dependency object made her sick with fear. She made Annette feel pity and suffer responsibility for the symptomatology she was exhibiting. Because Annette was also immature, the effect was potent.

Hurling guilt can be an effective strategy. Guilt is a projection of self-pity, a tool of some weak and dependent people. The mother/ daughter tie was a Gordian knot, until Annette was able to break it by getting married and moving far away from her mother. By joining her husband, she managed to shift her dependency and recover from abuse. Even so, Annette was to carry the feeling of guilt subconsciously in her brain, like a bullet in a spring-action gun. She couldn't feel comfortable asserting her own ideas because of lingering self-doubt. When her husband went away on duty in Vietnam, she was on her own. She got a job and went out on Friday evenings with some of the young women she met at work. It was innocent enough fun, but when her in-laws questioned these activities, she stopped immediately. She couldn't stand the guilty feeling she derived from their suspicions, and on the edge of her mind was the anxiety that she might make her mother-in-law ill.

The residue of guilt continued to haunt Annette. When her husband came back from Vietnam, she wanted to continue working, and aspired to a managerial position open in the department. He disapproved of her working, however, because he wanted her to have a baby, and to stay home and take care of the infant.

> I didn't feel I had any choice in the matter. He had it rough over there, and I felt he deserved some happiness. If I deprived him by not having a baby, I knew I wouldn't be able to live with him and bear such terrible guilt. I wanted to make his pain go away any way I knew how.

The guilt-tie influenced the way Annette raised her own three children. She knew how to react to old feelings of guilt—Mom's old "guilt trip." Annette felt it was her duty to make everyone happy. Her self-worth and identity became tied to fostering everyone's comfort and well-being. Whenever anyone was upset about anything, she'd wonder how she was to blame. It wasn't until her mother became seriously ill with cancer that the two of them began to alter the nature of their life-tie to each other.

> It's only by a lot of confrontation, as well as physical and emotional separation, that my mother and I have been able to let go of my subjugation to her. It's strange, but even though I lived two thousand miles away from her, I always felt connected to her will. I dressed, thought and behaved like an adult, but I really wasn't grown-up enough inside. When my mother got sick and admitted her overwhelming fears about losing me, I began to realize that she herself hadn't matured enough to be grown up. She broke down and confessed that she'd never felt good about herself, and that she wanted me to become the person she wasn't and wanted to be proud of.

In fact, 73% of the women in our survey stated that their parents' self-esteem influenced their own feelings of self-worth.

> My mother was chronologically much older than I, but we were both children emotionally. When my mother was recovering from a cancer operation, we both started healing that thing between us. I'm now forty-six years old, and my mother is seventy-one, but with new understanding, we both feel like full-blown adults for the first time. It was like a miracle!

Annette and her mother were finally able to change their relationship and began to establish separate selves without severing the family tie. The mother/daughter life-tie was reshaped by both of them. As a result of the process, both to be stronger, more independent, and instilled with new, positive feelings of self-esteem. Annette described the change:

> "I've started becoming selfish in healthy ways. I do things that may not please everyone, like buying myself a bottle-green convertible

and listening to old Pink Floyd tapes while taking long drives along dusty back roads by myself. My in-laws think I' m acting foolish and being selfish and scold me for not taking at least one member of my family along on these outings. That's okay with me; I'm entitled!

From Mother to Grandmother to Mother Again

The increasing number of divorces and the devastating financial impact divorce has on women has led to shifts in roles within families. It is hard enough even for couples with dual incomes to provide all the necessities for their families and to secure good care for their children while they work. A disturbing finding of White (1992) is that children of divorce, even after they have left home and their parents enter middle age, receive significantly less support (child care, advice, transportation, loans, etc.) than do children whose parents have remained married.

Divorced women with small children are under an even greater burden to find work. Increasing numbers of women are turning to their parents for financial support, child care and a place to live. A case in point is 30-year-old Marianne.

> My mother was divorced when I was seven years old. She had to work, so my two younger sisters were raised primarily by me. My mother's alimony income was sporadic and not enough to keep us all in decent clothes. It was in the mid-'70s, and there were a lot of TV family shows on the air. I used to be so envious of some of those TV characters! There was one show with Sada Thompson in it. She played the part of a divorced, traditional mother with a large, growing family. They had plenty of problems, but they always got worked out right away under the roof of this beautiful, big, old, shingled house. When I graduated from college I vowed two things: I was going to have a death-do-us-part marriage and some financial security to go with it.

In the 1950s, 1960s, and early 1970s, the media, including TV and magazines, continued to define the all-American family. Many families who watched these shows felt they must be doing something wrong, because their own family didn't mirror the media image at all. Many teens didn't see their own family measuring up to the ideal, and they wondered if the image was reality and whether they were being shortchanged by their families. Divorce and other types of family dysfunction led family members to believe that they were not "good people," for good people, as portrayed by the media, had good marriages, great parents, and a lack of real hardships, insurmountable problems, family secrets, or shame.

Marianne's hope of having an ideal family was a heavenly illusion. After a few years, her husband bailed out of the marriage and out of his job. He suddenly took off on his credit-financed Yamaha bike. Mike left Marianne 2-year-old Tracy to raise alone, a heap of unpaid bills, two months' overdue rent, and a used car that needed a new transmission. Under these circumstances she felt lucky to have a fairly well-paying job as a secretary in a defense plant with day care on the plant site.

But there is only one thing about life that is absolutely certain, and that is change. Six months after Mike left her, the defense plant closed down, and she was out of a job. There was no money for day care and only enough savings to last 2 more months. She lost her apartment and moved back in with her mother and stepfather.

> I was grateful that at least we had a roof over our heads. It was rough for my mom and me for a while. Being back home, I felt like I was a daughter again, not a mother, not even an adult. I had my old room back, and Tracy slept on the other twin bed. My mother had her usual routine and way of running her house. She did things differently from the way I ran my house. When I went out on weekends with friends, she wanted to know who I went with, where I went, and why did I come home so late. When I got another job, it was with less pay, but it relieved some of the strain. But there was an even bigger issue we had to deal with.
>
> While I worked, my mother took care of Tracy. This seemed ideal at first; I didn't have to worry about my child. However, it proved to be too much of a good thing. My mother had always worked, and I missed out on a lot of "mothering stuff." She remarried later in life and was financially secure with lots of time on her hands. Mom obviously felt she had a second shot at being the type of mother she was unable to be when she was raising us. She poured onto Tracy all this mothering stuff. It became the area in which she and I clashed. I also suspected she was trying to undermine my authority with Tracy. I felt that she might even be a better mother than I could be. When I

came home from work, I sometimes was too tired and drained to play with Tracy for any length of time. It seemed like my mom, step-dad and Tracy were the real family. I felt like an intruder, like a fifth wheel.

For about six months I was depressed. I didn't know where I really fit in, like a displaced person. I was no longer a wife or a mother with my own family. I felt I didn't have my own family, just a weekend sort of mom. I had a really good friend at work, though. She gave me a lot of support. I remember she told me I could keep feeling sorry for myself, or that I could start putting some money aside to get a place of my own. On her suggestion, I also sat down with my mother, and we had a good, civilized conversation—our first one in a long time. My mother realized that it wasn't good for Tracy to be so dependent on her and my stepdad. She also said that she wanted to do some traveling with him, and they might even move to a smaller house. Going back to being a grandmother with lots of special visits would be fine, she said. She helped me feel like an adult and a mother again. It took a few more months, and Tracy and I moved into a small apartment. The child soon realized that I'm her mom, that I'm her family, and this is her home. We're not the usual type of family . . . but I don't know too many of those anymore.

Mother/daughter/grandmother role transitions, such as the one Marianne and her mother experienced, will probably be more common as families break apart and stringent economics make it necessary to move back into the original family home. Families will have to explore new emotional territory and find the understanding, patience, and knowledge that will allow new types of family arrangements to grow and flourish. The crisis in Marianne's life put her in a position in which she gave up control of her child and became her mother's little girl again. Her mother was quick to react by becoming overly involved and unknowingly became another instrument of deprivation for her daughter. Eventually they reformulated a new mother/daughter life-tie that incorporated maturity and reality-based problem solving into their adult lives.

Good-Enough Daughter/Good-Enough Mother
Michelle, or Mickee, as she likes to call herself, is a product of "good-enough" mothering. This 33-year-old mother of a son and twin girls looks back on her own childhood with very good memo-

ries of her family, especially of her mother.

My mother told me how she headed off early sibling rivalry between my brother and me when I was first born. While she was still in the hospital, she made sure my father brought home a toy for my brother, Rob, every day, saying it was from his new baby sister. By the time my parents brought me home from the hospital, my little brother thought I was the best thing that had ever happened to him. Even now, as adults, we're very close, and he continues to be protective of his little sister.

We didn't have a whole lot of money in the family while I was growing up, but my mother made sure that a little money was put aside for books, our education, and a few family trips. I remember one time she made sure every one of us saved up money so that the entire family could travel across the country. She herself made arrangements to rent our house while we were away that summer. I think we must have visited every monument and museum in the country. Later I found that it came in handy with my history and geography classes.

My mother was smart, although she never had a regular, paying job while my brother and I were young. She was adamant that we get a good education and then a good job with a good salary. She wanted me to be independent. She knew I was smart and could go far if I wanted to. I did go to college, but I married soon after and became pregnant. For awhile I felt as though I let her down. She would have preferred that I see the world and be a part of it before I settled down. I really wanted that little white house of my dreams, with lots of kids and lots of pets. I guess this was some form of rebellion— being a traditional kind of housewife and stay-at-home mom. I knew it hurt her, because she had been frustrated while staying at home raising a family. She had put all her hopes and plans on her number one, smart daughter. I disappointed her, but she never said anything to me about it.

I think my mother knew that eventually I would use the education she worked so hard to give me to achieve something beyond prosaic domesticity. She was also wise enough to keep quiet about it and not nag me. While studying for a master's degree in gerontology, I'm juggling my husband, house, kids and pets, even including my 200-pound, pot-bellied pig who loves to go for walks with me. Home life still comes first, of course, but everybody is helping out and backing me up one hundred percent. My mom is my biggest cheerleader, and she helps a lot with the kids.

Mickee's life-tie with her mother didn't need a lot of reshaping; it was already the strong bond with her that gave her a positive sense of self-worth. She knew early in her life that having a family would be important to her happiness. Mickee's identity selection as a wife and mother was not as complete as she had anticipated. After the children were older, she felt a tugging for new achievement, a need to draw on her other strengths and integrate something more into her self-image. After her father died, she saw her mother get a job and then become active in community life, serving on a local political board and joining civic societies. Her mother blossomed with new vigor; thus she again set a good example.

It was after she watched her mother's life take a new direction that Mickee felt able to take the big growth step of going for a master's degree. She is naturally a little apprehensive about returning to school, but by taking one or two courses at a time, she is slowly and steadily building up her credits and her confidence. Mickee is reshaping her identity, adding new facets to an already complex lifestyle. But with her already strong sense of self, she continues to build both her castle in the sky and her self-esteem.

Adult Daughters and Fathers

My Father In My Dreams
I've been all things in
dreams and know myself
too well but you
whose flesh is spent, come scarcely, like a shadow
dark across the moon
and whisper past me warm
against my cheek
in tired dreams
night after night, I sink
beneath the weight
of wanting you

— *Susan A. Katz*

   This poem tells poignantly about a daughter's need for her elu-
sive father. What is known about fathers is relative to their absence.
Much has been written about the relationship between mothers
and their children, but there has been very little investigation of
how a father parents and how he influences the personality development of his children. Michael Lamb (1987) described fathers as
the forgotten contributors to child development.

   Where are the fathers and what is their role in relation to their
daughters? Are they nurturers or are they just financial providers?
The image of father conjures up words that have to do with disciplinary power, authority, money, and silence. Our culture does little to prepare men for parental involvement with their children. As
previously noted, since the 19th century, the activities of fathers
have kept them away from the home most of the time. This gender
split was due more to travel associated with wage earning than to
choice or other social issues. Was it nature's intention that fathers
be so peripheral?

   In the animal world, fathering is very important—perhaps essential—for group survival. As Johnson and Ferguson noted in 1990,
male marmosets assist with the birth of their infants. They carry the
babies around during the day, except when the mother is nursing
them. Siamang gibbon babies are cared for after the first year by
the fathers' grooming and sleeping with the juveniles. Male
macaques teach their infants to walk, and male rhesus monkeys
take care of their infants whenever the mother, is absent.

   From a human cross-cultural perspective, there are many different fathering styles. In Botswana, Bushmen fathers pamper and
spoil their children. Each parent works half the day for food and
spends the other half in leisure and family activities. The children
are close to their fathers and are never ignored. Melanesian fathers
take care of the children while the women work in the garden, and
groups of men gather together to play with infants and children.

   One characteristic stands out among cultures that have involved
fathers: Warfare is almost nonexistent. There are actually some
areas in the world where food and other provisions are so abundant
in the natural environment that rivalry and competition are rare
and avarice and warfare are unknown. Such places can offer fathers
more opportunity to be family oriented. The same probably is true
of animals.

In contrast, the nomadic Bedouins of Arabia are warriors; fighting is part of their culture. Their society is patriarchal, and gender roles are sharply divided. Fathers are not involved with children. Societies competing for scarce provisions and food engage in warfare and, adjusting to this, tend to differentiate the activities of men and women. It would seem to follow that discipline is more important for group survival in a warring society, and authority and its enforcement would be delegated to the physically stronger sex. By the same token, among societies that are not so heavily invested in warfare, the involvement of men in parenting increases. Paternal nurturing of children also increases when the society needs and values the work of its women.

What is a father's reaction when he suddenly hears the doctor's voice say, "It's a girl!"? Will he be excited, joyful, or disappointed? Did the father hope for a little warrior to fight by his side or a beautiful little female as a love object? Many women have wanted to give their husband a son, some keep trying until, luck be willing, they succeed. In our competitive society, "fathering" has implied being closely aligned with raising a son, but not a daughter. A father's expectations for a daughter could be summed up by the nursery rhyme, "Sugar and spice and everything nice." The concerns of fathers have revolved around providing security and safety and eventually finding a princely protector for a marriageable daughter. Whatever his intentions, a father—either by his absence or his involvement—will have a great impact on the positive or negative self-image a daughter will embrace well into adulthood.

There just isn't enough valid information in the form of literature and obvious tradition to decipher and analyze the daughter/father bond. We have discovered that women find it difficult to talk about their fathers. The daughter/father tie has been left in limbo for too long. There have been only two common ways that the father/daughter bond has been described. Freud (1935) looked at this bond in terms of the Oedipus complex; that is, the supposed sexual feelings a daughter has for her father. The other observation has centered around the *institutionalized power of fathers*, the system in which men have determined what part women in general (their mothers, daughters, and wives) should play in society.

In various and limited ways, fathers have been described as shadowy and obscure in the background, very attentive or completely

absent, overpoweringly authoritarian, gentle, charming but ineffectual, loyal to a fault, drunk and violent, or cloaked—in the dark-
est descriptions—of possessiveness and incest. Ursula Owens
(1985) has observed two important daughter themes: the need to
please father and the need to win his approval. Sometimes a daughter becomes the "chosen one" in her father's eye. In exchange for
being the chosen one, a daughter may have to return extraordinary
loyalty to her father for acceptance into his world and for being
under his protection.

Daughters who idolize their fathers tend to undervalue their
mothers as if blind to their qualities. A mother's world in the eyes
of her daughter is the everyday world, the meeting place of daily
needs. Even though some mothers work outside the home, their
children only see them engaged in the mundane images of nurturing and housework. The father's world is still the outside, exciting
marketplace, the field of action, the all-encompassing, "out-there"
world. In our society, motherhood is considered a necessary job;
fathering is considered an optional hobby. Fathers who may want
participation in nurturing and housekeeping activities find few role
models to emulate.

The function of male parenting a daughter, however underrat-
ed, is greatly needed to encourage and instill value, competence,
self-worth and respect in his daughter. For example, her image of
him can be the reference frame for the man she selects to marry. A
woman who has a close, healthy tie with her father can identify with
his good qualities, will entertain a healthy self-regard, and will be
more likely to form emotionally stable relationships. A father who
is emotionally connected with his daughter will lend balance to the
parental roles in the family

The NCWRR study found that almost 50% of women feel that
their father was, and still continues to be, a strong influence in
their adult life, but it is also significant that 23% of women believe
that their father was never a strong influence while they were growing in childhood or during adulthood. The adult daughters who
were interviewed and who perceive their fathers as a continuing
influence were split between those who see that influence as positive and those who see it as negative.

The Chosen Daughter

As past research shows, all too often what is written and heard about fathers relates to their absence and emotional neglect (Greenberg, 1991; Huyck, 1989). However, when fathers are involved in positive ways, their influence on their children proves to be a crucial factor in their balanced personality growth and personal development into adulthood (Bengtson, Rosenthal, & Burton, 1990; Matthews & Sprey, 1989). In short, a healthy balance of mothering and fathering is needed to produce "whole" men and women.

Judy, at age 45, says that it's about time she down-shifted her fast-paced lifestyle. She realizes she needs more time to devote to a new relationship and that she has to apply herself to doing some free-lance work in the country. Her midlife dream sounds like the dreams many men have described as they reach this place in life, only she is a woman who shares this similar vision.

> My grandfather and my father were the strongest and best forces in my life. Even though I had two younger brothers, I was the bright star that shined in their eyes. They actually believed there was nothing I couldn't do. They both played a very active part in my childhood: Storytelling, sports, games, and most important, the way they always listened to what I had to say. I was included in their life as an important person. They grew up to become aggressive, larger-than-life men with a "can-do" attitude that they passed on to me. I considered my mother to be a "rabbit." She was afraid of everything and everyone. I couldn't respect the weakness and timidity part of her. And I wasn't very nice about it. I often deliberately did things that would scare her.

This was a case of Judy being the chosen one of her father. In order to keep this prestigious position, she devalued her mother, and her pranks and contempt created a great deal of emotional distance between them.

> I was and still am a tomboy. In the late 1950s I was the first girl to get my own paper route. A paper route is traditionally passed on from one boy to another boy. I saved money and bought a route from another boy. I kept that route for a long time. I was fast, delivered the papers on time, threw them in the right spot and was friendly. I

got great tips and I got my first sense of independence through earn-ing money. I made more money than a lot of the other guys. I really liked to compete and be the best. Yes, I was and still am, a tomboy.

My father had a lot of faith in me and encouraged me to go to col-lege. He didn't believe that either of my brothers was capable enough, and they didn't seem interested in going on to school. I kept on competing and kept on winning. I was the "son" my father was proud of.

My mother always seemed to be in the background, always getting upset by my father screaming. My father is Italian and doesn't talk, he shouts or screams. I am also a screamer. My mother is quiet. She was always getting upset about my father yelling. I am also a shouter and not like my mother. Whenever my father and I got into one of our shouting matches, she just vanished into her garden to weed some peppers.

When I look back on my life I see so many accomplishments. After college I worked for several advertising agencies, and over the years started a small agency with a partner. For the last 15 years I have run my own company. I doubt if I could have achieved all I did without the influence and strong encouragement of my father. He was always there for me and behind me one hundred percent. He is close to eighty now, but is still strong, opinionated and full of robust life. When I look at him I see so much of myself. My confidence, identity, and personhood derive so much from his active presence in my life."

A father who encourages and participates in the personal events of his daughter's life will probably give her high self-esteem and a strong identity. As Judy sat in the office recounting her early rela-tionship with her father, she was very theatrical. Her voice was loud, her gestures were extravagant, and she would laugh forcefully, but she suddenly became quiet when I asked about her present life, and how she sees her future.

I want to get out of my business, get out of the city and I want to stop living in an airplane. I am in my late forties, I had one bad early mar-riage, but I have been in a really important relationship for the last two years. I find myself spending more time at my country home just wanting to be peaceful. The surprising thing is that I see myself taking on more of my mother's qualities, qualities I never valued when younger. I have a new love of gardening, something my mother would spend hours doing. I find myself digging up the earth, thinking about what I want to plant, all sorts of combinations of vegetables and flowers. I spend more time with my mother. I've come to realize that she was always the mediator between my father and me. I care about what she feels and thinks. I will always be flamboyant and competitive like my father, but I also realize that much of who I am becoming now is like my mother. I see myself as an integration of both.

Judy is very insightful about how her identity changed in adulthood. We found her identity and personal narrative heavily weighted with her father's image when she spoke of her early life. The shape of her identity altered as she grew older. Her sense of self-worth and ideas began to include some of the good qualities of her mother. Her story reveals the importance of good fathering as well as the need to balance and incorporate the qualities of both parents.

The Power to Wound

The family life-tie may continue to exert an influence and elements of control even after a parent dies. Alice, who works as a successful freelance artist, recalled the time when she first went away to college:

I was looking through the course catalogue and came upon one called Behavioral Psychology. I thought, Now there's a course for me. I assumed it had something to do with informing people how to become a well-behaved and successful person. You have to understand that ever since I was a little girl, my father drummed into my head the word *behave*. The word *behave* was inscribed onto my brain.

My father was a powerful influence in my life. Even though he is now dead, his way is still with me. The death of my brother sent my mother into a long and deep depression. My care was left primarily to my father and to a Polish maid who took care of me while my father worked. My father was authoritarian, a very Germanic character. To please my father I had to be totally obedient and obey his every word or suffer physical consequences. While growing up I was always afraid, but I thought everyone lived this way—that is, lived to be obedient.

> As a teenager I became totally afraid of him, my fear turned to hate because of the control he had over me. I tried very hard to get As; I tried hard to be a good student; I tried hard in my acting lessons and my piano lessons; I tried mainly to obey and please him. I never could. . . . I thought it was all my doing. I felt lousy about myself for so long. Any free time I had was spent working in his factory. For a long time he repressed all my feelings. Everything went inward. I was about eighteen when doctors diagnosed my severe pains were a result of ulcers. I kept it all in.
>
> Going away to college helped, but he was still controlling me. It was an emotional dance we were both locked into. My mother had emotionally withdrawn, my brother had died, so I was the target for his crazy need to control people. When I finally broke away and decided to get married, he died a month after my wedding

Alice was held in the emotional grip of her father for many years, even after his death. His influence contributed to her poor self-image. Early in her life, her father's authoritarian and abusive influence led her to blame herself for not being pleasing enough. She developed a pattern of choosing relationships with controlling men. Her low self-esteem continued from childhood into adolescence and into her married life.

Later in adulthood, Alice wove into her life the one positive aspect of her father's influence—discipline. This ingrained part of her personality helped her harness and exploit her creative, artistic potentialities. She became an accomplished artist; and it lifted her spirits and sense of self-worth. The destructive legacy of negative control that had held Alice emotionally captive for so long was finally defused by turning her father's one good influence, self-discipline, into a resource for positive self-development.

Phantom Fathers and Abusive Replacements

Often when a father has abandoned his family, the mother becomes an exaggerated "phantom father" to her children. She becomes overly strict, occasionally abusive physically, and emotionally distant. Until she remarried, Edith's mother became this exaggerated caricature of masculinity at its worst.

> My mother told me it was a man's world and each woman should

have the need to strive for independence. She was absent for many of my early childhood years and she was resentful for having to raise me and my brother. When I became very sick and had to be nursed for months, my brother was the one to take care of me.

You can imagine how happy my brother and I were when she remarried. It was a war romance. It was love at first sight. My mother became calm, gentle, she laughed again. My stepfather brought a good calm into the house. It was perfect, except for one thing: He fondled my breasts and continued to touch me until he grew too old to be interested. I kept it to myself. He was a saint to everybody. I rationalized it later by saying that he was from a big Russian family and they did this sometimes, it was almost cultural.

Edith had a very distorted and confused sense of herself. "Everyone loved my new father, but he made me feel dirty and I blamed myself." She reasoned that if everyone loved this man, what he did to her must be okay. She kept thinking that, if it was wrong, then it must be her fault. Edith kept the abuse a secret from everyone, especially from her mother. She didn't want to make waves, because ever since her mother's remarriage, she had became a contented and happy woman. She started showing affection, attention and care toward her children. Edith went on to state: "If I told her what my stepfather was doing to me, it would have destroyed her and maybe her marriage. I expected it would make her the miserably unhappy and abusive person she used to be."

Edith carried the secret of abuse into her adult years. The episodes with her stepfather negatively influenced her self-image and her identity. Her only means of defense in her late teens was overeating. She assumed, perhaps unconsciously, that if she became obese, he wouldn't want to touch her any more. Since then, Edith has had eating and weight problems. Her self-esteem was the first thing to be damaged, and it remained low for many years. After she married, she could never tell her husband or children about the abuse, for they also were very fond of the man. In fact, she remarked that her niece told her she didn't want to marry until she found someone like her uncle.

Edith developed in other areas of her life. She became professionally successful, establishing an independent nursing practice.

Even so, her sense of self is still influenced by her stepfather's misconduct. "It's getting a little better," she explained. "But even now, years later, when I talk about him, I feel as though I'm pushing something uphill. Keeping this awful secret has been such a struggle!"

Her stepfather is a very old man now, living in a nursing home. She rarely visits him and doesn't stay long. She finds it very difficult fielding questions from relatives about him. Some of them are perplexed and don't understand her obvious, relative withdrawal from his life. Edith began recounting her story in the privacy of counseling and now, at age fifty-five, and having let go of the secret, she is shedding pounds and feeling free of self-loathing.

The Legacy of Protective Daughters

As noted above, daughters who are the chosen one must sometimes go to extraordinary lengths to keep that favored position and maintain approval and self-esteem. Carolyn, now retired and widowed, was just such a daughter. She was the bright star in a family with six children. Her father, a wealthy man, emigrated from Vienna with his family. Her mother was from a poor family, but she was an extremely beautiful woman. Carolyn was the smartest of all her siblings. Her mother encouraged her to learn all she could and make something of herself, but it was her father's approval that really mattered to her. He kept telling Carolyn that he loved her the best.

> I was supposed to be a boy, so I behaved like a boy. I even tried to be like a boy to please him. I wore my hair short, and I rode my brother's bike. I did please him, for I was the only one he allowed to talk back to him.

The handsome and charismatic man lavished praise and attention on Carolyn, but it came with a price.

> My father was a charming man, but not responsible. He always had a job, but would get bored with it and leave. He was not good with money and what with eight in our family, my mother would have to go and pick up his paycheck so he would not spend it on alcohol. I'm afraid that's not the only thing he spent his money on—he was always chasing the women. My mother never knew this. I was the one who was designated to keep and protect this secret.

Carolyn lived in Greenwich Village in New York City. Her home was lovely and she credits her mother with maintaining and making it a place of love and joy. It would be her father's desecration of her home that finally broke that powerful father/daughter tie, but that would be much later. In her father's eyes, Carolyn was the "boy" of the family and was rewarded with many freedoms and encouraged in her independence. Her freedom, however, was spurious, paid for by the obligation to be party to the web of deceit that her father had created.

> I loved my home, my mother and my two brothers and three sisters, but in order to keep everything intact and my family together, I had to work like crazy to make my father appear like a loving and devoted husband and family man.
>
> It started when I was about fifteen. I would get a call from my father telling me to pick him up at such and such an address. I'd call a taxi and go there. Sometimes I'd have to wait in that taxi for almost an hour until my father came out. You see, he'd be bedded down with one of his several mistresses. I knew that. He couldn't get home on his own, because he usually had had too much to drink. So I would wait, he would get into the taxi, and on the way home he'd be thinking up some excuse to tell my mother. This went on for many years.

When Carolyn stated that this father/daughter relationship went on for years, it was an understatement. The aftereffects of this collusion persisted well into Carolyn's middle years. Besides being a confidante, she was an achiever, and her father had an important and positive influence on her later success in school and in the field of fashion design. But it was the darker side of this father/daughter tie that molded and shaped her sense of self for many years.

> I kept thinking it was my job to protect everyone who meant something to me. I saw myself as the angelic protector. If I succeeded in hiding or disguising somebody's secret problem, I felt good about myself. This complex I had continued way into my later life. You see, by sharing this secret with my father, I believed I was giving my family security and stability. It had become something good I could do and do well. This idea continued even after I was married, because

at that time it made a lot of sense to me. My husband loved my parents. We all became very close. There was harmony, and I felt responsible for it. As long as I was doing my job, I felt good about myself. I had a good family, and therefore I was good.

Carolyn's identity as the family protector was ultimately shattered when she was in her forties. Her mother was visiting some relatives in Rhode Island for 2 weeks, and father was supposed to be staying at home. Carolyn lived in a suburban town but occasionally went to the city to check on her father to see if he needed anything. She opened his bedroom door and discovered her seventy-something father intimately entertaining a woman in her mother's bed. In disgust, she threw the woman out. Then, still shocked and angry, she walked out, visualizing the destruction of the home and family that she loved, cherished and had grown up in. Having broken the bond with her father, she was now willing to accept the loss of her title, role and identity as the favored, dutiful and protective daughter. For about 5 years afterward, father and daughter didn't speak to each other.

It was during this interim that she discovered a lot more ability in herself than just being a "daughter-protector." As she continued her life narrative, she began to reveal aspects of her personality that included genuine achievement. She had let her siblings worry about the parents and concentrated on doing something with her own life. She established her own small design business. It took a lot of effort and time for her to get this business off the ground, but her investment in energy and diligence was well spent—and not only from a business standpoint.

Being on her own, Carolyn's self-esteem skyrocketed. She felt competent, comfortable, and proud of her accomplishments. She reconciled with her father, but her own growth as a person during the 5 years of separation from him helped to transform her relationship with him into one of caring and friendship. With her business success, independence and newly-oriented self-esteem, her ego no longer needed to lean on her father's favoritism. Nor did she need to function as the protector of her mother and her family's home. Growing with her own potentials and strengths has permitted the adjustment of the father/daughter relationship.

Adult Sons and Fathers

"There is not enough father."

—Robert Bly

That was a statement heard again and again by author and poet Robert Bly at his men's gatherings. Bly (1990) described this repetitive outcry as *father-hunger*. He sensed that boys and men must often feel a great void in their life because they lacked the presence of a father.

There seems to be a lot of internal grieving by adult sons for an emotionally or physically absent father. Since the Industrial Revolution, sons have been raised mainly by a mother. It usually isn't that fathers are purposely doing wrong by their sons; rather, the imbalance that has resulted from the clash of industrial and preindustrial values has left sons aware of a partial vacuum in parenting.

The relationship that was most harmed by the Industrial Revolution was the father/son tie. Before the Industrial Revolution, fathers taught and lived physically close to their sons. Sons were taught a trade, carpentry, or perhaps farming by their fathers. Sons knew where their fathers were during the day, they were able to understand the work they did, and could participate in the world of their fathers. Fathers were an actual physical presence; they were their sons' teachers, mentors, and life guides.

The Industrial Revolution took fathers away from the home every day, all day, to some distant factory or office. Their sons had no way of seeing or understanding the daily activities of their fathers. In this separation, sons necessarily spent more time in the company of women: mothers, sisters, female relatives, and female teachers. In the 18th century and earlier, a family's prosperity and a man's economic worth were derived from his property, particularly inherited property, and from what his property could produce; in the 19th century and later, his worth and status became dependent on his capacity to earn by industrial labor.

Gradually our society put more importance and value on mental work over physical labor. Sons learned to feel shame for a father who worked at manual labor for a living. To surmount the necessity of doing physical work, subsequent generations of sons turned to education to sharpen their reasoning ability and advance their knowledge. This movement gave them less in common with their father and diluted the tie. Since intellectual labor is taught in institutions, and sometimes at a distance, the father/son bond weakened.

These new generations of adult sons with families of their own now work in distant offices away from their home and family of origin. Unfortunately, the father/son split continues to widen, for men who work long hours in offices have nothing tangible to show and share with their sons. It is too difficult for a father to explain the world of papers, memos, files, and reports to young sons who like to hold, feel, and see things. There are very few adult sons who have memories of sitting on the seat of a tractor with the father, leaving at dawn with him to ride into town for supplies, or perhaps accompany and help him on his commercial fishing boat. A son who is not secure in the knowledge of what a father does, where he is, or who he is, may enter adulthood insecure in his own identity and self-image.

The image of the father has become obscured, set in a world that is ghost-like, with little form or shape. When a father returns home from work, the son can only vicariously perceive the man's tiredness, his remoteness and his shortness of temper. When a father is present, he can appear weak and insignificant. Fathers no longer fill the large, empty space in a room. Sons have grown into adulthood with an image of their fathers existing as shadows sitting behind a rustling newspaper.

Kupers (1993) states that many a son thinks that his father is powerful enough to make the world a safe and secure place for him. Disillusionment follows when the boy finds out that his dad is really not all that powerful. If this disillusionment happens in small ways, a son will be able to cope with the reality as he goes, and learn that all men are imperfect and that none are all-powerful. If abrupt and intense disillusionment occurs, such as a father's unemployment with resulting hardship, imprisonment, abandonment or abuse, a son's adult development may suffer.

Robert Bly (1990) believes that men must settle left-over conflicts with their father if they are to become whole. He also states that men need to accept and approve of their father's life in order to become whole. When sons grow up within the shadow of a father who is a bad role model, the son may face a challenge during his adult years to overcome the father's influence and behavior patterns that might make up his own.

Many men have grown up with a father who was physically and/or emotionally abusive. Such fathers may be substance abusers, workaholics, wife-beaters, brutish and punitive tyrants, or simply detached, rejecting and abandoning phantoms who leave the family completely. Growing up unhappy and grieving in the dark side of a father can be a heavy challenge for his growth in adulthood. Bly believes that in order for a man to continue to develop in adulthood he must learn to be empathetic with his father, to heal the wounded father by seeing him as handicapped, by accepting life without him and by giving up the wish that the father will take care of him. Seeing his father as humanly limited allows the son to accept his own frailties.

The father/son adult life-tie and the process of separating and connecting continues over the course of life. The stories, emotional responses, conflicts, joys and pains associated with the parent-tie are experienced the same way by men and women. Both women and men share this process of reshaping the tie and improving their sense of self within the family setting. The character of the changed and usually improved relationship will allow the sons' identity and self-image to continue to be reshaped and developed in adulthood.

The NCWRR study found that men, much like the women in our study, continue to be influenced and shaped in adulthood by the father life-tie. Their narratives demonstrated the incorporation or absence of the father/son bond in adulthood. Over 50% of men stated that their father was, and still is, an important influence on the character of their sense of self in adulthood.

Absent Without Leave

Often it is the absence of a father that packs an influential wallop on the development of a child, especially a son. Twenty-eight-year-old Joseph was raised by his Latino grandmother, mother, and one older sister. His life and identity have been marked by the absence of fathering and the absence of any predominant male figure.

Joseph's father never existed for him as a physical presence, but his abandonment has shaped the way he views himself and his masculinity.

The only fathers I saw growing up were on television. They were all white, could deal with problems in a half hour and they all lived in houses that some of my friends and I would have liked to rip off years ago. These types of fathers might just as well have been aliens living on Mars. That's as much as I could have identified with them.

"My mother worked as a seamstress, my grandmother was home taking care of us in our Brooklyn apartment. We were lucky, we had a two-bedroom apartment. My grandmother and mother shared one bedroom and my sister and I shared the other, until I got too old. When I was thirteen I started sleeping on the living-room couch. Money came from my mother's job and my grandmother's disability check. No father ever dropped any money off for us kids.

"I asked my mother when I was a little kid about my father. She and my father were just teenagers when they had me and my sister. He hung around for awhile when my sister was born, but when my mother got pregnant with me he got scared and took off for Texas. He never even stuck around to see what I looked like.

The lack of a male father figure and the heavy influence of females in Joseph's life produced in him a defense mechanism in which he emphasized the most extreme characteristics of masculinity. As a teenager Joseph's only male role models were thugs who hung out on the street, looking tough and acting tough. Trouble became the hallmark of masculinity for Joseph. After dropping out of school, he found plenty of it.

I was in trouble with the law as a juvenile and then after I was eighteen I was treated like an adult. Being treated like an adult meant I got a couple of short jail terms—no more juvenile halls. I was involved with stealing from stores, breaking into houses, and I mugged a few people. I never dealed [sic] drugs.

I grew up thinking that to be a man meant being tough. If I went to the farthest extreme from what my mother and grandmother were, then I would be a man. Having no "old man" around meant that I had to look for the most obvious signs of manhood. Those signs of manhood that I grew up with always involved some kind of violence—like getting in fights."

Joseph spent his early twenties in a correctional facility. It was here that he had some other male role models for reference points, but this time they were helpful. He got his Graduate Equivalency Diploma (G. E. D.) and acquired some insight through psychological counseling. Maintaining the prison garden plus some reading led to a job on the outside as a landscaper.

It has been five years since Joseph has been in any kind of trouble. He knows now how to select his comrades. He moved into a suburban community and has been working as a landscaper for three years. It took him about four tries to find the right job, but then he stuck with it. He married, and his wife's pregnancy has triggered thoughts about being a father and thoughts about his absent father. He hasn't stopped resenting the father who deserted him and his mother and sister. Becoming a father himself scares him. Joseph is still trying to build an image of himself that includes some respectable aspects of his phantom father. He learned a few things about his father by talking with those of the man's relatives who remained in the New York area. He found out that his father loved playing basketball, an enthusiasm that he has also come to share. His father liked to rebuild car engines; he finds himself tinkering with old cars.

In coming to terms with his anger by understanding that his father also had handicaps and was just a kid himself when he had a baby, Joseph has accepted the man's failings. This empathetic, mature perspective has helped him understand his own fears and accept his own limitations. He can see that he is in some ways connected to the man, yet separate. His identity has become clearer with the understanding of differences that exist between himself and his father. Joseph is not a quitter, and although he feels in the dark about fatherhood, he's not going to bolt from his family or from the job of learning the ways of husband and father. Joseph said it best: " I want to create a safe place for my kid to grow in, and that means his 'old man' is definitely going to be around for the long haul. It's not going to be easy—no television storybook life, but I'm going to give it a good shot."

Remote Fathers

Forty-two-year-old Paul recalled that, when he was a child of eight, his mother would take him with her to the train station every evening to meet her husband. At this time in the daily routine, she always admonished Paul: "Don't upset your father. He's had a hard day." Paul would sit quietly in the back seat while he watched his father start to unwind from a day in the city where he was occupied with charts with numbers in columns for reports.

> My father's unwinding consisted of ranting, raving, bitching and griping about all the people he had to put up with at the office. From the time he got off the train to our arrival home, he'd go from loud anger to quiet sullenness.
>
> At home before dinner, he'd finish reading the newspaper he'd started on the train and slowly polish off a few Scotches. I watched this man all the years of my childhood. Most of that time he was a mysterious person, like a stranger, sitting with a paper in front of him or watching the evening news on TV. On rare weekends he'd sweep up his family and take us on some kind of junket. Those times were adventuresome and interesting, but they didn't bring me closer to the man. Dinner conversation was formal and table manners were disciplined—by my mother. His inquisitiveness about my life was consistently limited to whatever I might have done in school that day. Most of the time I thought it best to stay out of the way; my problems were handled by my mother.

Paul had a father in residence, but he didn't have the slightest notion what the man was all about.

> I was trained to stay quiet around him. I remember listening intensely to see what clues I could pick up about him. But it just didn't happen. When I did screw up one way or another, I'd hear his angry voice rebuking me, but he wouldn't show me how to do better. He usually talked to my mother about himself, how he worked too hard, and when I made a mistake, he'd complain that he shouldn't have to cope with a troublesome kid on top of everything. He always seemed to feel real sorry for himself.

Remote fathers wake up to the realities of a son's life when it is time for the son to leave home, a time when decisions must be made. Such fathers tend to become suddenly active and involved. They try to direct the son down some familiar road that they themselves have taken. Recent research supports the contention that middle-aged fathers psychologically "rehearse" the departure from home of an adult child (Greene & Boxer, 1986) and are ready to help their sons (and daughters) as necessary; fathers are more likely than mothers to take pleasure in assisting their children to initiate adult undertakings (Huyck, 1989). Paul's father did have such an awakening. Paul was eighteen and ready to embark on life as a beginning adult. He suddenly found his father fully engaged in his life, taking charge much like a general planning a campaign. Paul listened to advice about colleges, business schools and careers. His father obviously wanted him to follow in his footsteps and become an accountant or, if not that, perhaps to go into the brokerage trade.

> I didn't know what hit me, suddenly I was showered with attention from my father. I guess to please him and keep all this new attention I had craved as a kid, I opted for college and then got an MBA. Big mistake! I drifted through college in somewhat of a fog, was scared to death in business school, but got through barely. It was as if I was on remote control with somebody else pushing the buttons. I didn't have a clue as to what I really wanted at age twenty-three. Who does?
>
> I started down the same path as my father, it was familiar and I was being pushed in that direction. The only difference was that I was going to be a stock broker—a manipulator of money instead of a bean counter. He was my only glimpse as to what being an adult man was all about—my father was it. It was like pretending to be somebody I wasn't cut out to be. I was mimicking a poor imitation of my father—he was never happy and I had become unhappy. If I had stayed with the world according to my father I would have had a very sad life.

Paul worked in the brokerage business for about 10 years. Then the recession hit and he was out of a job.

> For about ten years I pretended to be someone I really wasn't. When the recession hit and I got laid off I felt relief for the first time in my

adult life. My wife went into a tailspin. She worked part-time as a travel agent but her job would not support her in the lifestyle she was
used to. It got ugly for awhile. I was starting to downsize my life and
my needs; she couldn't adjust. We divorced and she eventually
remarried another fancy lifestyle.

His father never understood why Paul didn't go back into the
brokerage business. They argued bitterly about it. Paul finally
stopped talking to his parents altogether for about two years. He
was already thirty-seven years old when he decided it was time for
him to find out what he really wanted out of life. Although chronologically an adult, his decisions and choices had only reflected the
selections made for him by others.

One of the marks of adulthood is making your own choices and
taking responsibility for them. Paul decided to separate himself
from all the things that were familiar, easiest and safe. He had to
separate from his father's dominance. Paul moved out West for a
while and took odd jobs doing house painting, putting up fences,
working as a tour guide, and working with a stone mason. It took
him a couple of years to find out what he liked to do and was good
at. What he liked most was to work with wood. Soon after he started as a carpenter's helper, he discovered his love of building wood-
en things with his hands. The idea of making something fine and
beautiful from start to completion made him really happy. He loved
carpentry and slowly began to build a new life around it. In doing
so, he found his center, his sense of pride and self-worth.

As his self-esteem and fortunes grew, he felt in control of his life.
Because he was good at this work and prospered, he earned more
than his father and more than he had earned as an MBA. His father
is forced to respect him now for the progress he has made. Paul has
since healed the old wounds with his family. His father has a real
understanding of him for the first time.

My father and I had a heart-to-heart awhile ago. He admitted that he
was disappointed when I wasn't more of a success in the brokerage
business than he was as an accountant. [He had lost his job in the
early 1980s.] But at the same time, he quietly admitted that he is a
little envious of me for having made my own choice. He confided
that when he was a kid, he loved to tinker and build things and that

wooden sailboat toys and carved boxes were his favorites. It always got him excited to create something. While understanding myself more, I find that I can understand my father better. He seems to be changing, too, and he's happier in his new job.

Paul's improved situation does not mean that he will remain static. He will undoubtedly continue to be shaped and re-formed by circumstances, people, and events. The father life-tie may diminish at times or reappear with more force than expected at other times. For as Paul's father goes through reevaluations in late life about his own sense of self, so will Paul. This will happen through their interactions, reinterpretations, and exchanges of influence. Paul cannot avoid incorporating some of the features of the father who had once been so remote.

The Ties of Integrity

Fifty-year-old Allen had spent the last twenty years becoming a successful corporate attorney. A career move to Los Angeles, long hours, and frequent travel had taken their toll on his marital life. Although vastly wealthy and considered a success by his peers, two divorces had left him emotionally disconnected from his own life and his recollections of a former sense of self. An unexpected memory in adulthood will often trigger self-reflection and self-discovery. Allen experienced an event that led him to reevaluate and renegotiate parts of his own self-image.

> I grew up in a small New England coastal town with three other brothers. My father was one of two local doctors. Everyone knew him and certainly knew all of us. I was hell-bent on getting out of that town and making a big name for myself somewhere. I got along with my parents. We could tell they listened and basically I didn't have much to rebel against. They were fine people. My father was exceptionally bright and I couldn't understand how he could be so content practicing medicine in a small town when he could have gone further with his career. That was the one thing I was determined to do differently. I was going to go after the big brass ring in life, I was going to be better than my father. I guess I wanted to show him what success was really all about. At that time, when I was in my twenties, success meant money, a high professional profile and status.

Allen got the brass ring: He became a successful partner in a West Coast law firm. He worked the required long hours and married a woman who was on the fast track in law. They began acquiring all the trappings of success and socialized with all the people who could help their careers. He didn't return home too often; when he did, he felt as if he didn't have much in common with his family. Their lives were very simple and quiet. Allen wondered how they could have settled for so little, when they could have had a more successful life. For a long time Allen felt that his parents' influence—especially his father's—on his life was well over.

> I always carried around this image of myself that read "most important person." I always used my father as sort of a measuring stick of my identity. By my calculations I was light years ahead of my father in terms of success and power. That was all true until I had dinner with someone who set the record straight for me.

Allen's adult identity and sense of self-worth was totally tied to his success and power. Judging himself against his father's material success, Allen felt to some degree superior and in many ways a better person than his father. A chance encounter with a man who knew his father began to change his view.

> The law firm I worked for was firming up negotiations to represent a major client. Three other partners and I flew to New York to meet with the client and discuss terms about the representation. We met at a New York restaurant and when I was introduced to the client he acted like he knew me. I immediately thought my reputation as a hot-shot lawyer was what he was familiar with. Not so: He had summered on the Cape years ago and made an emergency visit to my father's office, as well as a number of follow-up visits. He told me how much he admired and respected my father. He knew him to be a man of strong character, honesty, and as a man who genuinely cared about the people who came into his life. He told me that he had met many important people in his life, but my father stood out as a man with a lot of integrity and kindness. Suddenly I beamed with pride, and at the same time felt very shallow and off-centered.

Allen never forgot that meeting. He continued to introspect and reflect on the motivations of his life. He wondered, what, after all, was important—what was of real value in his life, and what really didn't matter in the long run. With humility, he could now view his father's character and value system with new respect and understanding. In addressing parents' relationships with adult sons, Greene and Boxer (1986) indicated that renegotiation was a critical theme. Maintaining satisfying relationships while young adults establish independent households, launch careers, and form their own families requires both parents and adult children to reconstruct their relationships by reframing expectations, channels of communication, and occasions for interaction.

Alan didn't stop practicing corporate law, but he began to shorten his hours and take on *pro bono* work through a service organization. He began a new relationship, learned ways to relax, took time off to travel and spent more time with his parents and siblings. The hard and stressful terrain of his active lifestyle took on more curves and gentle slopes. Accumulating wealth and status took a back seat [to other priorities]. As he grew older, Allen embraced and successfully integrated into himself many aspects of his father's good nature. The man Allen had been in his twenties and thirties had changed. Many aspects of that prior self stayed with Allen, but he shed ill-fitting characteristics and integrated values and beliefs that were more harmonious to his changing self-image. He was able to identify himself with values greater than the acquisition of material wealth and the power of authority.

Allen's father died after a long illness. At the funeral, Allen's eulogy included story of his encounter with that client years ago that had given him a new respect for his father and had influenced his own direction and sense of self. Allen's self-views were framed in relation to his father/son life-tie and the meaning attached to it.

Adult Sons and Mothers

The NCWRR study found that close to 50% of men see their mother as a significant influence and a continuing influence in their adult life. Of this 50%, half of the men thought their mother made them feel guilty during their adult life. Thirty percent of those influenced said their mother contributed to their high self-esteem. The remaining 20% of those influenced who didn't know in what ways their mothers affected their self-esteem.

Sam Keen (1991) described the average man as spending a lifetime denying, defending against, trying to control, and reacting against the power of some woman. The life of a man circles around and then circles back to a woman—in particular, his mother. Men try to establish a separate identity first from their mother, and then from other women. A mother's power over her son can be experienced as terrifying, loving, guilt-producing, suffocating, abusive, caring, or combinations of these and other emotions. A small child automatically begins seeing expressions on his mother's face mirroring what he is. Like a mirror, she reflects his first glimpses of his interaction with the objective world. From moment to moment, she expresses for him whether he is lovable or disappointing, whether she disapproves or approves of what he is.

Dorothy Dinnerstein (1977) goes so far as to attribute male dominance directly to infantile fear and envy of a mother by her son. She also feels that this system is not created by men alone, for there is an unconscious conspiracy between men and women. Her central theme is that the power infants ascribe to their mothers creates a need in us for a more bounded authority. To Dinnerstein, male authority in adulthood appears to be a refuge from the more primitive and unlimited authority of the mother. Men have a need to defend themselves against dependency on women, and it's logical that they would compensate with dominance. It is probable that women in general acquiesce to this from fear of and need for his superior physical strength.

Yet a mother continues to have enormous power over a son's adult life—well beyond infancy, childhood and even adolescence—because many of her lessons are taught indirectly, wordlessly and so early in life. A mother shapes and imprints a child before it understands language. Her philosophy and belief system remain programmed in the adult human brain. According to Keen, a mother continues to be a shadow figure during her son's life. The burden on sons is greater than the burden on daughters. Daughters are encouraged to remain close to their mothers. Sons, on the other hand, have the psychological task of finding the means to separate from females, in particular their mother. This is difficult when a mother's belief and value systems are ingrained from birth. According to Freud, a son in adolescence has the task of transferring his identification from his all-powerful mother to his all-powerful father. Dinnerstein further states that males compensate themselves for the pain involved in breaking away from their mother by viewing women in a negative way.

Nancy Chodorow (1978) suggests that males show a tendency to define masculinity as that which is not feminine. Males in adulthood continue to wrestle with the threat of identification with females whom they depend on for adjustment. The further a male's behavior is from the model of female behavior, the more masculine he assumes he is.

Dinnerstein and Chodorow concur on the fact that fathers need to "mother." If and when they do, men see that masculinity involves nurturing. Male nurturing, however, is very difficult in our contemporary civilization, where over 30% of boys grow up in a fatherless home. Many fathers are not physically or emotionally present in family life. The absence and/or lack of involvement is bound to disrupt the mother/son relationship and the balance of male/female power in a way that will to influence the child. Boys, who are supposed to emotionally separate from dependency on their mothers, have nowhere to go for independence and masculine identification. In extreme cases, sons are cast into the role of a husband, father, provider, and protector. They can be pressured to involve themselves with family worries and problems and be required to listen to and console a needy mother.

A son growing up in this way may end up with ambivalent feelings toward his mother and toward women in general. The fatherless situation instructed him that, in order to be masculine, he must reject identification with his mother, separate himself from female behavior, and in the extreme, denigrate women, their beliefs and what they do. Our society has told males that the competitive world of business, competition, money, success, and power are the things to be valued—that this is the world of a male to which he should apply himself. Yet fatherless sons in today's world see their mothers working or seeking work for survival, being deprived, taking care of the home, and nurturing members of the family.

A fatherless son also realizes that the world of business, material possessions, and the power of authority—the putative world of his father—is not the world that has cared for him. He faces a confusing dilemma as he prepares himself for adulthood, unconsciously torn between his affinity for what women traditionally do and represent, and what the outside world defines as masculinity.

This identity issue for males doesn't always resolve itself at the end of adolescence or early adulthood. Stern (1983) suggested that the issue of dependence versus autonomy doesn't end at one particular, developmental stage, but may be resolved in different forms at different times during adulthood. The NCWRR study also found that there is no decisive event that shapes male identity, especially as it relates to autonomy and dependency issues. Men reared by a female single parent cannot avoid autonomy/separation crises and identification issues and must rework them repeatedly, especially those involving family ties, throughout their whole adult lives.

Sons Who Learn to Nurture

As Carl described his life during my interview with him, I was impressed by his level of caring for his wife and new home. He struck me as someone who was extremely sensitive to others' needs and feelings. The 32-year-old Carl explained that he had learned much about the feelings of others while being raised by his divorced mother.

My dad left the family when I was about eight years old. My mother, two younger sisters and I had quite a few rough years in Florida. My mother was devastated by the divorce and for awhile couldn't cope with us, the house, and was so depressed she couldn't get up in the morning. I took over, got my two sisters out of bed in the morning, and took them to the bus stop. My mother did fix us all breakfast, but then went right back to bed. My sisters usually played at a neighbor's house after school. I usually went right home after school where I would find my mother many times still in bed crying or sleeping.

I'd sit by her bed and tell her funny stories that had happened in school. I would make her hot tea and wait for a smile to come on her face. She would usually perk up enough to come down and get dinner and talk with the girls about school. She would tell me to make sure my sisters did their homework. By about eight o'clock she was back in bed with the lights off, sleeping or crying again. I would grocery shop and do errands with my mother. It was always good when she was out, but I was so acutely aware of her emotional fluctuations.

Carl was always listening for a change in her voice, or looking for a change in her facial expressions. He became aware of her distress or relief just by observing her. Carl was the same way with his sisters, making sure he was aware of their needs or problems. "I could tell as soon as my sisters walked in the door whether they were happy or upset. I would try to comfort and help any way I could." Carl's mother's depression lasted for about a year. She went for counseling and with the help of antidepressants was functioning at a normal level. However, the year of his mother's depression and subsequent years with her shaped Carl's attitude toward women and other people. He remembers the spring that she started to take back her life. "She would take us to the beach, I would watch my sisters and she would spend the afternoon swimming. She would swim every day for a couple of miles. I could see her getting stronger." As she got stronger she took a more active role in managing her home and family. Carl was still carrying the emotional weight of the family, but it was gradually becoming more of his mother's responsibility.

Carl went on to college and his mother and sisters developed their own lives. Education, career, and geographic locations all changed for Carl as he proceeded into adulthood. The one thing that did not change was his ability to respond, empathize and relate to other people. He was an avid sportsman, loved to fish, run, bike, play ball, joke around with his friends and do all of the "masculine" activities. However, at work and with his relationships he always had an understanding of the nature of other people. His colleagues, as he described, praised his ability to deal with tough situations and handle disgruntled workers. Carl's marriage has been based on mutual empathy and understanding. He and his wife are very attuned to each other's moods, needs, and emotions. Carl has no need to dominate his wife or prove himself as a man. When asked about his nature and ease with relationships, he responds:

It just sort of comes natural. I am comfortable in my manhood and I am comfortable with women and seem to be somehow wired to people. I understand others, but that doesn't mean I let everybody walk all over me. It just means that I can see myself, my needs and the needs of others. I guess I just kind of sort it out as I go along. It's just kind of natural for me.

Carl describes how his mother and his mother's situation influenced his life as a boy and continues to influence his life as an adult.

I guess I was thrown into a female world by default. By having to participate actively in my family and share responsibilities as well as looking out for the welfare of my mother and sisters, I had to deal with others. My mother needed me, my sisters needed me. I became a mother, a sort of weird husband, and major big brother to my family. There was no one else for quite awhile. My mother first influenced me and shaped me by her emotional absence. I had to learn to mother. In a strange way, she taught me to be aware of other people's needs by her absence. I had to deal with the dynamics and stuff going on in my family, the way many other mothers and women deal with not only their jobs, but their families. I have a lot of respect for women who mother and work. I guess men really don't know what goes on inside the world of their families and what their wives do. By the way, I think that the word *mother* is really not a noun, but a verb. It requires action and motion that should be done by both a mother and a father.

Carl's wife and her family consider themselves lucky to have such a jewel of a husband and son-in-law. Carl is a product of permission to nurture and mother, combined with a balance of personal need and autonomy. Carl doesn't know quite why he is the way he is, but he gives his mother much of the credit.

After my mother got back on her feet, I learned what it takes to balance a work-life, a family, and one's own needs. She managed our home, our personal needs, and provided financial stability. I admire my mother for her courage, her strength, and her empathy. Her influence and my having to pitch in to the family has steered my direction and probably the person I have become. A lot of people don't understand when I say my mother was a big influence in my life, that it wasn't my father, a movie star, or an athletic hero.

Carl's identity and evolving self-image is connected to his mother's influence and will probably continue to evolve within the context of his family life-tie. He is looking forward to starting a family and is committed to sharing child-care responsibilities with his wife. Fathering to Carl will not be a passive activity; instead, it will be an integral and natural part of his life.

Guilt Ties: Not for Women Only

It has been generally assumed that control through guilt is a type of exchange between females, usually in the context of a mother's attempt to control her daughter. The NCWRR study has found that guilt has been used by mothers to control sons, also. As cited in the beginning of this section, 50% of men felt that their mothers often made them feel unnecessarily guilty. The use of guilt by mothers to control their sons' behavior often persists into the son's adulthood. Adult sons may have moved great emotional and physical distances from their mothers, but those old guilt-ridden tapes from childhood can replay themselves in adulthood, shaping behavior, identity and self-esteem.

Seth had all the outward trappings of a successful man fully in charge of his life. He was a pharmacist who also managed a group of five pharmacies within the county where he lived. Fifty-five-year-old Seth had been married to the same woman for twenty-five years, had a sizable income, two children in college and a child in the Army. But Seth had major doubts about his own abilities. He had difficulty making decisions, and felt an overwhelming sense of duty motivated by guilt. His mother's childhood messages had remained with Seth throughout his adult life. He never edited or changed the psychological tape his mother recorded into his psyche.

First problem was that I was an only child. I saw my parents, in particular my mother, as all powerful. They had all of the answers, and boy, did they have a philosophy for life: "Do as we say and life will be wonderful." I ended up doing as they said and life was not wonderful. I have a whole lot of resentment in my adult life right now. My mother ruled our family. She wasn't Southern, but she acted like a Southern belle with my father and me. She was on the one hand dependent, and on the other controlling, a deadly combination.

My father was a kindly, distant figure in my life. My mother's ideas, thoughts, and way of life were what mattered. My father gave in to her whims, and I followed in his lead. During my teen years, whenever I questioned or rebelled against their authority, my mother told me how I was disappointing her and how I was causing her such distress. My father came back with an additional punch by saying that I was making my mother upset, how could I do this to her. Then my mother would counter-volley with, "You are going to make your father sick, you know how he gets angina attacks." This was the tactic throughout my childhood and it continues, subconsciously, to this day. Who I am and how I behave, to an extent, has been dependent on my parents' or I should say my mother's, influence. Although I am sure she would say that she was just trying to guide and protect me from bad choices.

I have a terrible time making decisions both in my professional and my personal life. I feel an intense sense of duty, that my choices and my wishes do not matter. Intellectually I know that I am still shaping my self and my behavior from some primitive childhood interpretation of parental whims. However, that parental tape, in particular that mother tape, is extremely forceful. This is especially true since she is now well into her eighties, widowed, dependent, but still wanting to control the show.

Seth has difficulty handling client, worker, and even family demands. He usually gives in, presuming they are right; or if they aren't, simply because it's easier that way. He sees his life as one long sentence of obligation and duty. Before he died, Seth's father told him to take care of his mother in much the same doting manner he did. Seth's father had always given in to his wife's demands, shaping his own life around that of his spouse. Seth's guilt has shaped his sense of self well into adulthood and his identity is ill defined as a consequence of trying to please everyone to avoid confrontation and the accompanying feelings of guilt.

Seth is in therapy and trying to rework a sense of self that does not incorporate the guilt that was measured out in large doses by his mother. In midlife he is trying to edit and change this life-tie that contributed to a poor self-image, to work some individuality into his identity and behavior. He examines his reactions so that his thoughts don't become associated with inappropriate feelings of guilt. He's becoming aware of the ways he unconsciously identified with his father's weakness, recognizing the values he has acquired on his own, and their positive effect on his self-image. Seth is starting to examine and meet his own personal needs, he is starting to say it is permissible to please himself. The self-work that Seth is doing is very similar to work that women influenced by feminist thought have learned to do. Feelings of guilt and the need to please others at the expense of oneself is not necessarily a women's issue. Seth's case represents one of quite a few examples the study found of a male whose adult life and self-esteem has been shaped in part by maternal guilt.

Motherless Son

A great deal of what has been written about deprivation of parenting has focused on paternal abandonment and the harm it can do to sons and daughters. Previously in this chapter, we discussed the long-term implications of a father being physically present, but remote, and of a father who has completely abandoned his sons or daughters. The recent book, *Motherless Daughters* (???), focuses on the plight of females and the consequences of a maternal vacuum during their formative years. Absence of mothering, although not often discussed, can also alter the development of males.

Frank was in his late twenties and had been living on the East Coast since he was about sixteen. His early childhood was spent in Oregon living with his father, who spent most of his time preoccupied old cars and motorcycles little time taking care of Frank. There was always food and a bed, but little else besides a steady stream of his father's bike buddies. Frank's mother had taken off with a boyfriend when he was about three years old. His father was bitter and resentful of his wife's desertion and projected much of his anger on Frank. Prudently, none of Frank's friends mentioned his mother. He grew up as if she never existed.

> When I was little I just followed my father around his garage where he repaired cars. I went to school for a while, but when I was about eleven started getting into trouble. I had a big mouth and would get in fights with other kids, and mouth off at teachers or anybody else who was in sight. The older I got the more fights I would get into with my father. I got hit and would take off and stay with friends and then come back home. Finally, things got so rough that my father

just gave up. When I was sixteen he shipped me to my grandparents in Florida.

I might have gone across the country, but it didn't change my bad attitude. I took that with me. I continued to mouth off and get into fights, I also discovered girls, or I guess they discovered me. I never thought of myself as good looking, but they did. My relationships with girls have been great in one way, and a complete disaster in other ways. I've hurt, not physically, a lot of girls. I can't stay with one girl for long, I get them to fall for me, then I check out of the relationship. . . .

Frank's feelings of self-worth were never high. His mother had abandoned him his father consistently ignored him, and the only ways he knew how to cope with controversy were to shoot off his mouth and throw his fists. He defended himself against dependency and the pain of possible rejection, by rejecting anyone, who started to care for him. His rejection of girls, especially, included misdirected retaliation against his mother. Frank could be charming, and, with robust good looks, he became a real expert at romantic relationships. He built hopes, made promises and commitments; then, without apparent cause, he would bail out. This type of behavior is sometimes exhibited by teenagers who are introspectively exploring their own, personal feelings with little regard for the feelings of other people or other unfortunate consequences. However, Frank continued in this pattern of behavior well into adulthood. His feelings of self-esteem and his sense of self were built on pillars of exploitation, control, and defenseivenesss. Control, for Frank, was being able to manipulate a relationship and decide when to leave it.

I know I am lousy husband material, so I stay clear of any kind of marriage commitment. The last thing I want to do is bring a kid into this world and check out like my mother did. I may not be a lousy guy with women, but I would never have a kid with the way I am right now.

When asked how he envisions himself later in life, he couldn't visualize himself being any different. He only felt certain that he would never allow himself to need the love of a woman. He liked to play with them, but he didn't trust them. Although rarely discussing his mother, her effect on him was always apparent in interviews. He revealed that one of his private thoughts was to try and locate her sometime.

Frank's personality is locked in a holding pattern that has been shaped by his mother's early abandonment of the family. His self-image and self-esteem may change later when and if he decides to locate his mother, or if he emotionally lets go in another healthy way. Until he is able to rework his feelings of loss, anger, and rejection within the context of his family life-tie, a component of his adult development may continue to be stalled.

SUMMARY

The family life-tie is one of the components of a person's identity, a part of the personal life story that starts in infancy and changes many times throughout adult life regardless of age or gender, although women and men may ascribe different meanings to their family life-tie from time to time. This tie influences the development of self-awareness and self-esteem. Although there may be physical separation between members of a family, there can never be a complete severing of the tie. The strength of this tie will occasionally expand and contract. A death, family dispute, or geographic distance may cause a contraction, which may dilute and blur the emotional influence of the life-tie for a period of time. Expansion of the tie in adulthood, perhaps through someone's illness, a joyful family reunion, or crisis, will bring the attachment of this family life-tie back into sharp focus. This contraction and expansion movement is circular and nonlinear.

Finding the self in the family life-tie is effected through imagery and recollection. Dan McAdams (1994) described how *imagery* is conveyed within the family. Infants and young children are inexorably and inescapably exposed to adult messages via *image messages,* onomatopoeia, and pantomime symbols. Children fuse and incorporate the images of their parents to mean "good mother," "cold mother," "aloof father," "powerful father," and other concepts. The early messages become incorporated into the adult identity, where they exert an influence indefinitely. Their meanings may be altered to some extent by the integration of later perceptions, new ideas that alter the old, associated parts of the individual's identity. Advancing age and emotional maturity, increased intellectual capacity and learning ability make impressions on this process through speech, schooling, and relationships, the latter especially within family life-ties. The fluid, progressing, and ever-changing parts of the individual's identity can be intermittently positive or negative in effect depending on the nature and character of the perceptive experiences. The process lasts throughout life. Those ideas and attitudes molded by experience in early childhood and imprinted are the most immutable areas of the identity memory bank. Images are mostly formulated by relationships within the family ties and shape the individual's self-image.

In this chapter the reader has listened to many of our study participants describe themselves using images that reflect the early family life-tie. Rita's image of herself as reflected by her "cold-blue" mother; Judy's image of being her father's "chosen daughter," Paul's image of his father's "remoteness," or Frank's image of being a "motherless son" were all powerful images that had been integrated into the person's identity and which affected his or her adult life.

The reader has learned how a guilt complex can affect the self-image and self-esteem of men and women alike. Annette was her mother's "pretty little princess" who had experienced guilt since childhood that could only be tolerated and temporarily assuaged by the neurotic pleasing of others at her own masochistic expense. We saw how Seth's mother manipulated and controlled her son by motivating him to obey her will and whim. In his life-tie, the son's obedience to his mother was his only defense against the infliction of guilt feelings via her subtle accusations.

Adults incorporate into their perceptions the effects of attitudes from within the fund of their identity. Both women and men have had to imcorporate into their adult images the effects of a remote parent such as Rita's emotionally distant mother and Paul's workholic father. The powerful and lasting influence of an absent parent such as Edith's father and the desertion of Frank's mother are qualities that can contribute to adult's self-conceit. The powerful and lasting influence of an absent parent such as Edith's father and the desertion of Frank's mother. The stimulus is altered with these emotional identity valences to form a resultant response.

The reader has seen how a parent's actions can influence a child to function in the role traditionally ascribed to the opposite sex. The powerful influence of Judy's father and grandfather led her to identify with instrumental areas of function during her childhood and gave her confidence and achievement orientation into adulthood. The crisis and subsequent depression of Carl's mother made a lasting and deep impression on her son in the span of one year by mobilizing his nurturing and caring qualities, character traits that continued to express themselves well into his adulthood. The very large blanket of familial influence, both good and bad, extends over the great divide that is often seen between the sexes.

We have learned that men and women continue to reshape and rework their identities at many different times, not at predictable stages or at a particular age. The family images of childhood that one carries into adulthood can be reworked depending on circumstances and social context encountered. Often a person revises the family life-tie during the later years, as Rita did when she began building a close relationship with her grandchildren. Sometimes it occurs in the early adult years: Joseph, for example, began to incorporate the image of his absent father into his identity after a troubled adolesence. It wasn't until Carolyn was in her eighties that she fully perceived the true meaning of the collusion that went on between herself and her father regarding his adulterous behavior.

The family history is a wellspring of experience to be drawn upon over a lifetime. The history itself is more than just a collection of facts; it is the product of perception and emotional experience. The relationships built within the family are fluid, circular and change over time, and even the family history itself is subject to revisions as life passes, and as personal growth and identity continue developing. In a sense, adult identity development is simply one's personal narrative, the expression of how one constructs and alters a personal image. If one sees the narrative as pleasing, self-esteem is high; if the narrative is not pleasing, self-esteem will be low. Selfhood is created in a social context full of personal meaning. Positive adult development and self-esteem only begin to develop when the life-tie ceases to be a controlling influence and begins to be a resource. This theme is central to growth within nonfamily life-ties as well as the following chapters will reveal.

CHAPTER 3

Education

> The human desire is permanent. All it really needs is
> the proper nourishment of education, and that
> education is merely putting the feast on the table.
>
> —*Allan Bloom*

To many, this would convey the idea that education means leading away from childhood and into adulthood. However, it may also mean to circle back from adulthood to nurture the judgments, curiosities and enthusiasms of childhood. Perhaps education should have no age boundaries, but rather be regarded as the key that unlocks a rich source of meaning for personal growth in adulthood for both women and men. Education can open doors for a reexamination and validation of what might have been neglected, buried, or misunderstood in childhood. Education should always be looked at as if it were unfinished business. A completed education, whether formal or informal, denotes the end of something, usually the end of discovery. True education is a deeply felt response to a need that may occur at any time of life to any woman or man.

The bulk of formal education is targeted and spent on the young. It has been assumed that most of the knowledge one needs for life can be crammed into the inexperienced and youthful brains of individuals between the ages of two and twenty-two. For adults, true learning through education requires the motivations of a passion, a sense of hunger and yearning. Young children often exhibit this passion, but learning frequently becomes robotic by the time an individual reaches adolescence. (That is not to say that all of today's youth are less than energetic and scholarly in their pursuits.)

Early education has been the site of a continuing battle. Feminists and social science researchers have documented the differential treatment of boys and girls during their formative years. According to the 1992 report by the American Association of University Women girls have been shortchanged and discriminated against within the educational system, while boys have been encouraged and favored. The study paints a dire picture of "educated" girls and the educational bias against them and supports the idea that boys are the ones society and the formal educational system back as winners in life. This favoritism may apply to youths in school, but our NCWRR study suggests that education and lifelong learning is the updated hallmark for self-esteem and identity in women during adulthood. Women may indeed have been shortchanged in their early education during youth, as supported by research. Some women may even have suffered from neglect and abandonment by the educational system in their early years, but this early neglect hasn't hindered them from exploring the depths and pioneering new knowledge during adulthood, at the same time enhancing their self-esteem.

As many a Saturday hero has discovered, when he fails to win or becomes disgruntled with choices, or when age overtakes him on the playing field, a fickle society abandons him without a second look or chance. The boys of summer then face a desolate winter with few provisions or life supports. Society may stand accused of shortchanging women in youth, but men are often shortchanged in adulthood. Men are just beginning to acknowledge and follow the lead of women in demanding a second chance. Many want exposure to the new ways of learning that can lead to fulfillment of new dreams.

Education, like the other life-tie components, is a major influence on adult development and self-esteem. Education provides a rich resource for the revision of meanings in adult life. Educational achievement can be of value in measuring success or failure. It can be a means for gaining personal knowledge about one's life and heritage, or a resource for financial security. Then again, it can be a vehicle for liberation and personal expression at any time of life.

In order to begin to understand the influence an educational Life-Tie has on adult development, it is important to review the history of education and the profound impact the system, the teachers, and the classroom have on girls and boys and the influence education and lifelong learning have on the development of women and men in adulthood.

OVERVIEW OF FORMAL LEARNING

It used to be that in the first five years of life the family was the child's main developmental environment. With the advent of nursery school, Head Start, preschools, and other forms of day care for tots, formal learning can begin as early as 2 years of age. The family of origin will influence these preschoolers, but the schools, including teachers, peers and the formal system, will be the center of learning for a minimum of 10 years. Formal learning may complement, contradict or supplement the family influence. The influence of various learning media beyond formal education will continue through adulthood.

The developmental influence of formal education on an individual's life is profound due to its sheer scale. By the time a child leaves school and is on the threshold of adulthood, he or she will have spent over 10,000 hours in a classroom.

The functions of the educational system have changed over time. The great teachers of ancient times were teachers who taught adults. Confucius and LaoTse of China, the Hebrew prophets, Aristotle, Socrates, Plato, Cicero—all were teachers of adults, not children. Their method of teaching was very different from the pedagogical method of today. The ancient teachers believed that learning required active inquiry, not the passive absorption of facts (Cole, Gay, Glick, & Sharp, 1971).

This enlightened way of educating individuals changed around the 7th century. It was during this time, particularly in Europe, when schools became organized for teaching children. Most of the teaching was by the church and mainly involved the indoctrination of young boys in the values and beliefs of the church to prepare them for the priesthood. This type of education continued for centuries before the advent of lay subjects and lay teachers.

Until the Industrial Revolution, the function of schools was to prepare a select few, mainly young men, for certain professions (medicine, law, etc.). Most other learning skills, such as the arts and crafts, were taught informally through apprenticeships. The Industrial Revolution created a need for skills that required formal education and led to compulsory attendance at school for males and females between the ages of 8 and 16. The post-Industrial Revolution era increased the demand for academic skills, because specific knowledge could become obsolete for working adults due to rapid social and technological improvements.

Compulsory education reflected the realization that the knowledge of parents in the family of origin and apprentice's masters at work was often not versatile and comprehensive enough and that such teachers could not be relied on for the adequate socialization of children. Schools became a place to teach societal values, self-discipline, personal interactions, laws, and the acceptance of group norms in order to preserve the status quo and foster industry.

Another function of the educational system has been to teach people how to improve society. Schools today are asked to correct racial and economic inequities and occasionally to become substitutes for poor and negligent parenting.

SELF-ESTEEM AND EDUCATION:
WHAT IS KNOWN

The factors that have been studied regarding the effect of education on the self-esteem of individuals have been limited and confined to children and adolescent subjects. The model of early education that has been used for teaching is known as the *pedagogical model*— meaning learning acquired through relatively formal teaching as described by Knowles (1973).

According to educator Malcolm Knowles (1973), this type of educational process assigns the total responsibility for deciding what, how and when one learns to the teacher. It is teacher driven, placing the learner in a submissive and passive role. Students only need to know what the teacher decides is necessary for them to pass and be promoted. This type of teaching becomes especially inappropriate and intellectually restricting by the time the child reaches adolescence and early adulthood. Pedagogy doesn't take into account a person's increasing need for self-direction and separate inquiry in learning. Low self-esteem—acted out through rebellion and resistance—and boredom have often been the end result of pedagogy.

When children enter school, they come with an individual, personal history derived from family interactions and other related social perceptions. A child will usually begin school with certain expectations about the classroom, the teachers, and their own performance ability. Based on what children are told about their performance, self-expectations will be built around school and teacher evaluations. Good or bad expectations, along with social comparisons, will lead the child to behave in ways consistent with the appraisal.

Classroom practices, including teacher characteristics, test methods for evaluation, and general class atmosphere, all have an effect on the self-concept and personal development of the child in school. The pedagogical method affects the pupils' self-concept. If the teacher's view of the pupil is that of a dependent person, the child's self-concept is in danger of becoming or remaining a passive-dependent personality.

There has been some disagreement over the ultimate significance of school success. Bloom (1987) suggested that a student's perception of his or her competence in learning is a major factor influencing feelings of self-worth. He concluded that a child's success or failure in school not only influences attitudes toward school, but becomes a profound instrument that alters the child's view of himself. Test scores, teacher evaluations, and the ability to get along with peers, all have a definite relationship to the self-perceptions of boys and girls.

The *andragogical model,* or adult-centered form of learning described by Knowles (1973), is one in which the adult is the motivator and driving force in his or her learning process. Before describing this model, it is important to understand the psychological meaning of the term *adult.* A person becomes an adult when she or he arrives at a self-concept of being responsible for her or his own life, of being self-motivated. Most men and women don't have fully developed self-concepts or identities by the time they reach early adulthood. The process of developing a full sense of oneself doesn't usually begin until one has left the early type of education-al system, after one has been employed, traveled, developed differ-ent kinds of relationships, has become committed to responsibility for a family, or has engaged in other forms of experiential learning.

The andragogical model is a need-to-know model. Adults ask questions and want to know why they need to know before they memorize something. Adult learning assumes that the adults have been through a transition from dependency to becoming a self-directed, mature student.

The adult years are often marked by changes in social roles. Changes encompass losses or gains in physical and emotional health, in marital status, work status, dependents, friendships or other meaningful connections that affect an adult's life. Adapting to events that change circumstances usually leads the adult to con-sider and appraise the possibility of taking a new direction in life. It is during these times of adaptation that new and critical learning takes place. These adaptations can increase the self-esteem and focus new meaning on the identity of both women and men.

Traditionally, it is thought that childhood is the time for learn-ing, and that adulthood is a time to apply learning to work, thus reinforcing the myth that adulthood is a time of mental sufficiency, passivity, stasis, nonlearning and working to maintain the status quo. This very narrow view impacts on one's sense of self, whether the person is male or female. The social message is that, in adult-hood, one has reached limits, that whatever you attained in youth is all you're capable of attaining and all you're going to be able to use. This is an outdated idea that handicaps both men and women. Actually, lifelong learning is a critical component of normal adult-hood. Self-directed learning in adulthood is a central feature of identity development and an important source of self-esteem.

The Implications of Education on Early Sex-Role Development

There is little dispute that both the family and the educational sys-tem have a significant influence on the development of sex roles. Some researchers have shown that schools actually teach gender roles; others maintain that schools free an individual from the gen-der roles developed within the family.

Whether or not institutions of education shape or mold sex roles, they do reflect sex roles as played out in the larger arena of society. For the most part, elementary education is taught by females at a lower salary than upper-grade teachers receive, while the majority of principals and school superintendents, who command high monetary compensation, are males. Schools apparently uphold and reinforce society's values through hiring and advancement practices.

Sex-role attitudes are also present in classroom activities. As early as Lee and Gropper's (1974) study, and as recently as the documentation of this condition by the American Association of University Women (AAUW, 1992), the known facts can be quite convincing that schools and teachers are treating girls and boys differently. Both studies found that teachers have well-defined, disparate expectations of boys and girls. The sexism may be subtle and is apparently not intentional or perceived by educators as sexism.

Research suggests that this differential treatment is associated with gender differences in achievement and personality. For example, observations in classrooms have shown that teachers had more interaction with boys in mathematics classrooms and more with girls in reading classrooms. The more interaction a girl had with the teacher in reading class, the higher her test score would be. Boys' verbal contact with their teacher in mathematics classes was similarly in reflected test scores. There were no apparent differences in the initial ability of the boys and girls. But by the year's end, girls were higher in reading achievement than boys, and boys were higher in mathematics scores than girls.

The personality of students may be affected by gender-linked treatment in the classroom. It has been observed that in a class situation, girls become dependent and acquiescent, while boys show motivation and independence. Boys sometimes receive a mixed message: School discipline demands quiet and controlled behavior, while life away from school is fraught with boisterous, loud and aggressive behavior on the part of males.

It has been strongly suggested that sex differences and self-concept are correlated, that sex-linked behavior of girls (acquiescence and dependency) results in low self-esteem and that the aggressiveness of boys correlates with high self-esteem. There is a strong tie between societal values and schooling. Formal education has an influence on identity and self-worth in the lives of school-age girls and boys. More important, the amount of education will continue to have a significant impact on identity and self-worth in adulthood. Documented research, however, has centered on education's influence on childhood and adolescence.

The following gender/education analysis will examine some of what has been previously observed about girls and boys before they enter adulthood and what the NCWRR found in its gender study concerning them.

EDUCATION LIFE-TIES OF GIRLS AND WOMEN

The Early Education Life-Tie: Shortchanging Girls

During 1991 the American Association of University Women conducted the latest and most definitive study on the effect of the current educational system on the self-esteem of young females. What they found is of grave concern to female development. Girls begin first grade with skills and ambitions comparable to those of boys, but by the time they finish high school, most have suffered a disproportionate loss of confidence in their academic abilities.

Contemporary culture deflates the self-esteem of adolescent girls by marginalizing females and stereotyping their roles in society. Unintentionally, schools collude in the process by cheating girls of classroom attention, by stressing competitive rather than cooperative learning, and by reinforcing negative stereotypes about limitations in the abilities of females. Teachers and counselors unintentionally dampen girls commercial and scientific aspirations, particularly in mathematics and science.

Adolescence is supposed to be a period of transition that should contribute features of adult life to a girl's identity. Dramatic changes in biology and psychology coincide with a girl's need to make a broad set of choices and decisions. The interpretations of gender differences that girls and boys make at this time have a profound impact on the future life of men and women in this society.

The AAUW report found that as girls and boys grow older, they both experience a significant loss of self-esteem. However, the loss is more pronounced and has the most long-lasting effect for girls.

In elementary school, academic achievement is the greatest source of their self-esteem. Preteen girls are relatively confident and assertive, and they feel pride in their academic abilities. Pride in schoolwork and in achieving skills rapidly declines during high school. By the time girls emerge from adolescence and are on the threshold of adulthood, they have much less confidence and a constrained view of their future. Fewer than half of the elementary school girls said they felt pride in their school work, and the figure drops to 17% by the time they reach high school. Their survey also found a strong relationship between perceived mathematics and science skills and adolescent self-esteem. Girls learn that girls should not be capable in these subjects. Hence their self-worth is lowered. The perceptions that girls have of their ability in mathematics and science had the strongest negative effect on their self-esteem of any subject area.

The AAUW study found that girls receive less attention, less praise, less feedback, and less detailed instruction from their teachers. Teachers initiate more communication with boys than with girls. They ask boys more complex questions, praise boys more, and most importantly, they track girls away from courses of study that lead to high-skilled and high-paying jobs.

The AAUW study has been praised as one of the first studies to correlate a girl's self-confidence and her future pursuits in the educational system with formal methods of teaching. However, as far back as 1925, Lewis Terman of Stanford University tracked the academic and subsequent vocational achievements of men and women through adulthood. He found that from first grade through college, females equaled or excelled males in academic achievements. In later life, however, men went on to achievements consistent with their abilities, while women failed to live up to their academic abilities and potential value. This question has been pondered by researchers for many years.

Some criticism has been aimed at the AAUW study. Critics counter that males also suffer from low self-esteem during the early years of education. The extra attention boys receive may be for disruption, rather than intellectual promise. Drop-out rates are, indeed, much higher for young males than for females. But it may be that boy drop-outs are yielding to family pressures to accept job opportunities that are not available for young girls.

Some past research has concluded that women lacked motivation and opportunity. Female physiology—designed for pregnancy and devoted to childrearing—has long ruled women's lives. In order for a woman to achieve status in commerce, she must abandon many traditional functions of the female role and adapt to a man's lifestyle. So the controversy continues. For a long time, the blame of not living up to academic potential has been placed on girls themselves, rather than on a rigid academic system that may impinge negatively on the psyche of both sexes. However, the AAUW report does underscore the idea that girls are not to blame for not achieving within the formal educational system.

Adolescent Girls, Education, and Identity

There is another issue that the AAUW and other research studies have failed to approach in comparing males and females. It is by all means important and necessary to have girls and boys receive equal attention, opportunity, and praise while being educated. However, society has placed far too much emphasis on both sexes to attain and crystallize an identity by the end of adolescence, which traditionally coincides with the end of formal education.

Erikson (1968) described the struggle for identity during adolescence as following a continuous, upward trajectory until the end of this time and age stage. From there on, according to Erikson, an individual strikes out on an independent path and with full knowledge of a self-concept and goals for the rest of life. But crystallization of an identity that will apply to adult life is undoubtedly an impossible task by the end of adolescence—not only from the standpoint of emotional maturation but, more pointedly, because of the pedagogical method of teaching. As stated in the beginning of this chapter, traditional pedagogy doesn't encourage independent thinking and self-directed behavior in young students. When learning is doled out as a passive-receptive activity that emphasizes rote memory in order to pass tests, the self-esteem and self-concept of students will not be adequately developed.

Furthermore, this psychological pattern of identity development by Erikson (and others such as Levinson [1978] and Vaillant

[1977]) suggests simplistically that life resembles a heroic quest on which a man (a) gains a sense of himself in youth, (b) puts on an armored suit of self-confidence, and (c) ventures forth pursuing the "Holy Grail," uninterrupted by character defects and untroubled by problems and deficiencies. Their psychological painting portrays a very narrow and gender-skewed image of growth that seems to culminate at the end of adolescence and at the end of traditional schooling.

The male bias of this psychology exerts great pressure to maintain the status quo in neglect of a full understanding of adult development. The quest paradigm is a handicap that has made women appear deficient. Erikson, and theorists like him, asserted that resolving the identity crisis of youth depends on striking out alone, becoming totally independent of others and making a firm individual commitment to a goal. Those who don't make strong commitments or become totally autonomous during this time are regarded as inadequate, weak, or confused. Females have been labeled immature because they haven't followed the male, linear trajectory of autonomous and independent behavior. By confusing normal interdependence with the idea of female dependency and normal emotionality with female irrationality, we demean females. By creating a clock marked with stages of identity development based on a male standard, we fail to honor what is most human and growth enhancing—the slow, normal evolving of maturity and wisdom through life.

It is still open to further study and debate whether females alone have been shortchanged and discriminated against during their early years by the educational system, with consequent low self-esteem. However, this is not the end of a gloomy story about female development; this is but one early chapter in a continuing saga about the unfolding of advanced female development. The NCWRR Study on Gender and Self-Esteem found that this same educational system that shortchanged women in childhood and adolescence is also providing support and encouragement in the adult life of women. This very important life-tie becomes a major source of high self-esteem and becomes part of the foundation for developing a strong identity for females in adult life.

The Education Life-Tie: A Tool of Change for Adult Women

The NCWRR study found that for close to 90% of women, education contributed a moderate to high level of self-esteem. Close to 60% of the women surveyed returned to school during their adult years. Interviews with women revealed that education was a source of positive self-esteem in adulthood and contributed to a strong adult identity.

Women have been the pioneers for continuing education well into adulthood. The educational system may have a negative impact on the self-concept of girls in childhood and especially during adolescence, but our study has found that adult women use the educational system as a tool to enhance self-esteem and personal growth. Women felt more confident and autonomous as a result of learning. They achieved an enhanced identity, sometimes for the first time during adulthood, and are now better able to engage the world around them and pursue future goals.

During the 1970s, and spurred on by the women's movement, there was an exodus of women from their homes and back to school. New centers for continuing education, the community colleges, and other institutions of creative expression have grown rapidly over the last twenty years. While raising children, in the postparental years, and even after retirement, women are going back to school. Some return for personal development and for the sheer joy of learning, others return out of economic necessity to learn new job skills, or polish old skills. Financial necessity is a driving force for many women. Some women need to gain skills to boost a family income. Many women find themselves in dire financial straits either through divorce or widowhood.

The study found that women have an intermittent pattern and history of being educated. This study backs up previous research that states more men than women complete formal education by their mid-twenties. Thirty-two percent of the NCWRR female respondents dropped out of college during their late teens and early twenties. However, 60% of women over the age of 26 returned to school in their adult years.

Often, with little emotional or intellectual difficulty, women pursue higher learning goals and begin to explore different values, philosophies and lifestyles as well as the practical applications of education. The study found women eager to study and experiment with new beliefs and practices as they move forward in their adult lives. Adult learners accept the existence of new trends, feel comfortable when asking and learning about them and are willing to seek out and embrace new ideas.

Continuing education, as this study shows, has a profound effect on the self-esteem of women. The majority of women agree that their self-esteem and identity have changed and vastly improved. However, within this shared framework, the content and intensity of meaning drawn from education is highly idiosyncratic and individualized. To one woman, education may be just a background for more personally enlightening experiences. To another woman, education may emerge directly as an important source of meaning around which a newly developed identity is constructed and themes of self are revealed. To still another woman, education may be the vital link that propels her and her family out of poverty. Whatever the reason, the relationship between the life-tie of education and self-esteem and identity development can only be fully understood within the framework of an individual life. The following narratives from our study will describe how individual women found education to be a powerful tool for personal development, and feelings of self-worth.

RETURNING FOR BASICS: PROVIDING
FOR ONESELF

Many of the women from the NCWRR study returned to school out of sheer necessity, but found an added bonus of self-esteem. After a divorce, a woman may find that alimony has become a dinosaur. The splitting of community property often means that the ex-wife gets the house, but she can't eat. A widow may find herself financially destitute after having health-care costs eat away her lifelong savings. A woman who hasn't been in the workforce for many years, or who only had a series of part-time-jobs listed on her resume, may find herself back in school out of necessity.

Meg and her husband divorced after twenty-five years of marriage. She had been accustomed to a comfortable upper-middle-class lifestyle in suburban New York. The divorce was amicable

enough. Her ex-husband agreed to a property division, and to see
their two teen-age children through college. Meg got the house,
but she soon found that her job as a substitute teacher didn't pay
enough to keep the roof over her head. She had only a dusty old
bachelor's degree from a liberal arts college. She decided to pursue
a master's degree in social work.

> I wasn't feeling very great about myself when I started back to school.
> I had spent that last twenty-five years cocooned in my family and
> marriage, being Ben's wife and Tess and Robert's mother. My mem-
> ories of school were not pleasant. Growing up I was overweight and
> teased by classmates. I never thought I was smart enough, and the
> teachers didn't either. I got A's in deportment, but for the most part,
> I was invisible with my "ladylike" C average. I used to cut classes. . . .
> Some of the teachers made me feel stupid. All those classes are a
> blur now. . . . I was nervous and ate too much.
>
> After I was graduated from high school, I went on to college any-
> way, not knowing what I wanted or what I could do best. My father
> wanted me to get the usual "MRS" degree, and he said college was
> the best hunting ground for a husband. During my senior year I got
> myself back in shape, and I mean that quite literally. The big task at
> hand was to lose all that weight. I should have gotten the class "MRS"
> award, for I never worked at anything as hard as I worked on getting
> a husband—dieting, clothes, cosmetics, charm—all that extra stuff.
> I left college in June with my diploma. By the end of August I left sin-
> gle life with a ring on my finger, and in January I left the church with
> a husband. I liked to think that as soon as I married, my life as an
> "adult" would really begin. I played at being a grown-up, but the real
> adult was nowhere—even though I had two fine little kids. Ben and
> I just didn't get along. I suppose it was mostly my fault.
>
> After the divorce, it was survival time for me. I had to face a lot of
> the hard stuff I didn't get done when I was younger. I always liked
> working with kids, but I didn't want to teach. I went for some voca-
> tional counseling and explored the field of social work. It was scary
> when I started the master's program. . . . I knew I had a bachelor's
> degree, but it was just about meaningless for a good place in the job
> market. I felt like a fraud.
>
> One thing I had lots of, and that was zeal and a capacity for hard
> work—with some desperation to fire it up. I studied all the time. My

nose was always in a book. I listened intently to what my instructors were saying. I worked diligently on my papers. I asked questions and began to feel smarter, especially when those A's rolled in. I had a deadline, for I had two years to complete the program and then get a job. My ex-husband was decent about it. He had agreed to support me for two years until I got on my feet. I was lucky; I know many divorced women who didn't get a break like that.

I finally got my MSW and started working in a children's shelter. I love the job! My own kids are proud of me, and at last I can be really proud of myself. It's as if I found my voice and used it. Divorce didn't do a thing for my ego, but college gave me something to be happy about. My master's is a godsend when it comes to feeling confident!

Meg had to go back to school in order to make herself job-worthy with a two-year deadline. Education was the appropriate tool to gain the skills she needed. Early education was decisively, though not deliberately, harmful to Meg. Her early school experience rewarded her mostly for obedience, silence, and passive behavior. Yet it left her unmotivated and without a thought of using knowledge and skill in her future. The educational system and the social norms of the late 1950s insisted on obedient behavior on the part of female students. It was only after many years, with the realization of a future financial crisis, that she mobilized her potentials and found professional dedication, security, and happiness.

It sometimes takes something unique in a female to surmount difficult odds and beat the system. Dr. Christopher Hayes , author of this book, writes the following account from his own family of origin:

My mother, the daughter of poor Sicilian immigrants, was raised in a tenement apartment where only Italian was spoken. Her father worked long hours in a barber shop, and her mother worked in a sweat shop at a sewing machine.

Living in a rough neighborhood of midtown Manhattan called "Hell's Kitchen," she was tormented by local children when she couldn't speak English. Her beginnings in school were also very difficult for the same reason, but some kind of flaming thing inside her made her determined to survive. Her motivation to overcome the stigma of being a "dumb guinea" and a "stupid wop" stayed with her through years of A report cards. Today, as a PhD with a state license, she has worked years as a clinical psychologist for a psychiatrist, has her own private practice specializing in the elderly, and works as a certified school psychologist. Along the way, she married a doctor, raised her four children and sent them through college.

Crisis-Driven Learning in Later Life

Maud was sixty-eight when she suffered a massive heart attack. A contented person, she had never questioned the life she'd led and the choices she had made. She had done her stint of work and now would take it real easy. She was even quite philosophical about becoming a widow. Her late husband left her with the loss of his companionship but with considerable wealth. Then rude reality struck hard against her placid complacency as she battled a life-threatening illness. The crisis made her review her previously unexamined life. She decided that if she recovered, she'd do something worthwhile with her life. After looking at her options, she decided to go back to school.

I never was one of those people who sat around reflecting about the meaning of life. School never meant that much to me while I was growing up. I was a "Depression kid" in '29 and had to leave school to help out the family. Until I married that fine man, the only thing that I knew anything about was working long, hard hours.

I married Joe just before he went overseas during World War II, and I worked in a defense plant while he was away. When he came back, we settled down in the Napa Valley. His uncle helped us get a hardware store started. I only knew hard work, for running a hardware store is a backbreaking, seven-day-a-week job. I was no little wisp of a girl; I was big-boned and strong. I could always carry and lift anything the men could. Joe and I were partners in that store. I worked right beside him while our two little boys played in the back. The two of them started helping out and ended up running the business. We lived in that store, barely took any time for vacations or developing a personal life. In fact, Joe and I seemed like one person, and that person's life was the business.

Joe died at the age of fifty-eight. I continued working in the store right alongside my two grown sons. They eventually took over the business, but I coped with Joe's death by working even longer hours. It took a toll on my health. Smoking didn't help, either. I had a very bad time when I got sick. When I was recovering, the doctor said it seemed like a miracle that I pulled through.

For a time, I wasn't able to go back to work, but then I didn't know if I wanted to. I was sitting at home, stripped of my work and wondering what was to become of me. I was still scared. Coming close to dying sure shook me up.

I started reading books while I was convalescing, but when I read about different kinds of people, places, and ideas, I realized that I had more questions than answers, and that I had a lot to learn. The old ways weren't going to satisfy me anymore. I took good care of myself, and when I was able to travel, I packed my bags and went to a retreat in Nova Scotia for about two months. It was a quiet place where I could isolate myself and do some heavy thinking about not wasting any more time. I slept, ate, read, talked with my counselor, meditated and made plans.

Back to California and steamed up, I enrolled in a community college where I found out I could be a hard worker being a student, too. I got my high-school equivalency, then with a no-nonsense schedule, I went on to get my bachelor's degree in philosophy. It was quite a stretch . . . in a couple of years, progressing from being the queen of nuts and bolts to a thinker of abstract ideas. An extra bonus of the project was discovering how much I loved learning about everything. I'm getting my doctorate in philosophy next year.

Some people I know think I've flipped. They just can't see any practical use for this academic stuff, especially, as they say, at my age. I don't think age need stop learning. Maybe it just makes it a bit slower in your seventies, that's all. This schooling has made me into a very different person. I'm certainly more alive and sensitive to things than I was as a business partner. Those things are important, of course, but I finished that part of my life. Sometimes I feel like I'm an archeologist unearthing new, fascinating fragments in my world and in my mind. The real tools I used weren't from my hardware store but from all those books, the people I've met and the schools. I love being a student. I may never stop studying till I can't anymore.

Maud was a late starter in life. Her frightening medical crisis was the pivotal point that made her examine her life and contemplate the future she had remaining. Late-life learning, as subjective as its goals may be, is still of great value in advancing age, for it can beautify the soul, open doors to brilliant light and sparkles of entertainment, inspiration and revelation. While it needn't be a hard ride uphill, it stands as the best alternative to porch-sitting, rocking-chair stasis and premature oblivion.

An Interrupted Life

Women's lives are often marked by interruptions. Interruptions such as pregnancy, early marriage, caregiving and/or financial responsibilities often detour women from an educational track. The NCWRR study revealed that over 30% of women's education was interrupted either during adolescence or early adulthood. Many women dropped out of school to get married or to support a new husband while he finished school. Some dropped their studies to work and give financial support to their parents, others lost interest and were bored, and some had to interrupt school because they became pregnant.

Forty-year-old Patty was one of those women whose education was interrupted by pregnancy. She was the oldest in her very large family and that meant she was often in charge of five siblings. Her mother cleaned houses when not running the house and taking care of the children. Patty remembers her mother as always being overworked and overtired.

> We got along, but my mother and I never talked about anything other than managing the kids, the house, and doing it with little money. If I wasn't taking care of my sisters and brothers or doing house chores, my mother just considered me in the way. I had no privacy growing up, but even though I was surrounded by my family I thought of myself as really alone. No one talked in my house. My father worked in a factory, but most of the money was spent maintaining his long-term drinking problem. He was physically at home, but had checked out years ago emotionally.
>
> I had a lot of questions when I was a little girl, I was real curious. However, no one seemed interested in my questions at home or even at school. I liked grade school, I had a few teachers who encouraged me and who thought I was a really quick reader. As I went into high school, I felt completely disconnected from this experience. I never

rebelled or was a troublemaker in school, I just never felt good about school. It seemed to be totally unrelated to my life and school never made me feel good about myself. I knew it was important, but it just didn't relate to me.

I just started my senior year when I discovered I was pregnant. I quit school and married my baby's father. He was nineteen at the time and working as a steamfitter's apprentice. When Mac was born we continued to live in my in-laws' basement that we converted into a small apartment. It's real funny: During my pregnancy and while Mac was little, I always read books. Sometimes those books were romance novels, but many were self-help and psychology-type books. My husband thought I was weird and saw all my reading as a threat to our marriage. I guess in a way he was right about the second part.

When Mac was about six years old I decided I didn't want him to have a mother who was a school dropout. So I went back and got my GED. and then enrolled part time at my local community college. When I went back to school as an adult, I was about twenty-five years old. School was a lot different than I remembered it to be. I was around other adults and people who thought like me. I was so driven to do well. Every A I got just drove me harder to get another good mark. I became so confident and so greedy for knowledge, it was like all these books were just adding to who I was. I had another baby during my transfer to a four-year school. Altogether it took me ten years to get my BA. I was thirty-five years old. My husband didn't like all these changes. We divorced and I got a job as a supervisor of the YWCA continuing education programs.

Right now I am working towards my doctorate. I probably will be close to fifty when I have that diploma in my hands. I am patient, tenacious, and look upon my education as a source of personal meaning and identity. I might have grown up as a child with education, but I didn't grow as a person with my early education experience. Going back to school as an adult has not just been an isolated event, it is quite literally part of my adult life and a large chunk of who I am and how I feel about myself, which is pretty darn good right about now.

Patty's life situation of being a young mother with little education proved to be one of the driving forces that led her back to school. She wanted her son to be proud of her as well as being able to provide him with a good role model. The most important and rewarding aspect of Patty's adult learning experience was that it was self-directed. By going back to school as an adult, she only needed to face her own approval or disapproval. She was also able to weave into her new learning early experience from mothering, informal reading, and managing a home. Life experience and the readiness to learn helped Patty over some rough areas of new course work. Newfound high self-esteem and her belief in her ability to succeed helped her tackle the difficult challenges of tough subjects. Above all, Patty had a tremendous need to find out about things, a need to know, and a non-stop curiosity about her world.

Whose Career Is It?

Sometimes selecting career goals and the curriculum to achieve them is usurped by some well-intentioned interloper. Decisions about one's life, education, and career goals can be overturned by interested others in the name of caring and knowing best. It is very difficult for any late adolescent to make life choices and decisions about higher education, but it can become a veritable nightmare when the choice is taken out of an individual's hands.

The story of Lilly is a good example of this dilemma. Lilly was sidetracked in her late teens and early twenties by an overly controlling father regarding her education and selection of a career. He presumed that his choice for her future career would be much better than hers. Since he was going to sponsor her financially, he assumed it should be his prerogative anyway.

Lilly grew up in what she described as a happy and loving home. Her mother had a modest education and had never worked outside the home; and her father, college educated and business-wise, was involved with his two daughters and helped them with their homework. He regarded Lilly as "the smart one" of the family, but she was also called "the different one," because of her strong individuality.

I remember how my father taught me to swim and play basketball. He was so involved in my life and my sister's. He coached my school's male basketball team. When I told him I wanted to play basketball at school, he patted me on the head and said I "should become a cheerleader." He always knew what was best for me.

Things really changed during my teen years. Once I got to age twelve things became difficult. I was skipped in school when I was in first grade, and was always younger than my school friends. There was a lot of screaming and crying in my family life at this time. I might have been smart enough to be a grade ahead of my age, but my parents didn't want me hanging out with the people I was in class with.

My parents didn't know what to make of me. They didn't validate me, and I was never able to make a decision about my life. My father jumped on the bandwagon when at a very young age, like ten, I mentioned that I wanted to be a lawyer. He never forgot that statement I made as a ten-year-old. His dream continued through my high school years and my first year at college. He wanted me to become a lawyer. When I expressed an interest in marine biology, he tried to discourage me from pursuing this interest. My years in high school and my college years really belonged to my father and not to me.

If I was bored in high school, I got real bored in college. I was not doing what I wanted to do. I took prelaw courses and did passable work, but my heart wasn't in it. The only time I got excited about my courses were the few required science courses I took, especially two marine science courses. Once out of college I finally confronted my father and told him I had no interest in going to law school. He was upset and said that if I wasn't interested in law school I should just get married.

I didn't want to get married, but I didn't know what to do with my life. I worked for seven years as a fundraiser for a nonprofit environmental group. It was a job that paid the rent, that's all it was. I married two years ago, and have found my best friend and mentor in my husband. He is the one that has encouraged me to go back to school and study marine science.

Lilly is twenty-eight years old and is studying marine science on a postgraduate level. Her father had chosen a different career path for her, because he underestimated "the smart one." He dominated her without considering her feelings or trusting that her trial-and-error approach to life would bring her experience, maturity, and good judgment. Her rebellion took the form of working and living on her own, and this helped Lilly mature. It was against the backdrop of this experience that she was able to marry well, gain security, support, and sufficient confidence to enter postgraduate school. With the encouragement of her husband, Lilly accelerated her studies with a heavy course load and finished the program in two and a half years. Completing an internship in a nearby marine laboratory has turned into a full-time, gratifying position.

Lilly was like many women in our study who admitted that they made far better students when they were mature and had life experience to contribute to their learning. They were eager, fully engaged and had incorporated the aspect of "life learner" into their self-concept. The women had many different reasons for returning to school as adults. No matter what the goal was, whether it was a new career or simple curiosity and love of knowledge, becoming an adult learner contributed to a more developed sense of self, enhanced self-esteem and created a stronger identity.

Challenge to the AAUW Report

The AAUW report has suggested that girls are discriminated against in school because of gender. It stated that girls suffer low self-esteem due to the way in which schools encourage and favor boys over girls. Gender-based educational favoritism may cause low self-concept in females during the school years, but other factors must be considered, then weighed carefully and cautiously before definitive conclusions are reached and accepted.

Perceptions concerning discrimination and support were very similar for men and women in our study. The NCWRR research findings state that 63% of women felt that their teachers didn't discriminate against them. Sixty-one percent of men also felt they were not discriminated against. Only 10% of the women surveyed stated that they felt teachers generally discriminated against them in school. This statement was matched by 10% of the men. Both women and men were equally split on whether they felt that teachers supported or in some way encouraged their goals in school. Twenty-four percent of women and 19% of men strongly agreed with the statement that teachers generally gave support to their personal goals. Twenty-four percent of women and 22% of men strongly disagreed with the statement that teachers supported personal goals.

The NCWRR study also found that both men and women suffered from low self-esteem during their teen school years. Thirty-eight percent of women and 41% of men said that their self-esteem was very low during the ages between 13 and 19. The AAUW report also looked at males and found that the self-esteem of boys diminished during the teen years, although not as sharply as for girls. However, the AAUW report doesn't interpret significance to the drop in self-esteem of boys during their teen years.

There are a number of possibilities that further research should examine in order to reveal the ways that education affects the self-esteem of boys and girls. The AAUW report stated that boys have higher self-esteem during their school years, so let us inquire why the high-school dropout rate is higher for males than females. Studies in 1992 revealed that 11.1% of white women aged 18 to 24 had not completed high school, compared to 13.3% of males. Boys more often cut classes, avoided homework and had more disciplinary problems. According to a U.S. Department of Education survey in 1990, 16% of both girls and boys felt "put down by teachers." The Department of Education survey also found that over 60% of female sophomores plan to go on to college, whereas fewer than 60% of males had plans for college.

No one has studied the effects of athletics and sports on the difference between male and female levels of self-esteem. Exercise, athletics, and sports have been known to release mood-enhancing brain chemicals. More males than females are involved in school sports athletic programs. So before any final, comprehensive conclusions are reached that can support the fact that existing educational methods of teaching are discriminatory and lead to low self-esteem in girls, there are other important factors that must be included in gender comparisons. For instance, is the pedagogical method of teaching in high school is essentially the same as it was in elementary school? To what degree, in what aspects? This method, without correction, encourages the development of passive-dependent personality features in both sexes. The next section will look at what research and men themselves have to say about their education, its effect on their self-esteem, and its consequences in their adult life.

EDUCATION LIFE-TIES OF BOYS AND MEN

Historically, adolescent males have been given more attention than females by being the subjects of intense psychological and social scrutiny. Professionals who have reviewed studies of students are quite right when they say that there has been a significant imbalance in projects studying the characteristics of human development, because they were only concerned with male behavior. However, males as well as females have been generally shortchanged due to many unrealistic, untimely and often inappropriate goals placed on the male population.

The NCWRR study found that 53% of males surveyed had their most negative educational experiences between the ages of thirteen to nineteen.

Formal education has been considered the testing ground, an initiation period or a rite of passage through which a boy is prepared for manhood. Instead of a jewel-encrusted medieval sword, battle shield, or kingdom, the modern-day knight is handed a diploma attesting to his preparedness to enter the world of adulthood. Modern adulthood meant following the modern sociological dream of independence and self-sufficiency, pursuing career goals instead of conquering new lands. It also meant marrying a modern-day bride, a mythical Guinevere, and raising children to fulfill a dream sometimes chosen by others. There is a dichotomy here. On the one hand, society expects self-sufficiency and self-direction on the part of men. On the other hand, the man is also expected to fulfill the expectations of parents, educators, and society as a whole.

Education is supposed to be developmental springboard that leads to a future through which a man can envision himself passing through recognized and honored stages of adult life. At the end of his life he expects to look back on a fulfilled life for, after all, he followed the "dream" and in later life he expects the younger generation to come to him for his years of wisdom.

In this dream a boy becomes a man based on social time, geared in earlier decades to the completion of his high-school education. This preparation has been considered sufficient to guide him and ensure him a proper adult role, fitting him into society with a well-cast identity of knowledge and skills to protect and lead him successfully through adulthood. However, the traditional rites of passage, including existing, compulsory, formal education, have mainly ensured his rigid conformity to the maintenance of the status quo. Schools have taught young men to be receptive and unquestioning, rather than inquisitive and innovative.

The "dream" decisions are made at an early age, often with little considered thought, worldly experience, or appreciable accumulations of knowledge. The standard message was to follow the prescribed social blueprint and reap promised prosperity in a stable career, a life-long marriage and children who would be respectful, loving, and caring. This blueprint was roughed out centuries ago, when the life span was around forty-five years, so that decisions that were made in youth could possibly be fulfilled. Career choices were largely hereditary: The wealthiest segment of society inherited wealth and property; the middle class inherited the family business; the poorest learned the family trade or took over occupation of the scion. Men were considered old and wise by the time they were fifty. A husband and wife could expect to live no more than a few years after the last child left home. There was very little time for activating a new life plan: The plans drawn up in late adolescence fit a life span that, for men, might average only fifty-five or sixty years.

The blueprint has to be revised, for life expectancy today is much longer for men, although not as long as a woman's life expectancy. Career, job, and marital decisions hastily made in late adolescence, during the school years, may become inappropriate, dull, outmoded, or financially unrewarding by the time that adolescent male becomes middle-aged. Suddenly, at the age of fifty, he may realize that he has a whole other life ahead of him, a life that doesn't fit with decisions he made in late adolescence. Feelings of being trapped, abandoned, deceived, and confused are often experienced by adult men who made life decisions too soon.

Women have been more flexible than men in reorienting their lives in adulthood. They are more likely to go back to high school or take college courses, to retrain for another career, or reinforce their skills and pursue goals within their career choice or just for personal growth. Many women in midlife never had to confront early career decisions and so are free to experiment with the second half of life. Many of the women back in school as adults entered with casual motives and discovered beneficial bonuses, such as enhanced self-esteem and a clearer identity.

Men in midlife who are discontented with the job choice they made during high school frequently find that they can't free themselves from the job that meets their financial responsibilities; they tend to remain in jobs they find dull, outmoded or unrewarding. Because of the handicap imposed by the role of primary breadwinner they pursue a lifestyle that is inappropriate during the second phase of life. Because their identity pool of knowledge and skill can't be revised and updated with the education they would need to prepare for a new career or for personal growth and expression, their self-esteem may fade, leaving them confused at this juncture of life, The NCWRR study found that only 35% of males returned to school during adult life. The men who manage to go back to school, however, have been gratified, for what they learned was enlightening, helpful in redirecting their energies toward new career goals, and they usually acquired new, life-expanding insights.

Education in Psychological Theories of Male Development

Erik Erikson (1978) believed that forming a vision of the self in the future is one of the basic tasks of adolescence and early adulthood. Educational institutions have been entrusted with the work of shaping an individualized curriculum to make this vision a reality— especially for young men. Erikson and his followers used a small sample of well-educated, white, middle-class men to gather data and draw conclusions. Erikson constructed a sequence of eight tasks that would challenge each individual continuously from infancy through adulthood. He believed that social and cultural forces determined the eight tasks, and that mental development progressed through a series of predictable, psychic negotiations between the individual and the social context.

The first task in childhood was to develop a sense of *industry*. A child's wish to become a productive member of a valued social institution engenders a desire to do well in school. A child who doesn't or cannot develop a sense of productivity and contribution during school years may develop a sense of inferiority which might continue to hinder and prevent his adaptation and growth through adulthood.

According to Erikson, adolescence holds the main task of developing an *identity*. This monumental task involves a process of intense reflection through which the adolescent finds his true capabilities and interests. After this intense period of introspection, this adolescent will be able to activate a plan for his future that incorporates his desires and proficiencies. The adolescent male who cannot activate such a plan successfully will be confused about what to do with his life and will be limited in adapting to adult situations.

The setting where most of these monumental tasks are supposed to be played out is the school system. Schools and institutions of higher learning have served as the basic framework for professional developmentalist observers of Erikson's theories. It is during the school years that one's basic fund of knowledge, attitudes and ideas—the identity—is supposedly shaped. Once gained, its loss or reconstruction are not anticipated.

Following Erikson's work, Levinson et al., (1978) described late adolescence and early adulthood as a time when a man forms his "dream," a fantasy of himself in the future. This dream vision animates his life, gives it meaning, defines, organizes and guides the choices that give structure to his life.

Peter Blos (1962) found that boys are oriented toward control and dominance over their environment, rather than being oriented through their feelings. In other words, male development is dependent on and identified with separation and control of the suppression of emotion. Development, for Blos, was a quest for competence, rather than contentment.

Education and Male Rites of Passage

American society gave its males the belief that psychological health, self-esteem, and identity depended on the qualities of individualism, self-sufficiency, and power. These were first obtained by separating from dependency on one's mother at an appropriately early age. It was deemed psychologically unhealthy for a male to become too attached to his mother. Therefore, it was necessary for the male to cut the mental umbilical cord, those "psychological apron strings," and to do it early enough so as not to damage his identification with maleness. With this warning label attached to male sons, mothers often distanced themselves emotionally and physically when their sons reached puberty.

What failed to be factored realistically into this social equation is that, when you remove the mother's influence, there often was no father or father substitute with whom the son could identify and find guidance. In many homes, fathers, grandfathers, and other male figures aren't available (due to separation, divorce, death, etc.). In such situations, modeling for young males is transferred to other males (e.g., Boy Scout leader, teachers, military officers, bosses, and gang leaders).

Society no longer provides many traditional rites of passage for males. What once was the task of ancient tribal rituals, family guidance, and community organizations, is now mainly in the responsible hands of overburdened educational bureaucracies and administrations. Actually, the educational system is ill-equipped single-handedly to lead either gender into adult roles. Educational institutions may have bypassed females, but they have given confusing and even harmful concepts to young males about manhood. For example, one of the social messages that has come down the educational pipeline is that males must keep validating their maleness. A man must be a successful competitor, a procreator, and a conscientious provider and protector. Schools, by default, have been left with the awesome task of guiding boys into manhood, and through them, men have been molded by myth as much as their sisters.

Education: An Umbrella for Mixed Messages to Young Males

The NCWRR study found that men had mixed feelings regarding their educational experience. On the one hand, their most negative experiences in school were during the years of 13-19 as reported earlier, yet 85% of males perceived education to be a positive contributor to self-esteem. This looks like a puzzling contradiction.

When examining open-ended questions and pursuing interviews with male subjects, we found some solutions to this puzzle: While they were in high school or college, teenage boys felt that schools were supporting them, especially in athletic programs, and this contributed to their self-esteem. However, they also recalled that sometimes they were singled out by teachers and administrators as being bad or disobedient or made to look stupid in classrooms. Yet many men who felt that their adult life wasn't very gratifying said they looked back nostalgically to their happier high school and college days.

The established themes of self-sufficiency and independence that have constituted the social fiber of man's life run contrary to the teaching methods of high schools and, to some degree, colleges. The pedagogical method of teaching that insists on passive-dependent receptiveness and a teacher-driven orientation is at odds with society's message to males and is often at odds within itself. For example, education motivates students by offering a predictable series of small but immediate rewards that are based on obedient classroom performance. But it isn't a realistic approach to adult life, because life isn't always like that. Some men spend the rest of their lives wondering why they can't achieve the success they achieved in the classroom and on the athletic field: Two different worlds with radically different expectations.

Males can be obsessed with individualism, the "man alone" image. This social theme of independence also encompasses the attitude that a man is either "at the top of the bunch" or he's "at the bottom of the heap" of a two-class social group. The man at the top is admirable, virile, powerful, heroic, worshipped; the man at the bottom is weak, inadequate, cowardly, ineffectual, humiliated and shunned.

The Passive-Aggressive Message
One indirect message presented to the students by the educational system is similar to that of society: There is only one way for men to succeed in life and that is through self-reliant behavior and successful coping with tough competition from peers. The educational system implies that it wants young males to assert themselves in order to become strong men. Yet the pedagogical teaching methods all through school demand behavior that is just the opposite. They are often required to function as passive, memorizing receptacles of information as it is presented by teachers. Students cannot be trusted to look for, find and use information; the aim of the

individual's education is to accumulate facts. Boisterous behavior is punishable, and questioning of content is not usually encouraged.

Yet under this same educational umbrella rests the physical education department, which encourages males to compete ruthlessly and, above all, win! Physical education, when left in its purest form, is healthy, invigorating and mood-enhancing. However, with the encouragement of the educational system, parents, and society, it is transformed into an ego-building mechanism based on destroying an opponent. It teaches the art of waging small wars against peers, friends, and strangers. In the words of college coach Vince Lombardi, "Winning isn't everything, it's the only thing!—from Little League to high school soccer to college basketball and football. Another important message that young males receive from kindergarten games on up is, "If you don't do sports, you don't do anything."

So one message teaches the art of passive/dependent behavior in the classroom: Be quiet; do nothing on your own, just listen and watch; and don't disrupt the process with questions and disagreement. At the same time this is going on in a classroom, there is another message being played out at the other end of the playing field. That message is to get ready to win at all costs; battle the other guy and do what it takes to get his trophy. The sports-trophy philosophy carries over into adult walks of life. Whether you are on the assembly line, sitting at a table with other board members, or out on an athletic playing field, the win-at-all-costs attitude prevails. Some competitive, lane-hopping fellows pilot a car as if they are in an aerial dogfight.

The educational system has played an important role in fostering this overly competitive attitude while instilling the double-visioned, mixed message of required passivity and silent self-control.

If a young male happens to lack physical coordination, strength, good eye-hand coordination, or an interest in sports, *he is stigmatized as a loser.* Self-esteem and status can be lost and identity confused for the boy or man who doesn't buy into the sports-hero mythology. He may get approval in the classroom for being quiet, smart and obedient, but he secretly knows that such behavior is not culturally valued in males. Schools, families, the community, and the nation rally and cheer their local sports heroes. Everyone knows the name of the local quarterback, but most won't know the name of the local boy who finished first at the less popular science fair. The mixed messages presented to both types of males are confusing and can be harmful to a balanced sense of self in adulthood.

Fraternal Messages of Humiliation

Originally, in ancient times, a young man's initiation into manhood was to prove his skill as a warrior, his ability to tolerate the pains of battle wounds and his skill in killing animals for food. In some primitive tribes, if a young man failed to surmount the trials of the initiation rite, he was officially regarded as a female, required to dress like a female, remain in the company of females and do female chores indefinitely.

Being part of the "clubby" teen and college campus culture involves, for a selected individual, initiation rites of a club, fraternity, sorority, or sometimes even an athletic team. These rites take place under the condescending and passively accepting auspices of administrators in high schools and institutions of higher learning. Ostensibly the rite is to prove the candidate's worthiness of the organization. Yet humiliation, mocking, hazing, verbal assaults, physical abuse, and sometimes death have all been assoicated with this supposed rite of passage.

Pledges and initiates are often forced to drink to excess. Some have been driven miles from campus only to be left with little or no clothing in freezing temperatures. They are physically degraded and suffer verbal abuse that can demolish what self-esteem is left. After days or weeks of surviving this type of nightmarish "Hell Week" assault, the pledges and initiates are embraced as family. The next year these same new members will have the privilege of participating in the torment of new pledges. Most high school and college administrations turn a blind eye toward this type of group behavior, perhaps rationalizing that it serves as a release of work tension, or minimizing: . . . "It's been going on for years, just a simple tradition." Only when there is a death or casualty from this rite will an institution take some temporary action, such as suspending or disbanding the organization; the rite itself is permitted to continue.

There are males who either don't want to belong to these types of clubs, or are rejected by them by being voted out. They often end up being socially isolated, or when generally disliked for some reason, ostracized. A student can be cut off from the mainstream of campus social life simply because he or she doesn't feel comfortable participating, or doesn't measure up to the distorted standard of cruel behavior. Some students who pledge and are rejected can suffer intense loss of self-esteem, can have their identity as a peer shaken and their status lowered. They can become confused about what male adequacy is all about.

The Mythological Illogical Message in "Boys Will Be Boys"

Pumping up manliness by putting down and degrading adolescent females is an attitude that hurts girls, but it harms males just as much. The locker-room, male bravado of "scoring," "telling all," and "bragging" or making explicit, derogatory remarks about sexual conquests are all peer-accepted forms of schoolyard and campus behavior. Most school and college administrators turn their eyes upward, shake their heads slowly from side to side, and then do nothing. This is tantamount to condoning this sexual and physical cruelty on the part of students.

The tendency of group security to become distorted and corrupt depends on the failure of leadership to control anarchy and mob chaos. A group of competitive and immature young men can degenerate to the point where the mark of maleness depends on the ability of individuals to degrade and objectify young, equally immature females as "scored points" of sexual conquest. Only when someone blows the whistle, such as the California Spur Posse incident, the Glenn Ridge, New Jersey, assault case, or the Navy Tailhook scandle, do families, schools and government authorities finally react and condemn this kind of group misbehavior. By the sheer act of not getting involved, schools indirectly show tolerance of adolescent male conduct that leads to a general contempt for women.

Institutions of higher learning can be incubation centers for negative male themes and ideals that often rob men of true self-esteem and a balanced sense of self. The images that tend to persist are ones of competition, aggressiveness, status, and the resort to violence, power and conquest at all costs. Mixed messages, starting in high school and continuing on college campuses, cause many males to have feelings that range from interjected anger to mild depression, and may lead to withdrawal, violence outward, and suicide. Adolescents' tendency to act out their intense feelings requires watchful supervision and guidance.

The notion that these intense feelings and acts are just a normal part of adolescence is false. Some institutions of higher learning bear a responsibility in this by tolerating contempt for females and allowing or supporting activities that induce negative characteristics in students. Supporting and encouraging young males to display attitudes that lead to misogyny and emotional and physical aggressiveness should not be tolerated. The long-term products of an educational system that houses and accepts such behaviors as the norm are men who, at their best, behave like "lost boys," who remain emotionally distant and lonely, who make lousy husbands and poor fathers, who suffer from midlife disillusionment and depression, and who, at their worst, are emotionally and physically abusive to other human beings.

Young males are consumers of certain images. It's unfortunate, but a lot of them tend to identify with uncouth, macho, bravado images portrayed *en masse* in such media as television, movies, books, and popular music. Boys entering adulthood are exposed to a world of mixed messages. On the one hand, women state that they want their men to be nurturing, considerate, kind, gentle, and emotionally expressive. On the other hand, young men receive societal messages that foster contempt and exploitation of women.

Following the Social Blueprint

The following case studies will describe young men who were exposed to and identified with many aspects of the "social blueprint" given them in high school and college. The raw fact is that using this blueprint for the good life can often backfire and shatter these men in midlife by the explosions of unanticipated realities. The collapse of the life plan that was designed for them in school can leave men confused, angry, and bitter. There are also some success stories about men who were able to adapt well in society and make successful use of the same educational system, after the blueprint failed. No mixed message is intended here; the intention is to explain how education in midlife can provide the means for new growth and reconstruction after such a failure.

When the Cheering Stops

Sports and athletic programs in schools and colleges can affect self-esteem and self-image in a positive way. A problem may arise when people, such as coaches, faculty, peers, and entire school systems base their collective pride and self-esteem and importance on one or two well-coordinated athletes or teams. Often an entire school's self-esteem rests on a single team or even a single player. The player may base his or her self-worth on game performance alone. But what happens when athletes have to move into the adult world without the cheering section?

Fifty-year-old Tom was from an Irish family outside of Boston. His family were working-class people who had settled in a factory town. He was the eldest son, and had a younger brother and sister. The academic side of school never captured Tom's interest, so he described his elementary school years as boring and unmemorable. He never felt at ease with teachers or many of his peers. However, by the time he got to high school everything changed. Tom became the local hero and source of the community's and school's collective self-esteem. It was a big burden that carried a big price for Tom.

I was 6'1" by the time I was a freshman in high school and still growing. Naturally I tried out for junior varsity basketball, and I made the team. I'd played a lot of basketball-type games on the streets, so I was able to play well in the school games. Soon I was being treated like I was some kind of a TV hero. I was only fourteen years old and had girls giving me the eye and smiling and wanting attention. When I made varsity, guys treated me with respect and wanted to be my friend. I kept hearing, "You're the greatest out there." It was the same all through high school. Sometimes, when I made a winning basket, the whole school went wild. I was never that good a student. Teachers let my marginal grades slide and just pushed me through. After all, I was everybody's number one boy. I got to admit, I felt great, too great. . . . My head swelled all the way through high school and into college on a basketball scholarship.

People I went with and the college coach thought I could make pro easily. I had a less than respectable D average in most things. Studying and classwork never did anything for me, but the idea of becoming a pro turned my head. I was a winner in everybody's eyes . . . I got to believe I was always going to be a winner. It was going to be easy!

Well, it was quick and simple: I got passed over by the pro recruiters in my senior year. The bubble in my head burst, and it was a shock. . . . It had never occurred to me that I could be in for a fall. Suddenly I felt like I was in the middle of a desert with nobody around except little old, just everyday me.

"I felt the attitude toward me change. Mine changed, too, like I let my *alma mater* down. Some people were still my friends, but I sensed disappointment all around me. I was angry and then bitter for a long while—like the quarterback who made all the right moves in the first quarter and then was put on the bench for the rest of the game. No one had told me there were new rules to the game and what the rules were to get in the pro field. I was just about failing, but then it was May and I graduated.

Left to my own devices, I didn't have a clue what to do with my life. I had put such thoughts aside thinking I'd get by as a pro. I came back home, maybe because that's where it all began. Everything else in the middle began to fade and didn't seem real anymore. Sometimes, though, I could still hear the cheering in my head while I was scrambling around looking for a job—any job. On the strength of having a diploma, I finally got a job with a local sporting goods chain as an assistant manager.

Well, I settled into a routine that became my way of life before I knew what was happening to me. In between all this, I sometimes felt sorry for myself when I'd think about all those what-could-have-beens . . . then about not making it. That started my drinking too much. . . . It made all the bad memories melt down some for a while, anyway.

The good part is that I married, and my wife stuck by me. . . . She's been real good for me. She made me believe that I'm no dummy and she helped me realize that I had a problem. After that, she was my cheering squad until I got over it.

It's not a bad life after all! We have two cute daughters. . . . I've moved up some, too. I'm one of the district managers of several large sporting goods chains. I live about thirty miles from my home town and can see my folks. My kids are computer geniuses—something I don't understand yet. But that's okay, I'm just glad the two girls aren't athletes.

I'm still kind of a hero when basketball season rolls around. The guys I watch the games with want to know my opinion about the different players and teams. . . . I play it up for all its worth.

Tom is an example of what happens to some youths who are athletic heroes in school, only to be left floundering after graduation, when the school moves on to cheer a new hero. All Tom's future hopes and his self-esteem were based on one facet of life—encouraged by his school, family and friends—but the singular skill he developed didn't apply to adult life.

When the Blueprint Fails

Jack is a fifty-one-year-old man who followed the educational/societal blueprint during his school years only to find out later that his life didn't work out at all the way it was promised. During his high school and college years, Jack studied hard, got excellent grades and was involved in several of the extra, curricular activities. According to his high school guidance counselor, his teachers and the notations in his high school yearbook, everyone expected him to be a success in life.

This "most likely to succeed" young man entered an East Coast, Ivy League college and continued to follow the blueprint that he had so far successfully managed. After all, his hard work and good grades in high school had landed him in a top college, so he felt confident about his future after graduation.

When Jack was interviewed, he was recovering from an ankle fracture. He said that his body was letting him down. He was obviously frustrated and depressed. He was asked about his schooling and his life since graduation.

> I haven't done well. . . . My life over the last 30 years has been a lot different than it was in the Sixties in college. It's not that I harbor any ill will now toward my schools and teachers. . . . On the contrary, I have a healthy respect for the schools and what they tried to do for me. I blame myself and my own shortcomings, but I also believe that the school I went through had something to do with the hard time I've had.
>
> When I was going to school, I worked hard, did well and thought I was a success. In school, it looked as if all I had to do to be a success was to get lots of As. Now I know that validation with As doesn't necessarily work, because it's an artificial gimmick and doesn't apply to what I ran into after graduation, and ever since.
>
> After undergraduate college I went after my MBA and finished

post-grad school fifth in my class. My family had helped me a lot and expected great things of me. I got married and didn't want my wife to work. She looked after our two kids. . . . I thought that was enough.

I was hired by a major corporation, but within a couple of years discovered I really wasn't prepared for the way things were run. I didn't understand or like the dog-eat-dog pattern of corporate warfare for one thing. Schooling hadn't taught me how to understand and manage employee relations, either. I had great difficulty trying to comprehend why it was, that year after year, after I kept working my tail off for them, I didn't get the bonus I thought I deserved or even a small raise. I got nothing, no A for all that extra, hard work they gave me or even a few, kind strokes from the boss. It began to look unrewarding. Yet there were other employees who didn't work as hard as I did, who got a bonus or a raise. I figured they knew ways to make the deals and work around the angles, and I didn't.

My wife and kids had to move ten times in fifteen years following company directives. We didn't have a chance to locate long enough to develop friendships . . . and our kids had a hard time switching schools over and over. Eventually my wife got so stressed out by that way of living, that one day she told me she had had enough. She left me for good when the kids left for college. I'm living alone in a small apartment, and after paying my own maintenance bills, I have all I can do to scrape the bottom for the kids' tuition and maintenance at college. Right now I'm trying to cope with the prospect of getting laid off like about 300 other people so far. . . . I hear the company expects to lay off another 500 by February.

I wish I could change myself or my job. . . . My ex-wife went back to school and is getting a master's in special education. She never worked much, but now she'll be starting a career of her own. . . . I feel bitter and burned out. This has been a much different world than I studied for and bargained my graying hair for. I played by the rules that I was taught in school, but the rules haven't worked out here. I look at my kids and see them playing by the same rules: "Get high grades and you'll get your rewards in the world of commerce!"

Jack applied himself brilliantly to the educational blueprint that was supposed to prepare him and individuals like him for a good, stable, and lucrative job. With this blueprint's promise for success in mind, he married and had children, but he wasn't prepared to cope with a recession, a poor job market, budget-cutting, staff-cutting, and unrewarded hard work for nothing. The collapse of expectations generated by college and the years of mediocre success in business left him feeling betrayed, anxious, insecure, angry, and cynical. He was in danger of sinking into the ineffectuality that comes with depressive psychopathology.

Jack excelled at following orders and being obedient and productive during his school years. He never questioned the authority around him, and he was rewarded for his passive, conforming behavior with excellent grades. He was made to feel he was a shoe-in for success. In the business world, employment made demands that school hadn't prepared him for: flexibility, creative thinking and discovery, enough assertiveness in the face of authority to disagree and make productive suggestions. Too much unquestioning conformity to the educational blueprint in the world of employment can, in fact, hinder adaptation and success.

Jack feels right now he has few choices and is locked into life by decisions that he made in late adolescence. The one thing he is trying to instill in his college-age children is that they don't have to make life decisions so early. His son is a sophomore and wants to leave school for a year. Jack, against the wishes of his ex-wife, is supporting his son's decision to leave school for a year to perhaps work and do some traveling. Jack, at this point in adulthood, is not ready to address the choices and changes that could open up new aspects of his life and sense of self in adulthood. However, by supporting new directions for his children that veer from the blueprint, he may be taking a first step towards making changes in his own life.

Lost Boys
Jason attended a private school for the elementary grades, a school that encouraged independent thinking, creativity, self-expression, and the importance of individuality. Since the private school didn't go beyond eighth grade, Jason entered a local public high school. It was a totally different and contradictory experience for him. He kept usurping his teachers' lesson plans by asking questions, expressing optional alternatives or disagreements. Conformity, rigidity, group consensus as opposed to individuality, and a mythical worship of all things connected with sports, were the themes that ran through the high school from administrators down to the hall monitors.

Fear of failure and disapproval, feeling out of place, boredom with memorizing, discomfort with the prevailing sports mentality, and intellectual suffocation were the major forces driving Jason's life in high school. He finally dropped out of school after his seventeenth birthday and sought stimulation and approval elsewhere. Never getting into serious trouble, he hung out on the streets with friends who also felt unconnected with school. He never was a real part of the street scene, though; he gravitated into the role of an observer, a thoughtful presence and a guide to those of his friends who were troubled.

I never felt part of anything in high school. I put up barriers against being called a nerd when I was about fourteen: I wore the peer-approved leather jacket, got my ear pierced and let my hair grow long. The guys I went with respected me, but inside I was scared. School didn't connect with me, and I thought I was somehow deficient. I built secure walls around myself. It was the only way I knew how to get through without scars.

I did want to learn, though! I dropped out of school and traveled through much of Europe with my parents, soaking up museums, cathedrals, castles, local culture and classical music. I got to be a history buff, and after spending a lot of time in libraries, I knew more about the two World Wars than my teachers. I also read most of Edgar Allen Poe, much of Shakespeare and some of Hemingway. I studied the artistic work of H. R. Giger and Dali, enjoyed the classics from Mozart to Tchaikovsky, as well as Guns & Roses stuff. Yet I couldn't diagram a sentence structure or understand mathematics symbols or shoot a decent basket in gym. I just didn't fit into the mold. I thought all along it was me.

Part of it was me, all right! I could have gone along with the crowd at school, but didn't want to. I just didn't have much confidence. Somehow I just couldn't conform to the academic side of school life, and I didn't have any excuse, like being an athlete.

Most of my teachers thought well enough of me, but they never quite understood where I was coming from. They might have found out if they'd taken me aside and talked with me. Their words describing me kept buzzing around in my head, "much potential . . . much potential." I remember being on a French class trip to Montreal and Quebec. . . . On the ship going up the St. Lawrence River, my French teacher and I sat together on the deck and really talked. It wasn't about a classroom or a homework topic; we met on some common ground. I enjoyed finding things in common to discuss and debate. Individually, my teachers acknowledged something special, something good and different about me. But it never seemed to fit the curriculum and class action.

I never could fit in with the program at school, so I dropped out. It was like I flew into a major, black hole in the sky. I'm nineteen now and still struggling to find my way out of it. If you don't fit the mold that they cast for you in school, you're a failure. I've worked cleaning up the laboratory of a major magazine photographer, then as a carpenter's helper. I dug up and shucked clams at the shore for a fishery, too. I'm planning to study art in London soon.

My education has been haphazard enough to resemble a patchwork quilt. I know I'm intelligent and pretty knowledgeable for school, but there is a world out there that I want to know about and find out what I'd like to do in it. I'm willing to go the traditional, compulsory route once I find out these things about myself and that world and its people.

People can easily perceive Jason as a modern-day James Dean, or just a troubled kid. He isn't alone; there are many school kids who don't connect with school, its system and methods of teaching. Many of them are bright, creative, eager with curiosities that the system doesn't satisfy, kids who like to use trial and error, think things through and express themselves.

The educational system has a difficult time connecting with boys like Jason. Although trained to identify exceptional boys, teachers are still failing to contribute inspiration and promote their affinity for learning and their yearning for information about the world they perceive around them. It's time-consuming, expensive and requires extra work on the part of an educational system to address the needs of the "other" type of student. Instead of providing "special education" for brilliant students as we have for handicapped children, the exceptionally bright youths are directed into the mainstream melting pot.

Jason may find his own way. His parents respect him and know him well. They'll stand behind him. Fortunately, they have the money to let him explore and experience the world around him.

But what happens to boys whose empathetic parents lack the financial resources to provide a private, stimulating growth environment? Budgets for some schools have been cut. The educational systems were forced to reduce guidance counselor staff in the Special Education Department and reduce the working hours of psychologists on the Child Study Team who could identify handicapped children and describe their problems. It's ironic that the next generation of handicapped and exceptionally bright children may be sacrificed for a financial bottom line.

It's Never Too Late to Learn

Ed was a rugged, dynamic type of fellow, calling to mind the movie star, Anthony Quinn. Now sixty-four, he has led a colorful and often chaotic life. Ed never followed the academic or social blueprint of school that promised him a successful life. He admits being a terrible student in high school, barely graduating, and always a rebel in trouble. He described his teachers as breathing a great sigh of relief when he left school each afternoon. In his youth, education meant nothing to him.

As a teenager Ed yearned to be a soldier, but by the time he was out of high school, World War II had ended. He didn't have any idea what to do with his life. He worked for a while pumping gas, got a job working on a fishing boat for a summer, then found work on an oil rig as a mechanic. This fellow didn't have the aura of a Harvard or Princeton man, but he had "street smarts" and was no one's fool. His ease with troubleshooting, solving and fixing problems on the oil rigs made his bosses take notice. The oil company recognized that Ed was someone special.

"By the time I was fifty I thought I had the best that life could offer me. It took me a while to get there. I put in long hours, and traveled extensively, and this put a terrible toll on my first two marriages. Three marriages and six children later, I thought I had it all nailed down just right. I had traveled the world over solving company problems, lived comfortably in South America with my family for a time, and worked my way up the line to be a supervisor of supervisors in the company. I had a successful ten years, and there were hints about a future vice presidency. I was privately proud of myself, but somebody said, "Pride goes before a fall." I fell.

I lived it up royally, spent too much money and never saved anything except my retirement pension money that I never saw. I
thought my situation would always be there, the money rolling in, a
great job. . . . I thought my family would never want for anything. It
happened so suddenly! I was politely informed that the company was
forced to downsize on staff. Something about "more global competition to contend with" and "corporate survival meant a leaner oper-
ation." They were very sorry, but my department and job had to be
eliminated. Just like that! Everybody said I had done a great job, but
the corporate world had its peculiarities. I got great letters of recommendation from the company, but looking around, I found other
companies were downsizing, too. Who needed another fifty-some-
thing supervisor of supervisors?

I went through a major depression, along with high blood pressure and cholesterol levels that were taking me straight into heart
attack country. My wife went back to work full time as a manager in
a department store, while I sat at home feeling sorry for myself. In
my mind, I was literally waiting to die. A year went by, and with the
help of a psychologist and a slew of medicines, I felt better. I then
made a commitment to change my lifestyle. It was at this point that
my engine fired up and I started to move again.

I always was a maverick, avoiding the well-beaten trails, but this
time I knew it would be necessary to go back to school and retrain
for something. No one in my family was surprised. "Better late than
never," they said. But I was really scared. My fifty-four-year-old
impression of school was one of boredom, strict discipline, refusal to
clasp my hands on the desk, humiliation, punishment, and anger.
Anyway, I knew I had to retool my mind if I was ever going to get my
life and my self-respect back again.

It certainly wasn't school as I remembered it. It was a revelation
how I enjoyed studying all the humanities. I went on to finish with a
bachelor's degree in psychology—quite a stretch from working on
oil rigs! I graduated with a summa cum laude degree, and for the
first time I felt book-smart. My wife was so proud of me! But a major
in psychology doesn't produce a job. I had gained a lot of my self-
confidence back, so I went ahead for an advanced degree.

"To make a long story short, I went for the 'big one'. I enrolled in
a program that combined a master's degree and PhD. I had my
doubts, of course. After all, what teen or young adult was going to lis-

ten to a sixty-something counselor? But I found out that there was a great need for diagnostics and psychotherapy for aging adults. I eventually got my PhD. in gerontology, the "in" degree of all degrees, and I can't begin to tell you how much better it was going to school as an adult. It's not only my professional status, but the realization of what I was able to do. I feel good about myself. That makes it a lot easier to help some old person out of the doldrums. I'm also in a good position to tell other lost people what they might gain from a return to school, even if it's just for the pure enrichment. Most of the adult students I took classes with were women. More men should try it.

Ed is an explorer and a pioneer in the gradually increasing trend of men returning to school to change, modify, or perhaps enhance a job status or start a new career. Education is not for the young only; it is the tool of choice for adults to combine experience with a base of new knowledge.

THE NEEDS OF OLDER ADULTS IN GRADUATE EDUCATION

As mentioned previously, adults come back to formal education for a variety of reasons. Unlike younger students, returning older students requires support and nurturing both in and out of the classroom. Faculty must be aware of their unique needs. The following case study addresses the collective experiences of the faculty in the Graduate Gerontology Program at Southampton College of Long Island University (LIU). The program has been in existence for over five years, has four campuses, with the average student age being 46 (the age range is from 34 to 74). The purpose of the program is to train students to work in the field of aging. The observations below are based on over 250 students in the program since its inception.

The LIU graduate gerontology faculty has found that returning older students demand and require that course content have applied relevance to their life and occupational experiences. As one faculty member noted in a recent departmental meeting, "If your lectures are not grounded in reality, you will find yourself quickly grounded." In general, older students have the following characteristics:

1. This student population enters the classroom with clearly defined occupational needs and expectations that must be addressed by the course content. Time that is spent in the classroom is considered a precious commodity. Lectures, reading materials, and classroom assignments must meet specific career goals and objectives. Students expect that faculty will apply knowledge to experiences that they can recognize.

2. Older students want any course (whether it is theoretical or applied) to include extensive time for discussion, interaction, and debate. One faculty member, asked to identify the most important component in making a given course successful for students, replied, "Our older students want to be heard; they want validation for their personal and occupational experiences; and they want a classroom environment that is conducive to the exploration of ideas and opinions; they don't want to be talked at, but talked with." In response, the faculty have adopted the notion that the classroom is an arena in which learning is a reciprocal process between student and teacher. Via discussion, both parties gain valuable insights and perspectives.

3. Students cooperate in mutual support. An overwhelming percentage of our faculty have noted that the classroom is not simply a place to gain knowledge but is utilized as a mutual support system among students. In over five years of reviewing our students' Integrated Papers (their final, culminating experience prior to graduation, which require them to reflect on what they learned throughout their course of studies), "student camaraderie" was noted as the second most beneficial aspect of the program (gaining skills and knowledge was first). Since most of our students are facing similar life transitions and challenges, their classmates become a support group. Such mutual support has been particularly helpful to older students when they find out that others in their peer group face similar anxieties about being able to handle the rigors of graduate education.

4. Due to the nature of the subject matter, students become very introspective regarding personal and career accomplishments, family relationships, caregiver concerns, and other

issues. A question that has consumed an extensive amount of time in departmental meetings is the role of the faculty member in assisting students with personal, nonacademic concerns. Some students look to the faculty for advice and guidance in handling such issues. Faculty have been required to draw a line between their role as a teacher and as a counselor. As one faculty member noted, "It is erroneous to believe that there is not some 'hand-holding' that goes along with your job description in teaching adults that are at a point in their lives when they are living the subject matter."

5. Returning older students (who may not have been in a classroom for 25 years) present to faculty a variety of academic challenges. It is not uncommon that faculty must refamiliarize students with how to write a paper, conduct a literature search, properly reference sources, and other academic skills. One particular faculty member recently commented that her biggest problem was making it clear to her students that graduate education is by nature different than continuing education (which is less academically rigorous). It has been our experience that faculty who face these issues with an attitude that part of their role is to assist returning students with academic and scholarly skills work best with this population. It is important to note that returning older students are quickly able to grasp and adopt the skills needed to write excellent papers.

6. Older students are constantly frustrated that the school bookstore is not open after work, library hours do not coincide with one's time off, registration and advisement procedures are not flexible, and other institutional policies. By nature, institutions of higher learning are not equipped or accustomed to dealing with non-traditional, returning adult students. Not only are faculty required to teach a given topic area, but also must "trouble-shoot" institutional problems.

It would be a mistake to state that all of the graduate gerontology faculty easily developed the right mind-set and skills needed to be effective teachers with returning midlife students. For those faculty that previously taught on an undergraduate level (where students ranged in age from 18 to 22), the adjustment process was quite noticeable. However, a fascinating process occurred with these faculty members as they became acclimated to this student population: At first, older students challenge of long-held assumptions and theories was somewhat disconcerting to faculty who had not often been questioned. Although painful for some, such faculty eventually welcomed the opportunity to rethink and reconceptualize their own beliefs and perspectives. Teaching students with greater life experiences promoted a high degree of personal introspection on the part of the faculty member. This has led to many faculty indicating that they have not only become better teachers but better human beings. Due to the nature of the subject matter and the age of the student population, some faculty reported that they had an opportunity to reflect on their own aging process for the first time.

As more older students return to the classroom, many faculty will need to re-think how they teach material, re-examine how they interact with students, and what is expected of them in making research and scholarship more relevant. It is our premise that older students offer faculty an opportunity to continue their own personal and professional development. Not all existing traditional faculty will welcome the opportunity to change a teaching style that has been cultivated and groomed for years. However, for those that do have the desire to teach older students, and adapt their teaching methods and perspectives, the experience is both exhilarating and unparalleled.

Intergenerational Learning

Just as institutions of higher learning are experiencing a deluge of returning older students into graduate education, the traditional undergraduate classroom is undergoing a radical transformation. Until recently, it was a rare phenomena to witness undergraduate classes that contained both younger and older students. Now, we are finding that undergraduate classrooms are truly intergenerational with a wide spectrum of ages and historical eras represented. The following are Hayes' experiences in teaching intergenerational undergraduate courses:

Initially, younger and older students sometimes interact based on entrenched stereotypes based on age. For example, Dr. Christopher Hayes' undergraduate class in Adolescent and Adult Development, several younger students once commented to me that they felt "awkward" talking in class about existing sexual practices of the "younger generation" with older individuals in the class. After several minutes on the topic, the older students (ranging in age from forty-eight to fifty-six) began to discuss living through the sexual revolution of the Sixties. In actuality, both age groups found that not only did they share many similar issues regarding sexuality, but that self-imposed age dichotomies vanished. By the end of the course, there was mutual give and take.

Students of different ages and genders can utilize the classroom experience as a vehicle towards increasing one's understanding of "self." For example, in a child psychology class that contains both students who have had children and younger students who have yet to experience raising a child, there is a unique learning opportunity for both to share actual versus anticipated child-rearing experiences.

SUMMARY

Education is a major life-tie that can affect the self-esteem of men and women in positive and negative ways. Women and men may experience the positive and negative effects of education at different times in life. Males may have received excellent grades and praise from the educational system early in life, contributing to positive self-esteem, only to suffer the loss of the plaudits during adulthood if the education isn't appropriate or applicable to their way of life. Women can suffer from neglect and consequent low self-esteem studying in an educational system too preoccupied with boisterous and athletic males, but they are often able to rebound in adulthood when they reenter school.

Education is a very important function in the life of people. It is a life-tie that affects self-esteem and is a resource for the enrichment of identity throughout an individual's life. Education figures prominently in the way individuals view themselves. Faith in the power of education has been widespread in America for more than a century. This faith is upheld because of two American ideals: first, that democracy requires an educated population to participate in public decision making; and second, that education brings economic rewards that enhance social status, individual prestige, and the pursuit of happiness.

When educational systems fail to prepare youth to meet their future individual needs, self-esteem is bound to suffer in adulthood. Early academic failures, fears, disappointments in status, rejections by clubs and college admission boards, consequent loss of pride and exclusions from activities can crush a young male or female's budding sense of self. Recognition for school achievement, individual encouragement, experiences with self-directed learning, and self-discovery can buttress an individual against future economic setbacks. They may also help assure social success and foster the intrinsic rewards of pride and motivation. Education is a structural factor that can interact with the adult life of men and women and with other life-tie factors and themes. Education provides a setting in which more meaningful aspects of life are realized, such as a locus of success, a means to maintain personal affiliations, an avenue toward financial security and a way to develop new, enriched, and enlightened aspects of an individual identity.

- Meg, a woman shortchanged by the system early in life, moved ahead from her early "MRS" degree to an MSW degree that has given her financial security and feelings of self-worth.
- Patty's development was interrupted early by a teen pregnancy, but she later went on to pursue higher education and become a good role model for her children.
- Sixty-eight-year-old Maud's quest for self-discovery was prompted by the crisis of a coronary condition, and learning gave new meaning to her life.

Many females have been shortchanged in adolescence by an insensitive educational system; males have been subjected to mixed messages early in life. Self-sufficiency and independence have been held as ideals that males must strive for, but contemporary education in the elementary grades of many schools demands passive-dependent, receptive, classroom behavior. Confusion and disillusionment are experienced by men in midlife when expectations don't meet the realities of their life.

- Jack had followed the social blueprint of obedience to those in authority through hard work, good grades, and achievement of honors, only to find later in life that getting a succession of honors and degrees doesn't protect one from divorce, financial shortfalls, industrial recessions and potential layoffs.
- Tom had great athletic ability, but his chance for a sports career was thwarted when, for some unknown reason, he was passed over by pro recruiters. When the cheering stopped, Tom found he had nothing else to fall back on for survival in the competitive world of business—until he discovered he could fall back on more education.
- Jason was a casualty in a system that failed to meet his personal needs. Bored and unchallenged, he dropped out of school.
- Ed is one of a few men who decided to go back to school in midlife. He has learned the value of being an adult learner.

Men are beginning to discover adult learning and its benefits. The trend of adults toward the return to school has opened new careers, has boosted self-esteem and fostered new aspects of identity. The educational system that was lacking or which in some way damaged the prospects of some young people can become the same medium that provides adults a second chance at a new career or personal growth. The reentry into education after a midlife failure can release a powerful force for rehabilitation. Retraining and the expansion of knowledge enable men and women to discover, develop and use potentials that were latent. Education enables people to reassess the requirements for a return to full life activity.

The approach through structured academic programs or informal group arrangements offers women and men opportunities to transcend the monotony of jobs they become locked into and in general can heighten awareness and embellish their identity with ideas, facts and opinions.

Education enables women and men to develop their potential and more accurately assess the requirements for a full life. Education in adulthood, whether through structured academic learning or informal learning, leads women and men to detach from the personal and private worlds of their family and social subcultures to heightened identity awareness. Self-esteem must come from the inside. Education contributes to self-esteem and growth when an individual enters the educational system with maturity and a background of life experiences. Unfortunately this happens for the most part only in adulthood. Early education may hinder self-esteem in both boys and girls, not so much on account of gender treatment, but because of education's very nature of total influence and control. It is only when this life-tie ceases to be an undue influence and ceases to exert total control on the individual, that it will become a resource that will affect self-esteem in a positive way.

CHAPTER 4

Friends and Mentors

To throw away an honest friend is, as it were,
to throw your life away.

—*Sophocles, 430 B.C.*

FRIENDSHIPS

Affective ties—based on the need to form friendships—are an important source of personal meaning, identity and self-esteem all through life for both women and men. Humans have formed social groups throughout history and most would agree that social bonds are essential to well-being. In ancient times, tight-knit social groups offered protection against the very real threats of an unpredictable and hostile environment. Although we don't live in imminent danger from predators, living in a stressful and often unpredictable world makes for a continued need for mutual caring. Social support makes women and men less vulnerable to the effects of crisis and stressful events.

The current emphasis upon personal connections and friendships as a touchstone of health, happiness and well-being is a recent phenomenon. According to Nussbaum (1994), the friendship relationship, which was virtually ignored by social scientists for the first seventy years of this century, has produced a massive and impressive amount of interdisciplinary research within the past two decades. Recently, a variety of excellent resources have appeared that report

137

upon both the latest findings and extensive original research into friendship during the mid-life and later years, (e.g., Adams & Blieszner, 1989; Blieszner & Adams, 1992; Duck, 1993; Matthews, 1986; Rawlins, 1992). Earlier generations would not have rated human relationships as highly, believing that the daily round, the common task, should furnish all one's needs and wants. However, friendships act as points of reference that help people make sense of their experience. Friendships represent one of the supporting pillars in human development. Friends can bolster our ego, self-acceptance, and self-definition (Tesch, 1983). Both women and men need a sense of being part of a larger community than that constituted just by the family. Friendships outside the family contribute in a large way to one's sense of self and identity.

Psychologist Leo Buscaglia once described friendship as a way of discovering another's unique world while at the same time receiving an honest reflection of one's own world. It is for this reason that it is so easy to love casual friends, and so difficult to love a lover. Our investment in a friend is far less revealing and demanding than that for a lover." The Greeks called friendship love *philia,* a rational and tranquil form of love between equals. Two friends are united by a shared truth or common interest. McAdams (1994) describes *philia* as an involvement for a friend. Good friends admire qualities in each other, sometimes seeing themselves, or what they would like themselves to be, in their friends.

Friendship Across the Life Cycle

Psychiatrist Harry Stack Sullivan (1949) believed there was nothing more wonderful than a close friendship. The intimacy experienced by two friends represents the pinnacle of human experience. Yet, Sullivan felt, individuals were very fortunate if they experienced such intimacy more than once or twice in their lives, especially as adults. He believed that a person is most likely to experience the beauty of an intimate friendship in the years before puberty, as a preadolescent whose sexuality has yet to be awakened. Sullivan assumed that life got too complicated afterward and that true friendship in adolescence and adulthood was very difficult to find. Adults are often left groping for connections with other people, longing and often frustrated by the limitations of human communion.

Fortunately, not everyone is as gloomy as Sullivan in their analysis of friendship patterns. John Bowlby (1969) did extensive work in the area of human relationships which he documented in three volumes on attachment and loss. Bowlby assumed that the most important need of human beings from infancy through adulthood is for supportive and rewarding relationships with other human beings. He considered that an adult's capacity for having good relationships with other adults depended upon the person's experience of attachment figures when a child.

A child who is certain of his attachment figures will develop a sense of security and confidence that will make it possible for him to trust and care for other human beings as an adult. In *Attachment and Loss,* Bowlby states his views on intimate attachments. He strongly believed that attachments to other individuals are centered to a person's life not just in childhood. Attachments are important throughout adulthood and old age. A person draws strength and enjoyment from others as well as giving these same qualities back to others.

Friends have been described as a central component of a social support system that accompanies women and men across the life course. Some friendships are maintained from childhood, other friends are added through life. Friends are found through school, work, professional associations, clubs, church, communities, travel and through other friends.

Age can influence friendship patterns. In young adulthood, friendship choice is often linked to such statuses as worker, parent, or spouse. In middle and old age many of these roles are relinquished and friendships become more expressive and less instrumental. Their formation and maintenance may be more problematic as one ages. Letters and phone calls may be a way to connect the hearts and minds of older friends. Over the life course, children and spouses may leave. Jobs, health, and locations all may change as women and men grow older. However, good friendships endure as the constant amid the many variables of life. Even when friends move on, either physically, emotionally, or intellectually, memories of that friendship and its importance remain.

Litwak (1989) indicates that the nature of friendship may change across the life span. He asserts that an older individual "in a modern industrial society is optimally served by at least three different types of friendship groups based on time" (p. 77). The long-term friend, the intermediate-term friend, and the short-term friend are structurally different, and they accomplish different friendship tasks.

Friendship and Gender

Friendship and the intimacy associated with friendship describes someone who is warm, compassionate, responsible, loving, gentle and nurturant. These communal characteristics have been used to describe women and not men. Women have been identified with being the better relators, as compared to men. According to Wright (1982) and Bell (1981), female friendships are more personal, intimate, and emotional, while male friendships revolve around shared activities. However, all people have a recurrent desire and need for warm, close and sharing relationships. The NCWRR study found that close to 40% of both women and men felt friendships have been important to them all through life, not at one particular stage of life. What is important is the fact that both genders value friendship and consider it important to their lives. Interdependence, a willingness to listen, offering counsel and nonjudgmental advice are important qualities in a friendship expressed by both women and men.

Males may lack the skills that females have when it comes to developing and maintaining relationships, but the need and importance is very much present in the lives of both women and men. Vaillant (1977), in a Harvard study, found men who showed concern for others early tended to adapt more successfully and happily to challenges faced in their marriages and work. At the same time females have been generally found to score slightly higher on intimacy motivation than males.

Contemprary female psychologists, such as Miller (1976), Gilligan (1982), and Belenky et al. (1986), have underscored that women's strength comes from their ability to relate and connect to others. They have suggested that men lack this quality. It may be that men do not lack the quality and the need to relate, rather they lack the means to express their needs to relate—more of a case of learned behavior than an innate gender quality.

One of the main defining characteristics of Western manhood has been that of rugged individualism and the theme of "going it alone." This attitude has produced generations of isolated and often lonely men. Men might have had the courage to stand alone, but lacked the awareness and societal approval to develop their needs for communion. Laurels have been awarded to those men who beat out the competition, climb the ladder of professional success and become "number one," but too often being number one means being alone. Ask any corporate CEO what price he has had to pay for going it alone to get to the top. Often he will admit he has been isolated not only from his family, but has few intimate friendships.

Past research has shown that patterns of friendship vary by sex. At all ages, females describe their friendships in terms of emotional closeness. However, many of the early studies were based on gender-linked social roles of the past. Men were in the workplace and women were at home. Over the last twenty-five years the roles have converged, with the majority of women participating in the workplace. The friendship patterns may be getting more similar, as social roles are becoming more diffused. The NCWRR study found that 53% of women and 43% of men stated they have a lot of friends, but few close ones. Twenty-nine percent of men have a few close friends; this was also true for 26% of the women in the study. Only 18% of males and 15% of females reported having many close friends.

The double shift—working all day and caring for home and family at night—experienced by many women handicaps their ability to maintain and make many close friends. Women's free time is hoarded and rationed out to only the most deserving, and in most cases this means close family and children. The era when women stayed home gave them surplus time to meet and form many close friendships with other women who had children and were also at home. Networking via the telephone, at the children's playground, at leisurely lunches, and cementing friendships over coffee served in the kitchen to ward off the sheer isolation of being at home became the backbone of long and lasting women's friendships. Just as time and work have been the enemies of males' forming many close friendships, they have now become the enemy of women as well. This equal-opportunity situation has proven harmful to social support networks for men in later life and could prove harmful to working women as they grow older.

Friendship and Self-Esteem

Friends help to affirm one's identity and self-concept in more ways than just sharing activities. As Tavris (1986) found through her research, old friends know each other well, they have a sense of history, they recognize and respect a friend's many roles, they understand one's values and personalities, and accept one's flaws. These ties can no longer be taken for granted. Friends reassure each other that they have a place in the world, and friends enhance psychological well-being by sharing triumphs, disasters, heartbreaks, and joys. Most importantly, friends validate identities and contribute to positive self-worth through the life course for both women and men.

The bonds of a truly shared self are a powerful source of self-esteem throughout life, but this is particularly true in adulthood as one ages. Betty Friedan (1993) found through her research that deep personal bonds with friends count more in vital aging than casual family ties, or attendance in social groups. A shared history is a powerful glue for an enduring friendship that may last through crisis, tragedy, love, children and geographic moves, for unrenovated ties can be lost or unsustainable. In their place new ones can be made or renewed.

Benjamin Gottlieb (1985) has identified three types of social support that are important to self-esteem and friendship patterns.

1. *Emotional support.* This refers to the ways that friends show how they care, respect and value each other. This support is important when life crisis and stress threaten an individual's sense of self. When one suffers a job, financial or another type of personal setback, friends can restore self-esteem by their concern, acceptance, and validation of the person experiencing the crisis.
2. *Cognitive guidance.* This refers to the ways friends help with actual problem solving and offer help in planning, coping,

and responding. Friends may offer concrete information regarding a problem and its possible solution. Illness and advice about seeking a particular doctor, advice about a legal problem, or information regarding emotional counseling may show the support of true friends. Such cognitive advice can help a friend overcome a difficult situation, restoring self-confidence and esteem.

3. *Tangible support.* This type of support refers to actual material resources that can be provided by friends. Money, food, driving, baby-sitting, or contacting family members in an emergency are forms of tangible support. This type of support communicates a friend's genuine caring and esteem for the friend in need. Often it is males who communicate care and friendship through this type of support. Tangible support sustains and supports a friend's need for value and human importance

As Friedan (1993, p. 290) stated so well:

It's important to keep alive and renew those life-enriching bonds of friendship as men and women get older. People form new friendships, if old ones lock them into stereotypes. Friendship across the life-span often involves pain, mistakes and uncertainties. The challenge in adulthood is to continually make the occasions to deepen the touching and shared disclosure that is friendship. It can be done trans-generationally, across hundreds of miles, in spite of poor health, loss of job or money." Friendship ties for women and men may change from childhood through old age, often barely resembling their youthful shape; however, friendships will continue to sustain, fortify and reassure an individual's identity and self-esteem through adulthood.

The NCWRR study found that having good friends contributed to positive self-esteem for 87% of females and 92% of males. Clearly, friendship is vital and just as important to men as it is to women as a source of positive self-worth. The following are a few of the stories that women and men tell about the importance of friendship.

Friendship Stories

Ties That Get Closer As the Years Go By

Even though it was February, Esther was thrilled to get the Christmas package from Alice, who lived about 60 miles away. Esther was not surprised at the lateness, for Alice was never known to be on time for anything during her 91 years. Esther was 90 and both had been close friends for over 70 years. They grew up as childhood friends in the same small town, and continued the friendship during the years they went to different colleges. In spite of the fact that Esther married and had children, while Alice never married, they continued to find not only common ground to continue their friendship, but each became a source of emotional support through adulthood. Lifestyle differences, geographic distance, age, and physical disability did not lessen their friendship ties.

> Most of my friends are gone, when you reach ninety there are very few familiar old faces. My friendship with Alice is an important source of who I was in my past and also who I am now. It is such a warm and secure feeling to be able to pick up the telephone and call Alice when I ache from arthritis or feel lonely and isolated on a snowy winter's day. We chat about the things we did as girls, foolish things, gossipy things and the problems we manage in our present lives. I never have to explain myself to her, nor she to me, we both can say anything to each other and forgive each other our occasional forgetful lapses.
>
> We have always been friends and have always been in touch; however, there have been times when the friendship has been more active and important. When I was raising my children and she was working, the friendship was more distant. Now that I am a widow and alone just as she is alone, we have strengthened our friendship bonds. As old and infirm as we are, we still try to visit each other a couple of times a year, and we write letters and keep in touch by telephone. The friendship grows more important the older we grow, her voice and words make me feel whole, make me feel valued."

Esther has been able to maintain and validate a strong sense of self as she has aged through her friendship with Alice. The impact of her loss of control in other areas, such as mobility and health, have been lessened due in part to her strong friendship bonds. The fear of age and isolation has been lessened to a degree by the maintenance of a strong friendship. Connecting with friends, whether by writing or talking about past events, good times, bad times, and the concerns of the future, can function as a tool to validate and cement an emotional reality and to confirm what is important about one's self as a man or woman ages.

The work of Arling (1976), Larson (1978), Wood and Robertson (1978), Mancini (1980), Beckman (1981), and Nussbaum (1983a, 1983b, 1985) has shown that interacting with close friends in later life is closely associated with positive psychological well-being than is interaction with other types of individuals, including family members. Nussbaum, & Robinson (1989) explored the various functions of friendship for elderly individuals and concluded that the most significant impact older adult friendship has upon individuals is the improvement of the psychological well-being and morale of the participants.

FROM SHAME TO STRENGTH: THE POWER OF A GOOD FRIEND

As reported by the New York State Children and Family Trust Fund's "Campaign to Prevent Family Violence", (1992) "Domestic violence is the single major cause of injury to women in the United States—more frequent than auto accidents, muggings and rapes combined. Women are more likely to be assaulted, injured, raped or killed by a husband or boyfriend than by a stranger." Reports from the New York State Coalition Against Domestic Violence in *1992* estimated that three to four million women are abused by their husbands or partners annually in the United States. The physical injuries and evidence of abuse can be readily seen on the bodies of women involved in such incidents. What cannot be seen are the psychological scars of shame, degradation, hopelessness, and lack of self-worth. Often isolated and alone, an abused woman lacks the social support of friends at a time when she most desperately needs guidance and the emotional validation from an involved friend. Mandy was an abused wife who was lucky enough to find a friend who helped her to make the decision to leave her abusive environment.

I am twenty-seven years old, and this is the first year of my life that I feel like an adult, I should say, a worthy adult woman. It's taken so long, it's been such a scary time for me and the kids, I couldn't have done it without Robin's help. You see, I dropped out of high school when I was sixteen, moved in with a boyfriend, had a kid; and then he left. I spent the next five years waitressing and trying to raise my baby. I was tired and wanted a way out. Well, that way out came by way of Brent.

Brent seemed to me the best thing that ever happened to me. He brought flowers, took me out to dinner, paid lots of attention to the baby and within six months we married. That's when hell broke out. I got pregnant the month after we married, then he changed. During my pregnancy he stayed out all night and started drinking. He would come home throwing things and before long he was throwing me around. At first it was just a slap, then I got pushed across a room and then his fists started at me. I was pregnant, alone with no family that cared, and I was so ashamed of what was happening. I thought it was my fault, I would hide in the house until the bruises healed so no one could tell what had happened.

You see, he not only hit me, but he made me feel like garbage. He used to joke about me to his friends, calling me names like "stupid" or "idiot." He said I couldn't do anything right, without him I was nothing. I believed it. If he didn't like dinner or the way I cleaned the house, it was my fault. I put up with years of humiliation, insults, and blame. I thought I could get him to stop hitting me, if only I could be a better wife, mother, and woman.

I was picking up my little girl from school, when I first met Robin. Her Alice was the same age as my Kelli, so we talked for a while and I found out she lived one street over from me. I told her I remembered her walking with the stroller past my house. She said she would drop by sometime. This scared me, for Brent never liked folks dropping by.

Well, she started coming by and I liked her so much. We laughed and found out we liked the same TV shows, had similar ideas on raising children, and had similar taste in clothes. However, this friendship went way beyond those things. She thought I was special, smart, and funny. No one had ever said anything like that to me. As the months of our friendship went by, it was inevitable that she would also witness the abuse carried out on my body by Brent.

At first I said it was nothing, that it was the first time it happened. But she knew I was lying and she pressed me to tell her everything. My heart and my emotions just poured out in sobs, it was the first time I told anyone. I was so full of shame. Robin saw things differently, she was outraged that Brent had done this to me, said it was his fault, not mine She said I was a victim and not to blame. While I cried she just held me and comforted me. I felt a little safe and little better about myself. I wasn't going to lose Robin as a friend, she didn't judge me.

Robin never blamed me for not leaving Brent, but she did urge me to take a step to call a local shelter for battered women. I was scared, but she was patient with me and after weeks of hand-holding she was there with me when I made that very important phone call to the women's shelter. Robin has continued to be there for me while me and the kids were at the shelter and she went with me to court to get an order of protection.

She has been there believing in me, believing that I could do anything I wanted. Eventually, I had to move out-of-state with my kids. I am at a local community college and still waitress at night. Although I don't live near Robin, we talk on the phone and see each other about once a month. She will be my friend for life. Without Robin's support, without her seeing me as a good and worthwhile person I don't know if I would have ever left. She helped to give me my life back, she helped me to see who I was.

Mandy's identity and validation as a worthy human being came not from her family of origin or her relationship through marriage, but from a friend. Robin's support of Mandy and nonjudgmental acceptance enabled Mandy to see a reflection of herself that was not the useless and helpless reflection she saw when Brent was humiliating and beating her. Through Robin's eyes, she saw herself as capable and worthy of love, and Robin's support helped to give Mandy the strength to take a first step in leaving a physically and emotionally abusive relationship. Mandy has a sense of identity and feelings of worth due in part to the friendship she shared with Robin.

War Heroes, War Friends

It has been during periods of warfare that men have formed strong and close friendships. Ironically, it is often during these periods of war that men who have for the first time emotionally bonded with other men often bear witness to seeing their friendships literally blown apart, their friends killed, maimed or psychologically destroyed. Lou saw action during World War II in France and formed close relationships with other men that have endured well into his later adult years. From outward appearances, Lou appears to be the typical local insurance representative in a conservative suit, who has maintained a contented family and middle-class lifestyle. However, there is another side to Lou's life: his enduring and loyal friendship to the men in his army company that helped liberate France.

> I have been going back to France every year for the past thirty years to meet with my old Army buddies. We usually rent a little farmhouse outside of Paris and spend two weeks every year reminiscing, catching up with our present lives, and having a good time over a few beers or good French wine. Our bonds are as strong as they were during the 1940s, even though we took vastly different paths after the war. I have my own insurance company, Frank is an engineer, Dave has a plumbing business, Jim is a radio announcer, Elliot is a lawyer, and Benny teaches high school shop. Some of us are married, some are divorced and one of the guys is widowed; some of us are college educated and some never went beyond high school; some of us are financial successes and a few are just getting by. The differences do not matter.
>
> Our friendship is locked in place by a past event that brought us together initially in fear, uncertainty and the need to protect not only our own lives, but those lives of our buddies. War is an intense time that brings together intense feelings for one another. A lot of people think that men can't show emotion, but I can tell you that during wars, men show nothing but emotion, empathy and caring for each other. Meeting with these guys once a year in France contributes significantly to the man I am and was, as well as giving me a strong and good feeling about myself.

Lou is a good example of a man who in later adulthood derives a positive sense of esteem from his friendships with his long ago war buddies. A bond was forged back in the 1940s that has endured in spite of social, geographic, financial, and lifestyle differences. This friendship, as Lou told it, was also responsible for healing the wounds of a traumatic war and also a means to acknowledge mutual fears and suffering.

According to Adams (1994), although gerontologists have focused more attention on friendship than any other discipline, the field has done a poor job of examining older men's friendships. The focus has been on friendship patterns of older women because (a) women comprise more of the older population than do men, (b) there is a perception that friendship is less central to the lives of older men than of older women, and (c) a gender bias exists towards a woman's perspective on the nature of friendship. A woman's perspective emphasizes what Wright (1982) called the face-to-face aspects of friendship (personalism and interpersonal sensitivity), whereas a man's perspective emphasizes the side-by-side aspects (instrumentality and activity centeredness). Lou's story of friendship challenges two of these assumptions. Although few researchers have focused exclusively on older men's friendships, it represents an area that needs continued attention and examination.

Young Males/Different Expressions of Friendship

This chapter earlier reported that males often communicate friendship in the form of tangible support. Denny exemplifies a young male who may have a difficult time expressing verbal and emotional support for a friend, but shows his concern and empathy in tangible ways. For the most part, nineteen-year-old Denny has found the meaning of life in his jacked-up Toyota 4X4 truck. If one mentioned the phrase "meaningful relationship," one would get a shrug and a blank stare. He has had numerous female relationships, his mouth has occasionally gotten him in trouble with the local police, and his verbal expressions are few. Yet this seemingly callous young male expressed care, empathy, and support for a friend who was deeply troubled over the breakup of a long-term relationship.

> I didn't know what to do when Jay broke up with Melissa. He was destroyed, he avoided his friends, dropped out of school, and took to sleeping away the pain. I knew the pain, but didn't know how to reach this guy who I knew as a great friend. We used to party, drive our cars to a pond at the edge of town and blare the music, we hung out at the beach, surfed, and skateboarded together. We were a team, invincible.

This new pain he felt, I didn't know how to connect with him. I was also scared I was losing him as a friend, I didn't have any good words for him. I guess I just parked myself on his doorstep and moved in with him. He lived with his parents, who somehow accepted the fact that I might be necessary to help him through this time. I don't know, but they didn't tell me to leave. We didn't speak about the breakup with his girlfriend, but I was there. We played music, talked about future stuff, worked and cruised in my truck. I remembered when he cried about what he was feeling. At first I was kind of embarrassed and didn't know what to do. I just sort of patted him on the back and said, "Hang in there, buddy, I'm with you."

He got through this pain. I'm no shrink, but I think I helped. My English and sentence structure is not terrific, but I got through to him, and whatever helps I'd do again. Of course when cruisin' through town, both of us look like the tough, cool dudes we think we are. We both know that there is a bond between us that has nothing to do with being cool.

Denny is a young male, perhaps a male that could be identified as an example of one of those males who can't communicate emotionally to other people. Perhaps he does not communicate friendship and empathy in traditional female verbal and emotional ways, but his story shows that Denny does communicate friendship and empathy in a different, yet important way that does connect and can influence a friend who is in need of support.

The importance of having a significant person bear witness to one's life is necessary for self-worth and validation of identity. Both women and men share a need to be totally honest, to be able to speak to another human being who accepts them as who they are, who believes in them, about what they have done and what was done to them, about what they hope for, think about, fear and feel. By having a province of friends who speak and listen with compassion, people validate each other's lives, make suffering meaningful and help the process of healing take place. Any significant soul-shaping event becomes more integrated into one's identity when one can express the essence of the experience and have it received in depth by a friend.

MENTORS: A NECESSITY FOR BOTH
WOMEN AND MEN

Mentor was the name of a friend of Odysseus who was entrusted with the education of Odysseus' son, Telemachus. Over time, the word *mentor* has come down to mean something much more than a mere teacher. A mentor is a guide or exemplar in dealing with the central concerns of an individual's life. The concept of *mentoring* has received considerable attention in recent years (e.g., Moyers and Bly, 1990).

Historically, a mentor has been an important guide to the young adult male setting out in the world. For a long time this figure had no significance for the young female in her life. Muses and mentors were seen as strictly belonging to males and a source of male inspiration. The only guide a young woman had was her own mother, who shared practical knowledge on becoming a wife and mother.

According to Nemiroff and Colarusso (1990), a major contributor to lifelong development is the continued possibility for identification. The process of identification is not limited to childhood or adolescence, but occurs regularly in adult life. The mentor relationship is an example of such a contributor to identity, self-worth, and continued development. These later identifications or mentor relationships provide added clarity and insight to the adult personality and can influence the choice of a profession or the quality of work achievement. The capacity for creativity can be channeled and nurtured by adult identifications with role models and mentors over the life course.

Men and Mentors

Throughout history boys were initiated into and confirmed in their sense of manhood and purpose by rites of passage that were administered by the elders of the community or tribe. Old men and young men defined each other through a process of teaching and learning. To grow old without wisdom and without being a mentor could strip the last half of life of purpose and meaning. The role of mentor has been redefined, limited and changed since those primitive tribal times.

Most of the social science research on mentoring has centered on the effect of mentors on males, particularly in early adulthood. The presence or absence of a mentor was said to have a large impact on adult development. Daniel Levinson and his colleagues studied personality change in males during adulthood and termed the future-life task as construction of the "Dream" (Levinson, Darrow, Klein, Levinson, & McGee, 1978). According to Levinson, the dream experienced by most men during early adulthood is the transformation of talents, goals, and interests into a life occupation. Early adulthood was the time to fashion new roles and a time to go about the business of creating a life. Early adulthood, as Levinson found, was also a time of uncertainty and forging ahead in unfamiliar territory, away from one's parents.

Searching leads to the formation of a framework for adulthood and the search process often involves finding a mentor or mentors along the way. The mentor is usually older and experienced, a protective guide who facilitates a young man's entrance into the adult world. For a man in his twenties, the mentor looks at him as a young adult, not a boy. A mentor is there to support his dreams and helps him to actualize them. The mentor is a nonparental role model, who can offer nonjudgmental assistance in helping a young man overcome the father/son polarity.

A young man's mentor represents skill, knowledge, virtue, and accomplishment—all qualities a young man hopes to someday acquire. The protégé hopes that someday he will surpass his mentor. The mentor relationship allows the protégé to identify with a person who stands for the qualities he seeks in himself. The mentor is an internalized figure who offers love, admiration, encouragement and self-esteem during the protégé's struggle with life tasks.

Forming a life goal, according to Levinson et al. (1978), happens to young men between the ages of twenty and thirty with relative consistency and orderliness. Levinson's developmental pathway was very similar in nature to Erikson's stage format, in that life tended to be a traceable progression from exploration in work to commitment to a lifelong work goal. The movement is linear; the need and role of mentor was seen as necessary only in early adulthood. Levinson believed that it was difficult for a man over forty to have a mentor and that a man who lacked a mentor in early adulthood could be handicapped developmentally. Levinson also felt that a person could not become an effective mentor until they were in their middle years.

Women and Mentors

Through time women also have had the "Dream." Unlike the dream described by Levinson that men experience, this dream usually centered around the relationships a woman would have in adulthood. This dream, in order to be attained, did not require a mentor; her investment was in the relationship with her husband and children. She assisted her husband in attaining his dream; she might, for example, become his muse.

Times have changed over the last thirty years. Women are in the workforce and are following the dream of their male counterparts. Following the inception of the women's movement, women in their twenties often established strong relationships with slightly older, more experienced mentoring figures. Their behavior during this period is almost indistinguishable from the males described by Levinson, one notable difference being that more women would have more cross-sex mentorships then males. Women seem to have just as many male mentors in their lives as female mentors. Traditionally men have had, for the most part, only male mentors as their life guides.

Josselson (1987) found that women who have made their careers an important anchor point in their lives have had mentors. Anchoring in work seems not to take place unless an important other takes an interest in a woman's career. She also found that only those women who obtained graduate or professional degrees, or who had apprenticed experienced a mentoring relationship. The mentor provided an entree into the field and a possibility of bonding in a personal way. When women have someone with recognition or stature in their field care about them, believe in them and encourage them, it is likely that they are more able to feel a part of a professional community.

The absence of a mentor has dire consequences for a woman's investment in her career. Josselson found that women without mentors work and achieve, but they are not bonded to their careers in an identity-forming way. For a woman to anchor herself importantly in her work, her work has to matter to someone who matters to her. When it does not, her work pursuits may be transitory as she searches for something else that will give her meaning, identity, and esteem.

The presence of even one person who validates the meaningfulness of her work can change an identity-distant job into an enriching aspect of a woman's professional identity. A sense that a person is "there for me" means that he or she can be expected to try to meet one's needs. A supportive presence assures a woman of being the object of devotion, attention and importance.

However, as Walker and Mehr (1992) found, mentors—either male or female—present certain dangers for women vulnerable to pleasing others as a way of life. Mentors can often expect their protégés to assume their values and enter into a hierarchical relationship. For women, trying to find a sense of personal identity, following a mentor may seem like submissiveness.

Male mentors may give a sexual edge to the relationship; that is, the relationship can get diffused with emotional and sexual attachment. In other cases, the relationship may resemble the parental relationship. Often the mentor relationship duplicates the relationship she had with her mother or father. Girls who never resolved the dependency issue may be particularly vulnerable. For sooner or later every protégé must challenge the absolute power of the mentor if he or she is to emerge the author of his or her own life. However, good mentoring, when it involves nurturing, teaching, and friendship are invaluable to the direction of a woman's life and the formation of a positive identity in adulthood.

NCWRR Findings and Challenges

There has been extensive research on the importance of mentors to men, and only recently has there been a focus on the importance of a mentor to a woman's life. However, most of the research has been centered on the premise that both women and men need mentors only in early adulthood. In particular, women and men need mentors only when they are formulating careers during early adulthood.

The NCWRR study found that mentors are as important to women as they are to men. Seventy-five percent of women and men in the study had mentors in their lives. Approximately 60% of both women and men said that a mentor influenced their direction in life. However, the NCWRR study also found that mentors are important to adult development well beyond the early twenties. Although the study found that 50% of men and 45% of women below the age of 26 had mentors, 31% of women and 25% of men found mentors important in their lives after the age of 26, continuing well into midlife and beyond.

Longevity, lifestyle choices, and workplace changes have created new demands and alternatives in the lives of both women and men. The predictability and stagelike qualities of life events are no longer applicable to our changing society. Throughout this century, especially during the 1950s and early 1960s, life decisions were made during early adulthood. Men made work commitments for life and women committed to home and family. The women's revolution of the early 1970s changed women's lives. Women entered careers in huge numbers, and their career lives and opportunities were tracked according to the old male formulas. If a man needed a mentor during early adulthood when he was making career choices, it became necessary for women to have a mentor during this phase as well.

Mentors are, of course, critical to men as well as women establishing work and career goals in their early adult years. However, mentors and life guides are important all through life, not just during a man's or woman's early adult years. Having a mentor during early adulthood fit with the old psychological stage theory, when men and, recently, women established goals for life. New social challenges, workplace upheavals, and everchanging lifestyle patterns present themselves as uncharted territory for women and men in the 1990s and beyond.

Women may be vulnerable and unsure of themselves when trying to make decisions in their thirties about whether and how to combine career with motherhood. A woman requires a highly supportive interpersonal environment to succeed and thrive on the challenge of sequentially ordering two major priorities, without sacrificing either. Mentoring is critical for women at this choice point in life. Often there are no role models or mentors to guide women through these murky waters.

Men who once made career decisions for life may find themselves in their middle years fired or laid off. Men need mentors in their later adult years when faced with changing careers, "retooling," and learning new skills that will keep them competitive. Men are also looking for guidance as to what it means to be a man today. Men can be seen gathering in the woods, behind drums, passing talking sticks, all in the hope of creating rituals that will enrich their lives as men. They are looking for fellowships, identity and a new meaning for manhood. Leaders and mentors are needed to guide men through their changing roles and societal expectations.

Both genders need new kinds of mentors to buoy self-esteem and to help make personal sense out of an ever-changing world. Both women and men face confusion and often believe that they may be losing their psychological footing. The world is full of uncertainty. World leaders and their ideas appear only to disappear as quickly as they came. Businesses and corporations that were counted on for lifelong employment fold, go bankrupt, or are lost to corporate takeovers. A college degree is no longer a ticket to a job and security. Relationships are no longer secure and are not always for life. Steadfast moral convictions and clear principles of action and behavior are constantly being tested and challenged.

The collapse of a predictable and secure world and the instability of cultural symbols and institutions can create a crisis of collective identity and collective self-esteem. These uncertainties and experiences are gender neutral, affecting both women's and men's sense of self-worth and identity throughout their adult years. The need for new directions, personal validation and inner stability can be partially achieved with the help of new types of mentors and guides who have forged these new roads and attained personal satisfaction.

The following are stories from some of the women and men interviewed for the study regarding the importance of mentors in their adult lives, mentors who validated feelings of self-worth and guided women and men in their search for personal identity.

Older Protégé/Younger Mentor

Fifty-five-year-old Ginger had grown up in a world that was stable, predictable, and highly structured. After 27 years of marriage, Ginger found herself dropped from the marital cocoon through divorce. Her husband lost his job after 20 years, decided to drop out, and disappeared with his rifle and brand-new pick-up truck into the mountains of Idaho. He had heard that a man could be totally self-sufficient and live apart from the world of taxes, nine-to-five work, and social responsibility. Part of that dropout from social responsibility included leaving Ginger with a large mortgage, unpaid bills and $2,000 in cash.

Until this happened Ginger had been cloaked in the cocoon of the social world she had grown up in as a young girl. Her responsibilities, she learned from her mother, would be finding a good provider and creating a stable home for him and his children. She followed the rules and soon after college she settled down with John in the suburbs of Chicago. He commuted to his job as an insurance adjuster for a large company for about 20 years, while she managed the home and children. Her life commitment, or dream, was her family. She also believed it her responsibility to help John attain his dream of career security through relentless entertaining and volunteering. Life for Ginger turned upside down. The old social rules were kicked aside, along with her financial safety net.

> I cried it seemed for months, I was scared, angry and desperate. I felt like I was at sea in a fog, I had no moorings or sense of place. My parents were elderly and outside of some financial help, couldn't offer me much guidance. This situation was so foreign to them—they'd been married for over 50 years. To my credit I had an old college degree, but nothing current as far as job skills. After months of denial and self-pity I finally got up the courage to go to a neighboring university and took a placement test. I did okay, which helped me feel a little better about myself. I entered a master's degree program in social work. My years of volunteering in a hospital, a local soup kitchen, and being a literacy volunteer paid off.
>
> I was so scared and so doubtful of my being able to handle graduate courses at my age. I thought my memory would fail or that I would be considered an old dinosaur. Although people were friendly and helpful in my classes I didn't feel like I belonged or had the right to belong. That changed when I took a class taught by Marva. Here I was, this middle-aged white suburban woman just in awe of this bright, young, black, and dynamic professor. Her class on women's history was stimulating and eye-opening.

I started talking to her after class about where I was personally and expressed doubts as to whether I could go further in my life as a professional woman. She so clearly had her act together. She took an interest in me and we started meeting for coffee after class. She was a thirty-something single mother of two high-school-aged boys, the father had deserted them in Chicago when she was in her teens years ago. Marva got her GED, went to college, and eventually through a series of grants got her PhD and began a career in teaching. Even her story at first made me wonder why this tough, street-fighting lady would take an interest in me, this "vanilla," mousy, middle-aged gal. All that's history. She took the interest, became a mentor to me and guided me through some pretty rough waters when at times I thought I would never make it.

Thanks to Marva's belief in me and a lot of work on my part I got my MSW and found a job at a shelter for abused women. Marva not only helped me with the practical stuff, like course work and job suggestions, she believed in me—that I could get a handle on my own life and succeed professionally. It didn't matter to her that I was in my mid-fifties and had never worked, she believed in the spirit of all women to make it in life when they have to. Those nights of endless cold coffee and self-affirming talks paid off for me. Marva and I are now colleagues and friends. I had to make the jump from seeing her as a mentor to seeing her as a friend and colleague—not an easy task, but accomplished. My self-esteem and personhood could not have come about as easily if it were not for Marva.

Ginger is an example of many women in midlife who needed guidance and mentorship when the predictability of her life changed. She was a woman in her middle years who found a mentor in a much younger and ethnically different woman. Because Marva is younger, she dose not conform to the expected picture of a mentor. Her protégé is much older, not a young and bright 20-something girl. Clearly, this type of mentor/protégé relationship is nontraditional. Nevertheless, Ginger's self-esteem and identity were elevated and clarified by the assistance and guidance of a mentor such as Marva.

No Road Maps for Career and Babies
Eileen had been the first female in her family to go through law

school. She was the eldest daughter of four other siblings. Eileen had a younger sister and two older brothers, one of whom went into finance and the other into law, their father's and grandfather's profession. Eileen was so full of herself when she graduated from law school and passed the Pennsylvania bar exam. She obtained a good job with an established Philadelphia law firm, married a lawyer in another firm, and began to build a very stable and pre- dictable life. They were a modern working couple, with similar interests and similar working friends.

Eileen was made a partner after 6 years of work in the law firm. However, she began having doubts about her life and the direction it was taking. Eileen felt unsettled and confused. She was 37 and wanted to become a mother, yet at the same time didn't know if she could manage both a career and family. Eileen didn't even know after 10 years of law practice if she wanted to juggle both. Nature made the decision for her: Eileen was pregnant.

Her working friends said she could do both, but many of them had no children of their own. Her husband was agreeable to any- thing she decided to do, which didn't help her decision-making process. Eileen found a mentor in her brother's wife, Jessica, who had given up a high-school teaching career to be a full-time mom for about 7 years, until her son was in third grade.

> Jess really helped me through a difficult time in my life when I didn't know which way to turn. Here I was a respected and smart attorney who couldn't decide what was in her own best interest. During my pregnancy I practiced law , but took a leave of absence after Henry was born. I was supposed to return to work after six months. I didn't want to leave Henry, I didn't want to give up my career. I had a real dilemma.
>
> After Henry was born, I spent a lot of time with Jess. She was calm, confident, and happy. I looked at this woman who had a teaching career and gladly gave it up with confidence. Before I became preg- nant I thought she was foolish to have given up a good career. My attitude at that time was one of superiority.
>
> Later, after Henry was born, she and I talked about priorities and things that really mattered in her life and in my life. Jess never felt she had to prove anything to anybody and was not ashamed of staying home with her baby. I learned not to be ashamed of my decision to

stay home with Henry and began to see what a full life I could have taking care of my family. Yes, I missed the practice, but I knew I would eventually go back to practicing law and in the meantime I became a legal advocate for women who were residing in shelters while seeking orders of protection from abusive spouses. This was very part-time and strictly volunteer, but it gave me the best of both worlds for a while. Jess was my guide in doing this, for she had become a literacy volunteer. This helped her integrate her feelings of needing to achieve at something outside the home while at the same time remaining at home with her baby. I don't doubt the decision I made about staying home, in large part because of Jess's example and her strength of conviction about remaining central in her baby's early life.

Eileen's mentor relationship was directly opposite of what one thinks of as a mentor. Normally one associates a mentoring, with career and work in the early twenties. Eileen's case demonstrates the need to understand that mentors are important to individuals at different levels and at different times during adulthood. Jess was a friend and a mentor who supported Eileen's decision emotionally as well as provided practical guidance in a tangible way; that is, by showing that Eileen could be at home with her baby while still satisfying a need to achieve. The mentor relationship established between Jess and Eileen help to restore Eileen's dignity, renewed her identity and feelings of self-worth.

Old Dog, New Tricks

Rudy was a plant foreman in Pennsylvania, who in his late fifties was terminated due to a plant closing. He became depressed and sat at home all day watching television, feeling that he was too old to get another job. He believed he had no marketable skills, and felt washed up. Rudy's confidence and self-esteem were at an extreme low point. He was resigned to sit home and wait for the next six years to go by until he could collect Social Security. That was until he met Barry.

I was full of self-pity and anger for about a year after I lost my job. My wife can tell you just how hard I was to live with. All this changed when I met Barry at the local lodge we both belonged to. Barry was close to seventy, but in many ways was younger than me. He was always full of energy, ideas and optimism. At first I couldn't stand the guy, but I guess a little of his gusto rubbed off on me.

We started meeting for lunch a couple times a week. I found out that Barry had a heart attack about five years ago and like me thought his life was over. He was depressed, scared and felt very hopeless. He told me that his work had been in construction, where he was physically active, strong and able to do a lot of heavy lifting even in his early sixties. This all ended when he had the heart attack. His whole sense of who he was wrapped up in doing physical kinds of stuff. Boy, his life sounded a lot like my life.

Barry showed me how he changed his life, how he stopped feeling sorry for himself and how he was able to get on with his life. He went from being an invalid to getting a handle on what he could do with his life. He is a fine woodworker and is making reproduction furniture from his workshop in his basement for customers. I spent a lot of time hanging around his workshop and I guess more rubbed off on me than sawdust.

He made me realize I had a full life ahead of me, I wasn't old and wasn't useless. I rediscovered my skills at electronics. I always was a tinkerer, so I opened a TV/VCR repair shop from my home. Barry helped me to turn a hobby into a business, by telling me how he billed customers, kept records, and how to keep track of my overhead costs. I never could have done it without his guidance. I'm never going to make a million bucks, but boy do I feel good about myself. I'm full of energy, I'm happy, just ask the wife!

Rudy went from a life of despair to a productive life with the help and guidance from Barry, who was both a friend and a mentor. Barry helped Rudy emotionally and provided practical assistance with small business concerns. The mentor relationship occurred at a time when it was most needed and often most neglected in men's lives. Men's prime, their time of greatest productivity, was previously ascribed to early adulthood. Mentor relationships were encouraged during this developmental period. Longevity, workplace changes and evolving social roles have required a rethinking of men's lives and their needs.

Mentors are vital to the well-being of men's later years, especially when many middle-aged men are being laid off from jobs or forced into early retirement. New skills, rediscovery of old talents, and emotional support during times of change can be attained and enhanced with the guidance of a mentor in an older man or woman's life.

New Men and New Questions

The rhetoric of late has blasted men for being too hostile, too soft, too macho, too wimpy, too aggressive or too insensitive. Clarity and insight into new roles is often in short supply. Old heroes and old myths of masculinity don't seem to work or help men in the real world they live in. Today's men are faced with an array of dilemmas and confusion surrounding new roles and expectations.

Malcolm was faced with a conflict between the old notions of masculinity and the social changes that were taking place around him at the workplace and within his family life. He was trying desperately to mold himself into this new image of masculinity, he was trying to be a man of the '90s. Malcolm was also a child of the '60s. His 48-year-old memory was full of protest marches, slogans and notions of equal rights for all women and men. At age 48 he began searching for a missing link that would bridge his old ideas of masculinity, which he had learned from his father, and the new expectations that he had been trying to live with for the last 25 years.

I'm of Portuguese descent, my father and his father before him were commercial fishermen. As a kid I would often go with the men out to sea to catch codfish. Of course I was all of about eleven years old, when these men including my father seemed bigger, louder, and more fearless than anything I could imagine. After all, they fought the seas and all the monsters hidden beneath the blue deep. In college I used to think that Hemingway had picked my father as a character for *Old Man and the Sea*. To me this was what a man was.

I went to a New England college and jumped right into all the social upheavals of the time, including rejecting all the things my father and family stood for. He had seen action during World War II, and I was protesting Vietnam. The relationship with my father was barely civil; it seemed as if we were from two different places. I had a short-term marriage during the early seventies, divorced, then settled into a career path as a computer programmer with my present wife and family of sixteen years. My father died five years ago, leaving me in a state of grief and confusion about who I was. I missed his significance, his "in your face" masculinity, his identity. I guess I lost part of my identity.

I had tried to be the "new" man. I supported my wife in her career goals, I was an involved dad, cooked, shared household responsibilities, and was politically correct at work around other women. I had a real empty space inside of me. I didn't know if this was the real me or just what the rest of the politically correct world wanted of me. There were great chunks missing from me and who I was.

I silently struggled with these issues for a long time, until I met Sam. He worked in a separate division within our computer company. At lunch the subject turned to a discussion about a group he was forming that discussed issues that face men today. I joked and laughed, but some of what he was saying registered in my brain. I felt like he was handing me a life ring.

We had many talking sessions before I decided to join him on a weekend outing into the woods with other men. I thought my wife would laugh, but she understood, because she had done this exploration much earlier in her life. The weekend became the first of many such weekends. Through the guidance of Sam I have learned to combine and validate the masculinity of my father with the new concepts of what it means to be a man in today's world.

I thought it was necessary to give up the hard, loud, physical world of my father. Through weekends in the woods, fishing, hunting and living off the land, even if it's just a weekend, with Sam as a guide, I have been brought in touch with my father's manhood as well as melding it with my contemporary notions of manhood. The real physical and hard world of men is just as much a part of me as the more cerebral world of comforting and listening to my wife and children. Sam was more than a friend, he was a mentor and spiritual guide, helping me bridge this gap between old ideas of masculinity and a new order of masculinity. I learned I didn't have to give up anything to be myself and feel okay about being a man.

Mentors and spiritual guides will be needed for men who are journeying across the uncharted territory of the new masculinity.

Many men are caught between two ideologies, the world of their fathers and the myths surrounding those lives, as well as the world they work and live in today with families and colleagues with different expectations. Mentors to men, whether they lead drumming groups in the woods, listen to men with relationship problems, guide men with career decisions, or act as role models to men who are aging, are as essential to supporting and validating new visions of manhood as men who settled the territories of the old West once were to carving an earlier male image. Masculine identity and self-esteem need modern-day guidance and acceptance of the questions and feelings that continue to arise in a society without a social road map.

SUMMARY

This chapter has tried to shed light on how friendship and mentors contribute to adult feelings of self-esteem and identity. This contribution is vital all through a person's adult life. Mentors and friends are relevant and necessary to the continued growth and development of both women and men.

The myth underlying the premise that women make better friends than men is just that: a myth. Men may not have the technique or the communication skills that women possess, but their need for friendship and the different ways men express friendship are realities. Although past societal roles have encouraged men to be "rugged individualists," thus ensuring that male identity that depended on isolation and total self-reliance, the majority of men in the NCWRR study said that friendships are vital and important to them. Friendships are as important to men as they are to women as a validation of self-worth and personal identity. Working women may have to be careful not to fall into the male trap of not allowing time for friends. Time once spent with a mutual friend is often what gets cut out of a busy woman's life. Women need the support and reflection that comes from a caring relationship with someone we call friend.

Age or stage of development, like gender, are not factors in the value of friendship as it contributes of feelings of self-esteem. A shared history is vital in reassuring one that he or she is a valued person.

- The example of Esther was a story of friendship between two women that spanned almost 90 years. Each other's voice on the phone bridged isolation and chased away thoughts of self-doubt and loss of control.
- Mandy found her friendship with Robin to be a vital bridge that led her from a relationship of abuse and degradation to a life that held value and personal worth.
- Lou formed a deep friendship with men during a time of war, a time when men usually are expected to be at the peak of their capability for violence and aggressiveness.
- Denny gave the outward appearance of arrogant youth, but was able to develop a caring and nurturing relationship with a friend who was in pain. Even without strong verbal skills, he was a friend who made a difference.

A significant person, man or woman, bears witness to another's life and reflects back value, care and self-esteem, and can help nurture another's a fragile identity. That person we call a friend.

Mentors can be called a friend, but the role of mentor is usually more formal. A mentor is a teacher or guide who helps a person develop in areas of work, achievement, creativity, or perhaps adaptative to a new role. Mentoring used to be the territory of men, supporting male dreams of achievement in early adulthood. Since the women's movement of the 1960s, women establishing careers have experienced the guidance of mentors. When women and men experience the presence of a mentor, self-esteem and identity can be elevated and clarified. The presence of even one mentor who validates the meaningfulness of another's work can change or reinforce one's identity and capabilities. As the NCWRR study found, 75% of both women and men had had mentors in their lives, and of those, and 60% felt that a mentor had influenced the direction of their lives.

Mentors are not just necessary to women and men in their early twenties or early adulthood. The uncharted territory of social change, changing life patterns, social instability, and the collapse of the predictablility of life events can create a crisis in the collective identity and self-esteem of many women and men.

- Ginger had expected a life of marital stability under the protective wing of a lifelong husband. Life changed for Ginger, as it has for many women, thrusting her into a new world without a road map or predictable rules.
- Marva, a younger mentor, helped Ginger secure a strong mooring for her own developing life.
- Eileen had been a career woman who suddenly changed gears when she became a new mom.
- Jess became a new kind of mentor, not in the area of work, but in the area of validating and supporting Eileen's decision to shift from career to motherhood.
- Rudy described himself as an "old dog" who definitely learned a few new tricks.
- Barry acted as a mentor when he guided Rudy through the rough waters of aging and feelings of uselessness to a life of renewed energy and productivity.
- Malcolm learned new images of masculinity and was able to sort out conflicting concepts of what it means to be a man in today's society with the help and guidance from Sam.

Friendships and mentors will continue to be an important source of self-esteem and identity validation for both women and men all through adulthood. Friendships and mentors contribute to continued adult growth independent of age or stage of development. Mentors, in particular, are crucial to individuals as sources of inspiration and as new age-guides to people as they grow older. Mentors are needed not only as traditional guides for young adults establishing careers, but also as guides to women and men during times of crisis, social change, and times of personal uncertainty. Women and men of 40 or 60 continue to need support and guidance from good friends and valued mentors who provide a sense of continuity of self after a lifetime of changes. Friends and mentors can help integrate an old self with a new self, can offer a different perspective and act as a mirror of a reshaped identity all through an individual's adult life. Friends and mentors are a rich source of self-esteem for both women and men, when this life-tie is used as a precious resource for growth in adulthood.

CHAPTER 5

Intimate Relationships

Love is a kind of madness, a divine madness.

—*Plato*

*I*ntimacy is a term implying closeness, but there are many kinds of intimacy. Some dictionary definitions stress a sexual connotation. Alternatively, intimacy may be defined in social terms, such as two close friends sharing secrets. In ordinary common parlance, *intimate* often implies erotic, heterosexual activity with all its preliminaries, contacts, emotional concomitants, and the nuances of sexual congress. A *romance* may be seen as the pursuit of intimacy, entailing all degrees of desire and frustration, from casual affection to desperation of desire without consummation.

Pedantic discussions of intimacy become entwined in such terms as "innate drives," "automatic impulses," "emotional bonding," and "automatic behavior with or without awareness of purpose." The whole question of instinctual drive is controversial and unsettled, with continued argument over meanings of terms. When the subjects are human, books tend to circumvent the topic of intimacy altogether.

Readers are encouraged to review the following classic and recent books: on the topic of intimacy, Former's *The Art of Loving* (1968); on the role of love in a relationship, Janus and Janus' *The*

Janus Report (1993); and on changing mores regarding sexual behavior, Tannahill's *Sex in History* (1980).

As a society we discuss love and intimacy as though they were things within one's control. Men and especially women want to know how to do it right, make it succeed. They want to know how to keep love alive and how to overcome its many problems. People expect love to be all things—powerful, lasting, healing—and that its power will make one whole. With these intensely high expectations also comes the equally intense risk of facing isolation, emptiness, failure and loss of self.

Thomas Moore (1992) described love as more an event of the soul and less an aspect or certainty of a relationship. He tells of how the ancient philosophers talked about love and intimacy. There were in early times no discussions about how to make relationships work or how to fix and patch love and intimacy. The ancients believed that concern should be for what love does to the soul. Freud (1935) spoke of love as an activity of imagination in which daily routines and concerns are drowned out. New-found love and intimacy with another expands the imagination into an emotional frenzy, causing hormones and brain chemicals to go into overdrive. Love cannot be roped in by guidelines and how-to hints, nor can love be totally relied on to restore or create a whole self, a permanent source of identity and self-esteem.

According to developmental traditionalists and stage theorists such as Erik Erikson (1968), issues relating to love and intimacy could be developmentally limited by one's age. In early adulthood, building on the base of adolescent sexual experimentation each woman and man was expected to find a heterosexual partner, learn to feel comfortable with his or her body sexually while developing the capacity for emotional intimacy, have children, and commit to that same partner for life. The midlife stage supposedly brought about the acceptance of a diminished sex drive in one's self and partner; late adulthood brought about the loss of one's mate and with it the loss of love, sex, and intimacy. This orderly developmental time frame may have been adequate to describe love, sex and intimacy years ago, but does not begin to address the many changes that have reshaped the developmental lives of women and men today.

Throughout adulthood women and men seek and need to

develop intimate bonds. There is never one right time for this to happen, nor is there one right way of expressing intimacy, nor a right type of partner. Many couples are marrying later than the traditional, "on-time" stage of early adulthood. Others plan on marrying for life, but find themselves divorced and in serial relationships all through their adult lives. Gay relationships, older man/younger woman, older woman/younger man, older singles marrying for the first time, and retirees living together make up a few of the many forms of intimacy people are developing as their adult lives expand. These ongoing changes in the intimacy life-tie create changes in self-esteem and in how women and men perceive their adult identity, and help reshape their self-views.

LOVE AND INTIMACY: A DELICATE BALANCING ACT FOR THE SELF

Strong cultural forces overemphasizing the importance of relationships can have a negative impact on a person's self-view. The prevailing social attitude can cause a person to look upon intimate relationships as a solution to all that is wrong with him- or herself. This can be a set-up for disappointment, disillusionment, identity confusion, and loss of self-esteem. Focusing too much on relationships leads to too many demands and expectations being placed on a significant other. Often our emotional eggs are heaped into one basket, burdening a partner with the impossible task of being lover, friend, companion, playmate, parent, and source of identity.

Men and women want unconditional love, protection, and assurance that the intimate partner will make up for characteristics the other may lack. By joining with an outgoing person, the shy partner falsely hopes that he or she will be made bold and the life of the party. Unfortunately, this does not happen and places an unfair burden on the partner.

The potential for pain and collapsing self-esteem are great in relationships. People are unprotected, vulnerable to hurt, defenses are down—especially if one's sense of self is riding on the success of the relationship. The closer we get to another, the greater the risks of intimacy. Women and men may chronologically be adults, but often during tumultuous times of high emotion and sexual arousal, they can be emotionally unstable, act less intelligently in areas where the heart rules the mind, and exhibit childlike needs of dependency. During the day people may be competent corporate managers and creative executives, but often by night and on weekends they turn into ultra-needy, immature, and overly sensitive children, unable to separate "I" from "we." Mature love depends on the ability to maintain one's personal identity; that is, to differentiate self from other in a relationship. The conflict between individuation and fusion is a central issue in human development, especially as it relates to intimate relationships. Remaining individualized, while trying to integrate and connect with another, is often like the a tight-rope balancing act. This awesome developmental feat is extremely difficult, and frequently impossible, when intimacy expectations and tasks are supposed to be accomplished and resolved in early adulthood.

The emphasis on the importance of intimate relationships as a primary source of self-esteem, health, and happiness is too unbalanced. There is a danger in believing that love and intimacy are the only paths to personal fulfillment. Freud, (1961) stated that psychological health depended on love and work. Unfortunately there has been an overemphasis on love and little attention on work. This very important intimacy life-tie is best when it acts as one point of reference helping to make sense and derive meaning out of one's life, rather than acting as the main supporting pillar of self-worth. It may happen that through a loss of that intimate life-tie, a man or woman discovers that the meaning of his or her life was bound up with partner to a greater extent than he or she had believed.

The allure and precariousness of balancing the power of love and intimacy can be best shown by retelling the Greek myth about the three sexes—hermaphrodite, male, and female. According to myth, male originated from the sun, female originated from the earth, and hermaphrodite from the moon, which partook of the nature of both sun and earth. Each human was a rounded whole, with four legs and four arms, and was able to walk upright or by turning over in circular locomotion.

These original humans were a threat to the god Zeus, who decided to bisect this powerful human creature. The outcome of this separation of the human race was that each half-being was compelled to seek out a partner who would restore its wholeness. The idea that a person gains wholeness by merging with another has been the main story line for romantic literature throughout history.

Falling in love and the associated pursuit of intimacy is one of the most compelling emotional experiences that anyone can encounter. At the height of being in love the boundary between ego and object threatens to melt away. Freud declared, "Against all the evidence of his senses, a man who is in love declares the 'I' and 'you' are one and is prepared to behave as if it were fact" (1933).

Thoughts of separation and acts of separation are part of the intimacy balance. Unfortunately, an act of separation may mean many things; most take it to mean the destruction or end of that particular relationship. But according to Jung (1957), separation meant an activity of the soul, a breaking into parts things that were too tightly packed, and that needed differentiation. The intimate relationship or joining of two people brings about a physical and emotional meshing, which often results in one or both partners trying to live out their lives through the other. Such diffusion of self represents a loss of individuality and loss of differentiation, hence creating low self-esteem.

Periods of closeness have to be balanced with periods of distance. A life apart is necessary. Expecting a partner to gratify all of one's needs is impossible, upsets the precarious balance and creates a life-tie that ends up a juggernaut, strangling two people. This life-tie must remain loose and fluid, able to change, expand and contract in order to allow for the continued growth of two autonomous adults.

What may be needed is a concept of *good-enough intimacy*. As was described in the chapter on family of origin, good-enough mothering refers to the imperfect, though adequate emotional care of children that is not harmful, and allows for growth and discovery as part of the maturation process of that child. In a similar vein, good-enough intimacy may be just what is needed to maintain the balance and developmental perspective on an individual's continued growth as an adult. Past perspectives and research have assumed that most important developmental tasks related to intimacy are accomplished in early adulthood. This study takes the perspective that just because a person reaches a chronological age of legal adulthood does not mean he or she is a finished adult product. A young adult, whether male or female, is an ongoing process—a creation in progress. A lasting intimate relationship may require a maturity that is often lacking during this early period, when most women and men have yet to define an identity and are basically unsure of their own needs and desires. So balancing separation and connection in a relationship can be an awesome task that has implications for maintaining positive self-esteem.

Roots of Intimacy

The flowering of adult intimacy depends much on the nourishment of an individual's early childhood roots. John Bowlby (1988), the foremost authority on human attachment theory, stated that once an attachment has formed between a baby and caregiver, that baby will become depressed, desperate, and emotionally disturbed if long-term separation from the caregiver is imposed. Bowlby found many links between disturbed adults and broken attachments in childhood. His findings show just how important the family of origin life-tie is as an influence on later adult development, especially in the area of relationships.

He describes how attachments are strongest during childhood, when children are completely dependent on parents for survival. In adulthood people continue to form strong attachments. Individuals tend to select partners who seem better able to cope with the world, who will "be there for us," "help us feel safe and secure." A child needs security to return to after small explorations into a strange, new, joyful, and frightening world. Children return to the caregiver as a home base after their small adventures and small experiences of separation. Ackerman (1994) reported on studies conducted on attachment in children in Baltimore. The Baltimore study found three patterns of attachment. If a caregiver is responsive to a child's need for contact and comfort, the child explores happily and will probably develop into a self-reliant adult capable of developing healthy relationships. If a caregiver rebuffs the child's need for intimacy and closeness, the child learns to keep its distance, and will distract itself with nonsocial activities and become compulsively self-reliant. If a caregiver acts inconsistently—that is, responsive some of the time and neglectful at other times—the child is likely to become "clingy" in relationships, dependent and unable to take healthy or normal risks in adulthood.

Children who have a trusting family life-tie, who can use family as a safe harbor, may be more stable and capable of developing loving, intimate relationships in adulthood.

Damage to the early bond between parent and child will have chilling emotional and psychological repercussions. A love-starved child may spend its adult life searching for a safe haven in an intimate relationship. Due to deficits from childhood, however, this adult will miss cues that might lead it to a truly secure and nurturing adult relationship. Instead, such a deprived adult may judge potential partners too harshly and be unable to trust, often becoming isolated or entering into abusive and destructive relationships. A deprived or neglected child is unwilling to take healthy chances or risks in relationships, often believing that he or she will be rejected or spurned by another.

Parallels were found by Hazen and Shaver (1993) between childhood attachment and loving intimate adult relationships. They found that childhood experiences trigger, garble or distort the experiences of later intimate relationships. However, damage done in childhood does not have to have a permanent effect in adulthood. During adulthood an individual will form different relationships, some good, that may neutralize and lessen the effects of a neglectful childhood. This is important, for it suggests that a person deprived in childhood can still develop into an adult capable of change and of developing an intimate bond with another.

Women and Relationships: NCWRR Study Findings

Approximately 60% of women said that marriage contributed to good self-esteem, compared to 76% of men. Only 56% of women, compared to 77% of men, stated that a partner contributed to feelings of positive self-worth. On a scale of 1 to 10, marriage and partners ranked fifth, well behind working, education, friendships, and raising children as a source of positive self-esteem for women.

The roots of intimacy have had many cultural and gender implications. The gendered self supposedly develops based on the need for love and approval that was established early in childhood within the family-of-origin life-tie. The love and approval sought and hopefully achieved will contribute to feelings of good self-esteem.

To win approval, most people and families are urged to conform to society's gender prescriptions by the demands and the expectations of significant others. These social demands and role expectations have traditionally burdened women with a relational overload; gender imbalance has steered women only in the direction of relationships, where they are supposed to gain identity and sense of self.

Women's lifelong socialization to prescribed relational roles has typically been labeled normative by developmental and other psychologists. Freud (1935) admitted that he did not understand women, but proceeded to describe female development as an aberration from the normative male model. He felt that women's lives were dominated by emotions of affection and intimacy, along with themes of passivity, masochism, and narcissism. Erikson (1968) proposed that a woman's *inner space* (her female organs and hormones) predisposed her to activities marked by union and care. He believed that women defined themselves through the selective nature of her search for a mate. Levinson (1978) believed that relationships were only a means to an end, that end being achievement for men. Maslow (1956) acknowledged the importance of relationships, but felt that a self-actualized person is independent of others.

Many of these early theories assumed inferiority and low self-esteem in women, assuring that women stayed in "their place" within relationships and that this relational model was the only source for self-esteem in women. Later, the new female psychology emphasized the same source of self-esteem and identity for women; that is, through relationships. Chodorow (1989) showed that females follow a pathway that allowed for the development of the self as an empathetic being in relationship to others. Miller (1976) believed that a woman's sense of self becomes organized around building and maintaining relationships.

Building on Miller's work, Gilligan's (1982) study of female identity development revealed that women define themselves with relational terms that imply growth in the context of intimate relationships. Belenky et al. (1986) found that female "connected knowers" experience growth when their "relationship" gives them validation and confirmation. In the absence of this validation women may feel emotionally crippled and incompetent.

New Women, New Challenges

The authors of these developmental models create artificial dichotomies between the identities of women and men. The revaluing of relatedness is central to creating inclusive models of personhood; however, the problem lies in defining women strictly with their affiliative capacities and men with instrumental capacities. Luria (1986) and Kerber (1986) expressed concern that the theories focusing on the superior nurturing qualities of women might create a return to the oversimplification of womanhood and the maintenance of a subordinate status, hence affecting self-esteem.

Relationship skills were the tools of survival for women. It was thought that men must *be* somebody and women must *find* somebody. Many women married to become wives rather than daughters. Adulthood was based on forging long-term relationships and marriage with men in the early twenties. Self-esteem and identity was embedded in the success of that early union. Although they had enormous responsibility for these relationships, most women had little power to control them.

Today women are no longer exclusively defined by men. They don't have to find somebody to be somebody; yet women still are considered the heavyweights when it comes to developing and maintaining intimate relationships. Many social changes have taken place for women, but much of a woman's success still depends on her being attuned to male culture, her ability to please men and her readiness to conform to masculine values in society's institutions. Whether working in a factory or working as a corporate vice president, a woman cannot easily afford to alienate men or be ignorant about their psychology. Many women who have learned to present a confident and professional face to the outside world often, in their minds and lives, think about and live with abuse, mistreatment, abandonment and misunderstanding. Deep inside they still feel it is their fault if a relationship is not working. Today, most women still do the "heavy lifting" in a relationship, and agonize over important decisions about their own lives. Women have been taught that it is selfish to even think of their own needs and are discouraged from putting their needs ahead of all-important others. Our findings report that over 72% of women felt that they have sacrificed too many of their own needs for the needs of others. Self-esteem for women has been equated with self-sacrifice. Nothing could be further from the truth: sacrifice does not add to self-esteem, it is a deterrent to positive feelings of self-worth. Self-esteem cannot be derived from society's expectation of what women ought to be doing and feeling. Men are struggling today to make decisions that will be beneficial to those they love, but they have not learned—as women have—to evaluate negatively the concerns they have with their own needs.

The NCWRR findings report that fully 35% of women, but only 15% of men, said that relationships with a spouse or partner produced low-self-esteem. And 27% of women, but only 11% of men, reacted negatively to the experience of living together or marriage. Forty-three percent of women felt that they had been in destructive relationships; only 29% of men felt this way.

It's not that loving and intimate relationships are unimportant or not valued by women. They are a very necessary and critical part of the joy and love women experience in their lives. However, the NCWRR findings suggest that when a woman invests too heavily in a relationship as a primary source of self-esteem, adverse consequences often result. Anything that makes the relationship less than perfect (e.g., if it is damaged by the destructive conduct of one partner, or if the intimate partner dies or leaves the relationship), the relationship becomes a source of negative self-esteem.

Women are prone to search for fault in themselves for any loss in an intimate relationship, be it by argument, illness, accidental death, or separation in war. The content of a woman's identity sets the standard for self-esteem, and the self-esteem is subject to experiences that shape her malleable self-concept. When a woman's self-image is evaluated on the basis of society's various expectations of her, she will fall short; and to this extent, she will suffer a negative impact on her self-esteem.

A woman may constantly monitor the success of an intimate relationship as the criterion from which she derives a sense of her own positive growth or a sense of some other variation in her self-concept. When the intimate relationships of some women deteriorate, they may derive, at some level a sense of failure of their own maturity. When a woman's ego is grounded solely in an intimate relationship, damage to the relationship or its loss can be devastating for her.

It is questionable whether, in marriage or living together, a spouse or partner can create or give positive self-esteem and identity to an adult woman. These aspects of life can enhance, bolster, and complement positive self-esteem that a woman may already have. On the same theme, it would be difficult for marriage or a partner to diminish a woman's self-esteem if she already has a positive sense of self built in from other areas of her life.

Positive self-esteem and strong identity do not mean dropping, avoiding, or losing the important intimate life-tie; rather, they require a woman to emotionally separate herself from dependence on the relationship, and to build other areas of self-worth. For instance, no one would ever consider investing money in just one financial stock. No one wants to put all his or her eggs in one basket. Security and strength depend on diversification and mobility of investments. The same holds true for self-esteem and a strong adult identity. Women must continue to gain self-esteem from many different areas, not just from relationships.

Past developmental theory, social expectations, and even new female psychology have stacked the deck against women. The relationship life-tie is important, but it is not the supporting pillar of adult identity and self-worth in women. Theory would have one believe that relationships are the primary work of women, and that this work should be accomplished early in adulthood. Women have been encouraged to channel the impulses of early adulthood into the making and preservation of relationships. But relationships, as culturally determined primary sources of self-esteem, can be precarious and false means by which a woman can feel power, effectiveness and importance. Problems arise when relationships substitute for activity and actions in other areas.

The following are a few stories from women interviewed that describe how balance, or lack of balance, in the relationship life-tie can create enhanced self-esteem or completely destroy a false sense of self that was primarily built on the shifting sands known as love and intimacy.

The Wilderness Years

Kay is now 49 years old and had been divorced for almost $3^1/_2$ years. She has maintained her North Carolina accent in spite of the fact that she has lived away from the South for over 20 years. Before her divorce she had been married for 26 years to Phil. Kay had married in the early 1960s at the age of twenty. She followed the path that many of her generation and generations before had embarked upon—a path that led to long-term commitment through marriage and managing a home and family— all in exchange for the "princely" protection and security that a husband could provide.

At that time, a woman's ticket to adulthood was based on her becoming a wife and maintaining a family, as Kay believed. Identity and self-worth were tied to issues of intimacy and relationships. During her high-school years, Kay had been an outstanding student, her test scores were high, she was a leader, an editor of her high school newspaper and yearbook. Her parents were pleased with her grades, for they would gain her entrance to a good college. Their hopes for Kay were that at a good college she would meet a good provider as potential husband material. However, through a family reversal, college became out of the question for Kay.

My father lost his business and had to declare bankruptcy. There was no money for college. I had to get a job when I graduated from high school. I was devastated, but never told anyone because I thought I was selfish in wanting to go away to college. I also had a distant dream of becoming a psychiatrist some day. Instead, I moved to Charlotte, found a job in a bank and began living with my aunt. I had been there a year when I met Phil. He was in his last year at North Carolina State. He was an outstanding engineering student, very, very bright, with a great future ahead of him. Well, after Phil and I had dated for about eight months, my parents were pushing me to get that wedding ring on my finger. I was more infatuated with the idea of being in love than actually in love with Phil. He eventually proposed. I had some second thoughts, but my friends and family felt that a guy like Phil would never come along again in my life. The message I got was I had no life without someone like Phil in it.

I supported Phil through grad school by doing secretarial work at a lumber company. He got a great job offer, but we had to move to Oklahoma, away from family and friends. Of course I soon became pregnant and in the course of two more years was pregnant with twins. I was isolated, frustrated and suffered from headaches and stomachaches that no doctor could diagnose. The doctor told my husband to buy me a badminton set and play badminton every night with me. I did feel better for a while—Phil and I were doing something together. That silly game made me feel alive and spirited. It didn't last. Phil went back to his workaholic ways and I went back to my headaches and stomachaches. My only comfort turned out to be food, and lots of it.

We were like two ships passing in the night. I knew our marriage was in trouble, so I decided it was up to me to make it right, that was my job. I read every magazine and book on the art of the successful marriage. The more I tried to make it right, the more he turned away to his own private life. I felt like it was my fault. I felt lousy about myself, so I continued feeding my misery to the point where I gained about 50 pounds. The kids had been the glue that kept us civil and polite to each other, but that glue dried up when the kids grew up.

Close to my forty-sixth birthday Phil said he wanted out of the marriage. He wanted a new life and had found a new and improved model to replace me. He was so calm and professional about ending our marriage. I felt he was ending my life. I tried being calm and adult to the point where I suffered a major depression from keeping everything bottled up inside. I wouldn't leave my house for 6 months. I slept all day and was up all night. I had my groceries delivered.

Through a good neighbor friend I went to see a doctor first, then a psychiatrist, who put me on antidepressants and started therapy. I get angry now, but that anger is good anger. I am angry for trying to define myself totally through my husband, kids, and family. I'm angry at how I was so stupid to have bought that package about a woman's job and worth are through marriage and a husband. Of course most women of that time did the same thing that I did. For 26 years I didn't have a self, I was invisible; a non-event.

My anger has been channeled into good things. I am finally going to college. It may have been delayed by about twenty-six years, but I'm doing it. I love my classes and I am just absorbing every book and idea my mind can inhale. I lost the weight, am exercising and nurturing my body and my soul with self-love for a change. I am beginning to find out a lot more about Kay and I like who I am becoming. It will be a long time before I am ready for any kind of relationship; if I never find one, that's okay, too.

Kay, like many women of her generation, equated adulthood and identity with intimacy. Finding a husband and establishing a family in early adulthood, particularly before the age of 25, was considered to be a hallmark of on-time development. Intimacy ties established too early in adulthood can lead to a false sense of self if they are entirely enmeshed with significant others.

Young females who anchor themselves in relationships as a main source of self-esteem before they have developed and pursued other important activities and actions will suffer a loss of self-esteem and identity when and if those relationships end. After the loss of a love-tie, women have been thought to feel not only impaired, but full of inner loathing and bad feelings. However, sometimes it is through the loss of a love-tie that women have found a new sense of self, a sense of energy, direction and spirit. Through such a love-tie loss women have learned to live through themselves, rather than living through that other person.

New Times, Old Messages

Chelsea is a nineties woman. Unlike Kay, she has deliberately stayed away from making any commitments that resemble marriage—that is, until she met Neil. Chelsea is thirty-five and feels comfortable with her life, who she is, and what she does. For Chelsea, getting seriously involved or married while she was in her early twenties would have been a disaster, but she feels confident that a commitment at this time is right for her. She is an example of many women today, who find it necessary to define themselves first before they commit to a long-term relationship. One of the strongest forces in creating a strong sense of self is the ability to make choices. Women now have opportunities to explore and make many choices that can add to self-worth and identity prior to committing to marriage (see Block, 1980; Cockrum & White, 1985; Doherty & Jacobson, 1982).

> I was brought up in a suburb of New York City, went to college in New Jersey and when I graduated I headed for the "Big Apple," open to what ever came my way. Sure, I had my share of boyfriends in college. Some were serious, but not serious enough to thwart my plans at a career, meeting new people, and doing different things with my life. My mother married right after college and had me and my brother and was satisfied with her choice. But I also see that if any-

thing happened to my dad she would be so lost. After my brother and I left home, he is her entire life. That's scary to me.

I have been a TV producer for the last eight years. I worked my way up from a college internship, to being a coffee "gofer" to my present position. I have two assistants, the respect of colleagues and financial security that has enabled me to feel comfortable and secure with myself, although there was a short time when I was about twenty-six when my family and back-home relatives started putting pressure on me to settle down and find a husband.

My mother and my aunt were worried that I would never marry. They believed that the older I got, the less my chances were for finding a husband. My two cousins who were younger were both married with babies on the way. I used to dread the holidays, the questions and not-so-subtle remarks about my being unattached. Their panic for a time caused me to panic. I began to believe that they were right. I began attending college friends' weddings—"Always bridesmaid and never a bride." The excitement and acceptance that swirled around my women friends who became brides was rattling my once-secure life. For a time I would read the wedding announcements in the papers, would thumb through *Brides* magazine and look at potential dates as potential lifelong partners. For a time I thought I would only be valued for who I belonged to, rather than who I was. Deep down I knew this was silly, but I played into a lot of old stereotypes about women and how they are identified.

I had a wake-up call when I got a promotion at work, a chance to travel and produce some documentaries, which I had always wanted to do. It was a chance to grow in another direction. Suddenly those wedding announcements and bridal magazines paled by comparison. I plunged into my work and advanced and learned a lot about my craft and myself. It's scary to think I might have married someone earlier out of pressure and a need to make my family feel secure.

I am now 35. Maybe I don't fit the image of a new bride, but after 2 years of living with Neil, we feel it's a good time to make that long-term commitment called marriage. He is comfortable in his work and life, and I am comfortable in knowing what I am all about and what is important to my life. There will be no long white dress for me, no bridal shower, no 400-person guest list, nor a reception with band and free-flowing champagne. We plan to have a simple, no-frills chapel ceremony and an intimate dinner with close family at a small restaurant. The marriage ceremony is but one small experience of many that Neil and I will go through as a couple. I know that my feelings of self-esteem are enhanced by Neil, but he is not the source of my self-worth.

Chelsea realized that an intimate relationship is one part of an identity and one part of her life—not representative of her whole life. This intimate life-tie can act as a resource, rather than a controlling influence. This is due in part to Chelsea's developing a life outside of relationships. Instead of building self-esteem and an identity solely on relationships, her identity encompasses many facets. This development took time and, as she said, would probably have been cut off if she had married in her early twenties. Society, along with developmental psychologists, has prescribed too many packaged roles for women, without allowing them to define themselves. Defining and shaping an identity takes time, and often is never quite finished. Chelsea took the time to develop self-esteem and an identity from many different reference points in her life.

When Love Hurts

Domestic violence is the single major cause of injury to women in the United States. An estimated 3 to 4 million women are abused by their husbands or partners—the men who promised to love them—as reported by the New York State Coalition on Family Violence in 1992. When love is tied to physical and psychological battering, the pathological association of love and hurt creates a relationship life-tie that all but eliminates any vestige of self-worth a woman may have had. Self-loathing, shame, blame, and fear immobilize many women and prevent them from taking action on their own behalf. Close to 20% of the NCWRR women said they had been physically abused by a spouse or partner; 30% of women stated that they were emotionally abused by a spouse or partner.

This life-tie of intimacy can become a knot of power and control. The partner in control—usually male—begins with emotional abuse that begins to undermine the other's sense of self-worth. Constant criticism, belittling one's abilities, name calling, insults, manipulation of emotions to produce guilt, as well as attempts at isolating that partner from friends or family, are part of the repertoire that a batterer uses to emotionally strip the other of dignity and esteem (Water, 1979).

Emotional abuse can very easily escalate to physical abuse once the partner has been worn down emotionally to the point of having no self-worth. Often physical abuse starts with shoving, grabbing, slapping; then can escalate to hitting, punching, throwing, or kicking. Sometimes, although not in the majority of cases, the abuse will end in the death of a partner. Margaret was an emotionally and physically abused wife, who endured this pain for 12 years before she was able to seek help and leave the relationship.

I never knew what would trigger his rages. One evening he spotted rotten lettuce in the refrigerator and threw me to the floor, all the while yelling about what a stupid fool he had for a wife. In the beginning, it was great, he made me feel like a queen. He was smart, had money, and a lot of people respected his talents and thought I had a real "catch." I was a young secretary when I met William, who was on the rise in a large commercial bank. Everybody said he would make bank president one day and thought I was the luckiest girl to land such a guy, even though he was about 15 years older than me. He told me I was pretty and young enough to have his kids, and that we would have a perfect life.

It started with small insults at parties we attended. He would put me down in front of his rich friends, or he would say my family was nothing, I was nothing without his direction and help. Pregnancy ensured that I didn't get out of the house much. I tried my best to be the perfect wife and perfect mother, but I never seemed to get it right. He would make lists of things I did wrong. I remember the first time he hit me. I had put a cassette into the tape player backwards. He grabbed me by the hair and threw me against the wall, saying I was a know-nothing who destroyed one of his prized tapes.

I felt like it was all my fault. He was smart, respected; we lived in a beautiful home and he made a lot of money. My own family didn't want to hear about what was happening to me. They felt I was lucky that such a successful man married me. So for a long time I believed it was all my fault. I felt responsible for making him happy, for making a loving home for him. I thought if I was a better wife he would stop the hitting—after all, he was the success and he was the respected member of the community; it must be my fault if he wasn't happy with me. I thought I still loved him and for a long time had hope that the relationship would get better, I guess, if I only got better. I became a nonperson, a terrified animal who quietly went around my own home in fear that anything I would do would set this guy off. For survival I knew and avoided the things that would trigger his hitting.

It was a funny thing, but it was at one of these required cocktail parties we had to attend to better his career that I got help. I met a woman who was a volunteer at a shelter for battered women. I was so tired and worn down that I didn't care how I shamed him or me at that point and I told her what was going on. She was horrified, didn't take his side and started telling me that it wasn't my fault. That was the first time anybody said that to me. She gave me a number and I got out of the house with my kids and eventually got a divorce. It was a long process to start building a life and trying to see who I was, that I was worth something and worth saving.

Margaret had been the quintessential good girl, bright, with some education, overprotected by family and without a particular career path. She happily gave herself over to her partner's needs, subsuming her own identity to her that of her husband. This process led to a loss of self-esteem whereby she blamed herself for her husband's abusive behavior. With no self-esteem or identity, Margaret was able to deny the abuse, rationalize and make excuses for her husband's behavior, and had little ability to assess the risks. Feelings of misguided love and the societal message that women are responsible for relationships helped to lead Margaret down a silent path that could accept such outrageous and destructive behavior on the part of a spouse all in the name of love and intimacy. The physically and emotionally abusive relationship is the extreme example aspects damaging and controlling of the relationship life-tie.

Turning Age and the Meaning of Adulthood Upside Down
Marylou, now forty-four, is another woman who attempted to establish a lasting and loving intimate relationship when she was in her early twenties, only to see it dissolve in midlife. Then she entered into a relationship with a man, in which she has taken the role of the "older/wiser" woman. She describes her youthful self as the "good girl of all times." Marylou went through a parochial school

system where every thought as well as every article of clothing was controlled. She describes her self in her teen years as being afraid of doing the wrong thing and characterizes her years in parochial school as controlling, guilt-ridden, and demoralizing. She was afraid of boys, always fearful of any attempt at sexual advances and was consumed with guilt at being labelled a bad girl.

"Peace and sacrifice at any price" was my motto. Soon after high school I met the man who would be my husband through my cousin. I was infatuated with him. He was neat, clean, and handsome. I thought he really cared about me, but later the care was really control. Before we married, he took my cigarettes away and gave me one when he felt I should have one. For our honeymoon, he told me how to pack my suitcase. When I wasn't home at a particular time he would call and demand an explanation. I can only describe those early years as being on this giant conveyor belt that was leading me to the altar. It was expected, my parents liked him, they were planning this big wedding and I was getting attention, gifts, and feeling envy from girl friends. I did have doubts a few months before the wedding. I didn't know if I really cared, I was afraid. My mother told me everyone went through these jitters—besides, the invitations had been sent out.

The reality of my marriage left me flat. I was so young and so naive. I had ideas of love, communication, doing things together, growing together—it was so disappointing. I became a good Navy wife, had two babies right away and played house. The roles were a little warped: He played daddy not only to the kids, but to me. I was still the good little girl who obeyed and let her husband control her life, right down to telling me how to fold diapers. This behavior went on for years. I was so young and so unready for marriage.

As the kids got older I went back to school nights, taking a couple of courses at a time. My husband and I used to have fights over my leaving his dinner warming in the oven, while I went to class. By this time, I was thirty-seven and had had enough control. My first steps at creating an independent life, a life that was important to me, rocked our relationship right to the divorce court. I had stopped asking, How can I make this better for him? and started asking, How can I make it better for myself?

Eventually I finished college, passed a civil service test, and got a job in a county agency. I had my own apartment, was in charge of my own money, traveled on my own, and made all my own decisions. At about the age of forty, I finally became an adult. It was also the time when I knew myself well enough to be confident in a relationship without losing myself. I know what intimacy is about, what it needs for two people to make it work. It's hard, rough, but so rewarding. I can't imagine any twenty-something kid getting married or being involved in a long-term commitment.

John and I started as friends. He is younger than I am by fifteen years, and had dropped out of seminary school when I met him. In a way he had divorced the church and I had divorced my husband—both of us had been in controlling relationships. I've had more with John in two years than I had within my twenty years of marriage. I can't say that it's totally because of John. This type of intimacy I have now I could never have gotten when I was twenty years old. I am a person, I have ideas, and know what's good and what's not good for me.

The age difference was hard on my parents and kids, but he has made them feel comfortable, especially the kids. He listens and has proceeded slowly, using caution and care in entering their lives. He knows these people are important to me. It was not easy for me to live with someone so young. Everything that I thought when I was twenty has been turned on its head. John loves me for my own qualities, but even as secure and happy as I am, I don't know if I want to get married. I am happy with John just living together. If I have any regrets, it's that we can't have children due to my age. That's a reality that both of us can live and deal with. Right now I am content to have been a bud that is finally in full bloom.

Marylou contradicts many of the social ideals and behaviors that have been prescribed for women in relation to adulthood, marriage, and intimacy and aging. Psychologists have believed that marriage and the development of relationships have supplied women with a sense of self (Erikson, 1968; Jordan et al., 1991). However, as Marylou described, marriage, particularly when it is entered at too young an age and before the self begins to take shape, can draw a woman away from that budding sense of self.

Many women like Marylou tuned in early to cultural expectations of the female ideal. It became all but impossible for them to become themselves. Instead, they reshaped themselves to suit other's expectations. Even though there have been many changes occurring in women's lives over the last thirty years, women are still defined as dutiful daughters and well-behaved students. They are encouraged to cultivate a pleasing personality, and it is assumed that they are the ones who will sacrifice and be selfless as a partner or spouse. Women cannot be totally understood according to the male model of development, but theory cannot overlook the importance of individuation and separation as it relates to the development of a human identity for both women and men. It may be necessary to differentiate one's self and create a balanced life as an individual before one can become the intimate partner of another in a relationship capable of maintaining the emotional health of both partners.

Marylou found a balanced intimacy during her middle years, a time when she allowed herself to grow before committing to a new relationship. Her choice of a much younger man with whom to develop an intimate life-tie may confuse and upset traditionalists. But in many ways it is a very complementary relationship. She is secure, self-assured, self-defined and still in need of personal exploration. John is sensitive, bright, empathetic, and not controlling. The relationship is a relationship of equals, a relationship that is full of movement, space, and acceptance.

Men and Relationships: NCWRR Study Findings

In addition to the data reported in the preceding section on women, our study revealed other interesting attitudes of men.

Sixty percent of men strongly felt that emotional intimacy was as important as sex. For men, "being a caring person" ranked second on a scale of 12 items as a source of positive self-esteem. This was also true for women. Eighty-three percent of women agreed with the statement that emotional intimacy was as important as sexual intimacy. Both women and men ranked "being loved" fourth as a source of positive self-esteem.

Before the social changes of the 1970s, women often demanded little from men in their relationships, either in terms of emotional closeness or who cleans the bathroom. Women have tolerated behaviors in men that they never would have tolerated from a close female friend. Males have never been expected to be "scholars" in the realm of intimacy. Parents encouraged and allowed boys to be physical, tough, independent, and removed from emotions.

Masculinity themes usually begin to shape males' intimacy and sexuality at an early age and may continue to affect male sexuality throughout the life span (Marsiglio & Greer, 1994). Marsiglio (1988) noted that traditional gender socialization during males' formative years encourages men to be competent and assertive; and willingness to assume the initiator role with women may contribute to older men's anxiety about sexual performance.

A man's ability to connect and be intimate has depended to a large extent on the father-son life-tie relationship. Most men were raised by fathers who were physically or emotionally absent or were taught to dismiss notions of emotional connectedness. There has been very little social reward for men investing in emotional intimacy. No accolades are given to men who value emotional ties at the expense of their professional investment. A national football player who missed a game to be with his wife when she gave birth to their first child was derided and fined for his behavior. Cultural gold stars are not given to men who seek to develop and maintain the intimacy bonds of their life.

Men have been more inclined to express caring and commitment through concrete acts. The verb "to husband" means to take care of the place with which a man has been entrusted. To husband is to practice the art of stewardship, to oversee, to make judicious use of things. These are concrete acts that men have been socialized to believe signify love and care. Psychologically, the husband is a man who is able to make commitments, to forge bonds, put down roots, and turn feelings of empathy and compassion into acts of caring. Tangible acts of caring have symbolized male intimacy.

Daniel Levinson (1978) gave his approval to the life pattern of men as it relates to intimacy. He believed that the goal of a man was to find a partner who would be lover and a friend, and who would help him in search of his dream or life goal. The attainment of the dream or life goal would express and symbolize his love and caring for his partner. In early adulthood men cement the bonds of intimacy through marriage. However, even Levinson noted that intimacy and love are strained when a man is giving his dream of work or career the higher priority.

Before Levinson's theory, Erikson (1968) believed that a man was supposed to establish his career/work path and still be able to resolve the intimacy-versus-isolation crisis during this early phase of his life. According to Erikson, the young male adult emerges from the adolescent search for an identity ready for intimacy. He is eager and willing to fuse his identity with that of another and is prepared to commit himself to concrete affiliations and partnerships and to demonstrate the ethical strength to stand by these commitments. The stress and conflict that this life task puts on men is considerable. Forging a career and establishing a long-term relationship commitment all during the early adulthood years is burdensome and often unattainable. Men's comfort with issues relating to intimacy, in fact, often doesn't develop until the middle years.

Women have complained that men are neither desirous nor capable of emotional commitment. Part of the reason may be due to unreasonable expectations. Men may lack the maturity level in early adulthood to deal adequately with intimacy ties. Our NCWRR study found that intimacy and love are important to men; however, the majority of men who responded this way were over the age of thirty. Their self-worth and identity are partly invested in their relationships, but at a much later time than early adulthood. Developing the skills and communication necessary to maintain the intimacy life-tie is a learning process that women have been taught from childhood. Not so, men.

New Roles and Challenges for Men

Men, along with women, have been bombarded with change over the last thirty years. The sexual revolution of the sixties, the birth-control pill, feminism, women at work, gay liberation, and changing gender expectations have all contributed to confusion and bewilderment on the part of many men. Love and intimacy, once the sole domain of women, are qualities that men find very fulfilling to their adult lives. Being able to open up and expand emotionally can channel men into new areas of growth and development at any time during their adult years. Liberating both men and women from the constrictions and demands of establishing this intimate life-tie only in early adulthood has led to new forms and expressions of intimacy for both women and men.

The transitions in social behavior in this new era of intimacy are without precedent for men, and altering established customs and traditions hasn't been easy or quick. These turnabouts in acceptable behavior, particularly for adults conditioned to the old ways, are still full of frustration and ambivalence. Men and women have been bruised, shaken up and sometimes handicapped by the new gender system. Unanticipated conflicts attending these changes upset the well-being of many men as they wrestle with the enormous role innovations required of them.

Contemporary men are juggling contradictory role expectations. They should be aggressively competitive in business, but gentle with children and women; ruthless and punishing with criminals and enemies in war, yet tender in ministrations to the sick and wounded; efficient, cautious, conservative, and obedient with social systems, but adventuresome with the risks of invention; responsible for employment and the support of a family when most things cost five times more than they used to, yet expected to share all domestic chores with a working wife; required to work to exhaustion and still have reserves in physical stamina, consideration, and sensuality to gratify the enhanced sexual desires of the liberated woman. In these ambiguities, men have frequently been blamed, made to look the villain, even portrayed as "the enemy" when they fail to meet either end of these dichotomous and contradictory obligations successfully. These new-era men can struggle conscientiously with the complex requirements they are confronted with, but when they fall short of adequacy, they suffer loss of self-esteem. The situation mirrors the dilemma of women in previous times.

Men of today have been described as "fleeing from commitment." They are sometimes portrayed as unwilling and emotionally unable to give up their cosmopolitan, bachelor condo and freewheeling lifestyle of entertainments and compensatory, transient, erotic pleasures. They are criticized for resisting the long-term, encumbering disciplines, responsibilities and considerate sacrifices incumbent upon them in an intimate, cohabiting and compensating relationship with an adoring wife and children.

These characterizations may be more fantasy than reality. What may be a reality is man's ambivalence about what he wants from a woman in a relationship today. Men still want intimacy, but the old rules and roles have changed so drastically that no one is certain about what intimacy is. Women are out of the house, in the work-place earning money, and the change in power relations that fol-lowed the economic shift have changed the rules of engagement surrounding areas of intimacy.

These continuing role struggles have left the definitions of male and female ambiguous, leaving both sexes uncertain. Men are pleased that they are no longer the only breadwinner and solely responsible for all major decisions concerning home and family. They are happy to be with women who are true companions. But at the same time men feel a sense of loss. They have suffered, as Goode (1982) suggests, a loss of centrality, a decline in the extent to which they were the center of attention. They must now compete with women as well as other men for status, prestige and money. Most men spend their days working long hours, often bored with little financial or job security. Society still blames the man, not the wife, for not making enough money or not being able to support his family. Faced with many conflicts, men resent their losses while taking advantage of their gains. They may express anger with women; at the same time, they don't want to live without them. They struggle to reshape their relationships, but their identity and sense of self often seemed threatened in the process.

Men's inadequacies in relationships have been pointed out by women. Women lament men's inferiority when it comes to deliver-ing sublime intimacy, unequaled passion, undying devotion, and eternal security. No man can deliver all of this, nor, for that matter, can any woman. Yet these qualities remain in the minds of many women in search of "Mr. Right." Women's unrealistic romantic notions, imagination, and "love will conquer all" attitude create impossible standards for men to meet and hold men responsible for their shortcomings. Often the tyranny of intimacy, that is, the belief that closeness between persons is an emotional necessity for wholeness, can be used as a conduit to promote superiority of one gender over the other.

The reality is that men are beginning and trying to learn to be more open and expressive in areas relating to emotional closeness and intimacy. They are seeking new ways to be loving, caring and sharing human beings. Their personal lives are becoming as impor-tant as their work lives. Men are beginning to like displaying the gentler parts of themselves, and developing their spiritual and nurturing qualities. Men's changes may be slow, unsure, vague at times and perhaps contradictory, but change is occurring in men's lives as it relates to intimacy. Often emotional closeness develops for the first time late in a man's life, or during the middle years, after a personal crisis or lifestyle change. Sometimes intimacy develops as a result of a second marriage or relationship, or with a different type of partner.

What men have described in interviews and through the NCWRR survey is that intimacy is a part of their ongoing development through the adult years. The development of a close and intimate relationship with a partner does not necessarily occur during the early adult years; rather, men frequently find themselves more comfortable and more committed to this life-tie later in adulthood. The narratives that follow describe how men feel about issues of intimacy and also how this life-tie has contributed to their own growth and development.

Getting It Right the Second Time Around

It is during late adolescence and early adulthood that issues of love, sex, and lasting commitment to a significant other are encouraged and expected. Men as well as women have gone along with these early expectations, even though many are full of self-doubt and immaturity, know little about their own or their partner's needs and desires. Men and women who followed the tradition of early role expectations for marriage and long-term commitment often felt like actors who had been handed a script without stage directions.

Roy, age fifty-two, is a divorced father of two grown sons. He has been divorced for eight years and has been in a relationship with another woman for the last three years. Roy feels that his present relationship reflects a deeper sense of intimacy and feeling on his part than was present during his first marriage. He is now able to express emotions better and feels he has been released from an earlier and constricting gender role. He was never able to feel good about himself during the first relationship. He admits that he falsely blamed his wife for not making him feel good about himself.

I married Patsy for all the wrong reasons, and I think that today she would say the same thing. I was 26 and she was 22 when we married. It was like playing house—only we couldn't pack up our toys at the end of the day and go home, we were home. I married to have a stable home and establish a family. Although I was older than a lot of men who marry, I didn't know much of anything beyond dental school. I was smart, had lots of degrees, but college and then dental school didn't teach me a thing about loving, feelings, and sharing a life with someone. I knew that I was about to join a dental practice and was expected to marry and settle into the community and life would take care of itself.

Patsy was extremely traditional and wanted to be a wife and mother, like many women of her generation. As the years went by I found out that I really didn't want such a traditional life, I wanted to have a marriage based on more equality. I guess I was becoming more affected by women's liberation than she was. She mirrored her life according to mine and the children's. I used to offer to take care of the kids on the weekends and some evenings if she wanted to join an organization, find a hobby, or take some courses. She refused and said she liked being home with the kids.

I used to want to go on trips with her, just the two of us without the kids. But the only vacations she would go on were with the kids. She said she didn't get married to not be a family. I guess that's what the problem was, she stopped being an individual, she stopped being Patsy, and just identified herself with being a family member. From the outside it looked like we were doing everything right—we had a house, kids, and money in the bank, but there was no reality or feeling inside that house. We were all playing a part. I was miserable and for many years felt too guilty to leave. I stayed until the kids were older and established in college, and then Patsy and I agreed to divorce.

During the divorce I felt like a cad, a failure for not making the marriage work, and just for putting up with being miserable. I know many guys who just exist within the shell of a marriage. My self-esteem was not good at this point, but I had a job that I liked and kept a good relationship with my kids. I started going for therapy. This helped me work through a lot of bad feelings and helped me to shed a lot of old ideas about roles and relationships. I kept blaming Patsy for everything, for being too traditional. But when I look back on my life, I guess I wanted it both ways, I wanted that traditional life while at the same time I talked a good game about equality.

I might have been 26 when I married, but I never explored my own needs or spent any time examining what I wanted from myself and a relationship. I was supposed to get married, so I got married; I was supposed to be a husband and father, so I filled up that space, but it was still hollow. Lately, I feel I am in sync with my emotions, my desires, and what I need and want in a relationship. Jen and I have been together for about 3 years; she was previously married also. We both have a maturity about ourselves, we know who we are and we are comfortable with ourselves as well as each other. Our life together does not follow any prescribed role, we sort of invent it as we go along. I have discovered a deep sense of intimacy with Jen, but most importantly I've discovered a new intimacy with myself. I never was ready or could have experienced this profound sense of love years ago.

During his early adult years, Roy experienced both intimacy and isolation Erikson's descriptions of success and failure for this age stage. Roy and his wife were unable to develop a deep intimacy, because neither one of them had a sense of their own individuality and self. They created hollow roles that just intensified the feelings of personal isolation within the marriage. Both were acting out parts of a social script that neither one quite understood or was prepared to handle. Early adulthood was the prescribed time to settle down and establish an intimate, loving and long-term relationship with a partner. This life-tie, if entered into before either partner has established an identity and an individualized sense of self, will not become a positive resource, but will remain a stifling control over that person's life, fostering low self-worth. Both Roy and his first wife had entered into a relationship with each other before becoming separate people in their own right. Roy's time alone after the divorce, along with introspection, therapy, and maturity, contributed to his ability to establish an authentic intimate relationship.

When It's Better to Be a Tortoise than a Hare

Brad is an example of a man who postponed marriage and a major commitment to a partner until he was in his middle thirties. His early adult years were full of frustration, he was unsure of himself, felt physically awkward, and had a difficult time being confident and knowledgeable around females. Brad's growing pains stretched into his twenties. His confidence was low; he didn't feel

he measured up to his male friends' accomplishments in the relationship arena or to the expectations of family and relatives who
awaited an introduction to a future daughter-in-law.

> I grew up hunting and fishing with my family in a backwoods area of
> Massachusetts. To many of the people in the small town I grew up in,
> my family was considered to be "poor white trash." My family were
> considered dumb folk, however, I was not. My life changed dramati-
> cally from my family's life when I was in high school. Teachers knew
> I was smart and encouraged me to apply for a scholarship to college.
> I did, and the result of all of this effort was that I ended up a docu-
> mentary producer for one of the major TV networks at a very early
> age—in my twenties. Professionally I was sophisticated, but socially
> and emotionally I was still in the backwoods.
>
> You see, the backwoods represented an alcoholic mother, a father
> I never knew, and a stepfather that was sexually abusive to my sister.
> This was not exactly a "Brady Bunch" family. Feelings of love were
> never expressed, I had no training on how to relate to girls. I grew
> up in a sexually inappropriate household. We lived in silence and I
> was wrapped in shame. I never dated in high school very much. Girls
> were interested in me, but I could never follow through. I had all
> those urges, but was scared of myself and my memories. I was
> wrapped in self-doubt. It wasn't until I was twenty-three that I lost my
> virginity. The relationships I had were with older women.
>
> Living in a big city creates all sorts of pressures, especially with
> women. I have found that many women have put their more femi-
> nine side on hold, due to career and corporate pressures and com-
> petition. Through my twenties and early thirties I had relationships
> with women, but never any I considered serious until I met Lin. Lin
> is Oriental, eight years older than me, and a computer software
> designer. We have been together for two years. She is bright, talent-
> ed as well as intuitive, sensitive, and caring. Through therapy, self-
> awareness, and time to mature, I feel I have been able to commit to
> Lin and our relationship has evolved into something I feel will be
> secure and long-term. I am comfortable with my manhood around
> Lin. I never would have been able to even contemplate marriage or
> commitment in my twenties, I was still a pretty mixed-up kid. I
> haven't met too many mature twenty-something men who are able to
> establish a lasting connection with another person.

Brad, a smart and talented man, knew better than to attempt to establish a long-term relationship in his twenties. He had psychological issues to work on that stemmed in part from trying to accept and let go of his family-of-origin life-tie. Until he resolved and came to terms with his own family, identity, and self-worth he would never be content and secure in a relationship. He is comfortable expressing his emotions and feelings with Lin, for there is a genuine sharing of feelings on both sides. The age difference between Lin and Brad is a complement, rather than a barrier, to their relationship. She is secure in her work and her concept of womanhood, and Brad is mature enough in his masculinity.

Masculinity, Intimacy, and Sexual Orientation

Men have difficulty understanding and working on issues related to intimacy, emotions and definitions of masculinity. In addition to this confusion, some men must also confront and accept a different sexual orientation than they had been living with for most of life. When a man has lived in a traditional heterosexual relationship, where part of his masculine identity rested on being a husband and father, the doubts surrounding his manhood, identity, and self-worth can be shaken when he comes to terms with his real sexual orientation. Colin was a 55-year-old man who had been married for over 25 years and had a grown son. His early identity rested on being a husband and father; his other identity came from being a minister, a role traditionally identified with masculinity and strong male leadership.

> I feel good about myself now, but 10 years ago I was confronting one of the biggest challenges that shook the foundation of my being. It was 10 years ago that I acknowledged I was gay. I had been doing a pretty good job of hiding my sexuality for many years, I even hid it from myself.
>
> My background is 100% New England WASP. I grew up in a loving family, but also a very traditional and conservative one. I dated in high school and was quite comfortable, although my comfort also came from very little knowledge about sexuality. Everyone was awkward, fumbling, and exploring their feelings and physical needs in a youthful and ignorant way, so in that sense I was no different from any of the other boys my age. Ignorance was bliss.

Church was important in my family and became of central importance to me in college. I went on to seminary school and completed
my education and training to become a minister. Protestant religion
encourages and expects ministers to marry, especially before they
acquire a position as clergy in a particular area. So the pressures
from the church, my family, and society brought me to my wife. I was
attracted to her physically and intellectually. Mostly it was her personality that attracted me. Marriage was going to make me a complete person and contribute to my identity and sense of who I was.

For the first 5 years marriage was good, especially when my son
was born. Everything was normal and routine. But I got older and
experienced more of the gray areas of the world and became more
seasoned myself, I had tremendous doubts about who I was and what
I was feeling. I began acknowledging to myself physical needs and
feelings that I never brought to the surface. My wife and I continued
to be cordial, polite, and good friends with each other. Sexually and
emotionally we both drifted apart. I wasn't meeting her needs and
she wasn't what I needed.

We divorced amicably, and although she found someone else we
both kept our friendship and shared the responsibility of our son.
Those years—after my wife and I divorced and when I came to terms
with my sexual orientation—were painful, full of shame, and filled
with a sense of failure. I felt I had failed my marriage, my son, my
family, my church, and society. The blackness that hung in my life
was at times unbearable.

Ironically, it was an older retired minister who helped me regain
my sense of humanity, worth, and dignity. He had counseled many
men and some ministers who had struggled with sexual identity.
Through his help and meeting other men with similar issues I
worked through some very tough stuff. I think after ten years I have
successfully dealt with and clarified intimacy issues such as love, masculinity, roles, social expectations, and differing sexual orientation
for myself.

Right now I feel good about myself, I have interior strength.
Coming to terms with my sexuality has had an added benefit of
being able to relate to others better. I am comfortable being affectionate and tender, I have been released from being trapped by old
notions of masculinity that required an edge and a hardness. I know
how to be intimate and how to be comfortable with intimacy. This is

much more than just a sexual issue.

Most important, I have learned that I am proud to be a man. I am completely happy with my gender. My sexual orientation has nothing to do with masculinity. I have been a good role model for my son, my father was a good role model for me. My father was a strong man, yet affectionate. I learned that a man could be a strong presence in society and still be tender and that sexual orientation has little to do with masculinity and gender.

Colin has had to confront many issues relating to gender, sexuality, role expectations, and areas of intimacy. He has learned that being masculine has nothing to do with sexual orientation. He has developed and maintained a nurturing relationship with his son, maintained a respect and friendship for his wife, and has brought to his own life a new perspective on the meaning of intimacy. This perspective encompasses the idea of masculinity that includes love and intimacy that moves beyond and does not necessarily depend on one's sexual identity.

Double Standard of Aging Applied to Men

Establishing ties of intimacy in later life often bear little resemblance to those forged during the early years of adulthood. All too often false limitations are imposed on both women and men by standards that are geared to twenty-year-olds. Older adults need to know and feel comfortable with new ways to touch and love each other that evolve away from early sexual pressures.

Older men often feel they can no longer measure up to old images of manhood. Just as women have been defined by aging stereotypes, so too have men. Early definitions of masculinity emphasized sexual prowess, "scoring," and physical capacity, and discouraged the expression of emotions and intimate feelings. The man alone image makes men especially vulnerable as they age. When age alters their sexual capacity, men's self-worth and identity, which have been tied to the physical aspects of intimacy, suffer the consequences.

Unfortunately, research on older men's sexuality is very limited in the gerontological literature. Overall, studies based on nationally representative samples deal with sexuality in a very narrow context (Marsiglio & Donnelly, 1991), and studies that do inquire about a range of sexuality issues are based on small and/or nonrepresentative samples, often with low response rates (Brecher, 1984; George & Weiler, 1981; Starr & Weiner, 1981). The most sought-after data in the existing literature involves the frequency with which older persons remain sexually active. Contradicting popular myth, available findings indicate that many older adults remain sexually active, although with decreasing frequency compared to earlier life periods (Brecher, 1984; George & Weiler, 1981; Marsiglio & Donnelly, 1991).

Jake is seventy years old and a former high-school coach who became a widower two years ago. He is in the process of redefining himself, coming to terms with loss, exploring new ideas of what it means to be a man, and discovering new meanings of intimacy.

If I had to use one word to describe my life as a man, that word would be "physical." As a kid I was a championship football player, I went to college and became a quarterback on the college team. I thought about becoming a professional, but although I was good I was never that good. As a teenager and in college I always had my pick of girls. They threw themselves at me. Boy, what an ego trip that was; I had just about any girl I wanted. At that time, being a man depended on all that was physical, my ability to throw a ball and the frequency of having sex. This went on while I was in my twenties until I met my Janie.

We married, I got a job as a high-school coach, had six kids and settled into a good life. We had a good marriage, although it was securely built around pretty traditional ideas. She never worked outside our house except for volunteer and church stuff. She was happy raising the kids and taking care of me and the house. My world was one of sports, hunting, fishing trips, poker games, and staying physically fit. My idea of being a man rested on championship games, the biggest fish caught, card games won, and my sexual performance. Six kids was sort of the proof of my performance.

My wife and I had a good marriage, but I regret not saying things to her I should have said while we were together. Two things rocked my world and changed me. The loss of Janie made me feel like I was hit by a wrecking ball. I always thought I was the strong one, but her death made me feel like I was nothing at all. Everything was empty, including myself. The second thing that leveled me was being diagnosed with diabetes. It created problems sexually for me. I couldn't perform, and for a man who based a lot of his identity on his performance it was devastating. I was depressed and wanted to die.

That changed when my kids started forcing me out of the house. I joined some senior groups and started traveling with a group of men and women my age. It was on one of these trips that I met Adele. We had a lot in common and much to talk about. Adele had been a professional swimmer years ago and still swam with a senior women's group. I was at first scared and felt stupid even considering a relationship. I felt too old and felt I couldn't perform anymore sexually. Adele persisted and had a lot of patience with me. I began telling her things about the way I felt, things I never could talk to anyone before about. I told her I was scared about being alone and scared about not measuring up as a man.

I started listening to her, I mean really listening and feeling a lot of her pain. We laugh and can poke good fun at each other, we go for long walks holding hands, we rub the sore muscles and aches and pains we have in our backs and legs, and we can stretch out on the couch listening to music while embracing each other. Sometimes we don't even say any words, our thoughts just reach out to one another. My love and feelings for her have nothing to do with whether I am able to perform sexually. My life is full and my feelings about being a man include many of the things I once considered unmanly like touching without sex, crying, showing scared feelings, and expressing tenderness. I only regret that I never was able to be like this with my first wife, Janie.

Jake found that earlier definitions of masculinity only encouraged feelings of powerlessness and fostered low self-esteem as he got older. As older women have been judged by unrealistic standards of youth and beauty, men have been wrongly judged by double standards of sexual potency and virility as they age. Women are given permission to express emotions and feelings, whereas men have been taught to deny and hide such qualities. Aging men become trapped when their sexual performance becomes diminished and they have learned no other way of expressing intimacy.

Jake was able to get beyond the stereotypes of masculinity and began to learn about other forms of intimacy. Allowing himself to express feelings, allow to be vulnerable, to listen to another, and to touch a woman without worrying about performance, he allowed himself to find a new kind of intimacy later in life.

SUMMARY

The NCWRR study has found that through adulthood women and men both seek and need the intimacy life-tie. Weaving this life-tie is important to both genders throughout adulthood. It is not necessarily a task to be completed in early adulthood, but is an important tie that threads throughout an individual's life. There is no gender distinction in the quest for intimacy; however, women have been encouraged to seek relationship ties more consistently and earlier, whereas men have been encouraged to express them through concrete actions and abstract symbols.

Strict developmental time frames do not address the many changes that have reshaped the lives of women and men today. Past perspectives assumed that the most important developmental task related to intimacy occurred in early adulthood. However, a well-seasoned maturity, which is needed for developing intimacy, is one quality that is lacking in early adulthood. Mature love and intimacy depend on the ability to maintain one's personal identity, to differentiate self from other.

The maintenance of the intimacy life-tie requires a balanced relationship between oneself and one's intimate partner. This balance reflects a coming together and a pulling apart. The balance is maintained by a flow alternately toward and away from each other. A positive sense of self-worth begins to develop when the intimacy life-tie ceases to be an influence and begins to become a resource. If a man or woman sees the intimacy life-tie as a control or power imbalance, development is hindered which will also hamper the development of positive self-esteem. If a man or woman feels, however, that the relationship is a resource, a source of mutual support to be drawn from when needed, personal growth and positive self-esteem will be enhanced.

Women

The NCWRR study found that for women, relationships are not a primary source of positive self-esteem, and have often contributed to negative feelings of self-worth. Many women had been in early relationships that were controlling influences and represented power imbalances that produced low self-esteem. When women in the study learned to establish separate selves, independent of relationship ties, and began to view relationships as resources and not influences, self-esteem rose.

- Kay is an example of a woman who early in adulthood was defined and controlled by her marriage. Kay equated adulthood with intimacy and marriage, however, she never developed a separate self independent of the marriage. Kay's divorce caused her to lose the identity that had been built around her husband and family. Depression was the result. She is working on correcting the imbalance by developing a primary relationship with herself through personal exploration and learning, before considering entering a relationship with another partner.

- Chelsea is a good example of a woman who defined her sense of self first, before committing to an important relationship. Her identity encompassed many facets, including a stimulating career. She was comfortable being single and realized that giving into family pressures in her twenties to marry would not be in her best interests. Her relationship with Neil is a balance between two mature and self-defined adults. The relationship acts as a resource for both partners, one that will support and allow for the continued development of two separate individuals.

- In Margaret's story of domestic abuse, the pathological association and of love and hurt created a physically and emotionally damaged human being. The control through emotional abuse by her husband undermined what little self-worth was present in Margaret. Emotional abuse escalated to physical abuse. Societal messages that women are responsible for the nature of relationships only fostered self-blame in Margaret, leaving her unable to assess the risks to her own life.

- Marylou, not unlike Kay, married early as tradition dictated, only to see her marriage and identity fall apart in midlife. Although she described herself as a "good girl" whose motto was "Peace and sacrifice at any price," the price for Marylou was too high: For a time it robbed her of an identity and positive feelings of self-worth. After getting divorced, being single, going back to school, and getting a good job, she found herself ready for a relationship. This intimacy life-tie is untraditional in many ways, but it draws its vitality from the relationship of equals. It is a resource, not a controlling influence, as her first relationship was.

Men

The NCWRR study found that men get more satisfaction from relationships than previously thought. Men, unlike women, were never encouraged to gain a primary identity through relationships. Rather, men have used relationships more as a resource, hence fostering better feelings of self-worth. The identity and self-worth of men have been tied to life goals, with intimacy just a means to an end. Intimacy was needed to complement a man's main task of career and work achievements.

The social changes of the women's movement brought about changes for men. There has not been a road map to guide and direct men appropriate to behavior in this changing world, and there have been no specifics outlining new definitions of masculinity. For the most part, men have been trying to become more expressive and sensitive to areas of intimacy, but along with change has come conflict, confusion, and ambivalence. Whereas women plunge headlong into relationships, men meander and plod along slowly, sometimes only beginning to feel comfortable with intimacy during their middle years.

- Ray was divorced after many years in a marriage that was characterized by tradition and strict gender roles. Instead of resolving Erikson's intimacy-versus-isolation stage in early adulthood, he only achieved a hollow form of intimacy and lived a real life of isolation. It was only during his middle years that he was able to explore real feelings of closeness and express a genuine form of intimacy in later adulthood.
- Brad's early adult years were marked by memories of shame and self-doubt traceable to his roots of intimacy. Deprived emotionally and shameful about sexual family secrets, he was wise enough not to develop early relationship ties until he had worked

through his own psychological and emotional issues. For Brad intimacy had been tied to shame, which resulted in his seeing intimacy as a controlling and bad influence. Eventually, with much work, he gained a perspective on intimacy and love when he could see it as a support and resource with Lin.

- Intimacy does not always mean only one right type of partner, or one right way of expression. Colin acknowledged and accepted his homosexuality later in life, after years of being married to a wife and fathering a son. His old ideas of masculinity, reflecting society's ideas of manhood, at first attached feelings of low self-esteem and low self-worth to his homosexuality. Colin found that masculinity had nothing to do with sexual orientation. Coming to terms with his sexuality has actually enhanced his ability to relate and be intimate with others.
- Double standards of aging and sexuality are not only aimed at women. Men like Jake also experience this double-edged sword. Jack had grown up with masculine definitions that revolved around sexual prowess, physical strength, and the invincible strong-man images society projects. The death of his wife and loss of his sexual capabilities through diabetes left Jake with little self-esteem and an image destroyed. He was able to move beyond the stereotypes of masculinity and old forms of intimate behavior and establish a late-life relationship with a woman that was defined by sharing, tenderness, listening, and new forms of expression.

An intimacy life-tie that fosters feelings of human value and worth is a relationship that allows a man or woman to be who they want to be in a relationship, and allows the other partner to do the same. Lerner (1989) believed that being who one is requires the capacity to talk openly about things that are personally important, to take a clear position on where one stands on important emotional issues and to clarify the limits of what is acceptable and tolerable to the partners in that relationship. Allowing the other partner to do the same means that one can stay emotionally connected to an other who may think, feel, and believe differently without needing to remake the partner.

A balanced intimate relationship is one in which neither party silences, sacrifices, or betrays the self and each partner is able to express strength, vulnerability, weakness, and competence in a balanced manner. It is this precarious balance between maintaining the "I" in a relationship while connecting with the "we" that determines whether it is a life-tie based on influence and control or a life-tie based on support, a resource that fosters positive feelings of self-worth in both women and men.

CHAPTER 6

Children

Parenting, the greatest single preserve of the amateur.
—*Toffler*

Probably no other life-tie experience demands as much—physically, emotionally and mentally—as parenting. Parenting is like looking into a circus fun-house mirror. The image one sees in that mirror can easily distort and magnify faults as well as strengths. Parents, through a child's eye, can view themselves as all powerful, benign protectors, or mythic monsters and evildoers. Both men and women often face the dilemma of losing perspective on oneself and being consumed by the task of parenting. Raising children requires adults to confront and review their own past. Parenting can make a man or woman more focused about personal beliefs, can reaffirm or disavow early roots and can yield new discoveries about an old self.

Until recently, many developmental psychologists assumed that the child was the only one that underwent change and that parents stood by as unchangeable, stable and resolute fixtures. Parents were thought to be a nondescript backdrop against which action took place on the child-centered stage. The idea that inner change is a prerogative of youth is a logical conollary to the theory that adults have fixed identities by the time they enter early adulthood.

Just as a baby, a child, or an adolescent undergoes vast developmental change, so do their parents. The developmental tasks for parenting are awesome and challenging. As parents, individuals have to learn new ways to interact, to abandon their parents' poorer practices and to incorporate their good ones. An adult's boundaries are automatically expanded beyond their previous individual world to include a child. The family, in the act of parenting, undergoes many changes.

There are new forms of parent/child attachments. The nuclear family with dad at work and mom at home no longer represents the majority. New forms that make up this life-tie interaction include solo and single parenting, stepparenting, shared/joint parenting, and gay couple parenting, to name but a few. These new forms of parenting create new ways of viewing the self, for both women and men, in the context of parenting a child. Having children no longer means having them at a prescribed time in early adulthood. Because of career and educational pursuits as well as financial stability, many couples and some single mothers are having children later, in their thirties. Many more than ever before are having them when they are in their forties.

Children become an integral part of a woman's and a man's adult life. Parenting and ties to children do not end when the last child leaves home or when a parent enters midlife. Parenting throughout the life of the child involves many new and ever-changing states of thinking and action. What applied in raising a toddler, does not apply as a teenager. People who parent find themselves in a constant state of ebb and flow, always modifying behaviors to meet the demands of being a parent. Nowhere is the process of developmental contraction and expansion more evident than in parenting.

"What is self, what is other?" This question, often analyzed in psychology, comes to the forefront when discussing children and parenting. A parent provides the context in which development of the child takes place. Growth of the child and growth of the parent is a constant push and pull, straining between a state of embeddedness and a state of differentiation. The psychological dance between parent and child is a pattern of expansion and contraction, of holding on and letting go.

Kegan (1982) believed that healthy holding lays the foundation for healthy separation, a shift from embeddedness to differentiation.

If a parent has difficulty letting go at the proper time, that parent may be experiencing and feeling a loss of self. For when a parent cannot let go, but sees the child as a major source of identity and worth, little development can take place for either. The NCWRR study may not altogether agree with Erikson's linear age/stage developmental sequencing. We agree with Erikson's (1968) idea that the degree of autonomy children receive from parents depends on how independent and autonomous the parents feel. Erikson (1968) also believed that a parent who has been psychologically deprived will have a vested interest in not psychologically letting go of the child.

A child has to pull against embeddedness from the "terrible twos" to the teen years. The newly developing sense of differentiation demands a parent who is flexible, secure, and patient to allow this process to take place. The parent must develop the flexibility to contract, to expand and, also, to know when to remain in place within the context of this fluid relationship. A child can have at times both a positive and negative impact on their parents' self-image. Problems arise with an adult's self-image and self-esteem when that parent has difficulty accepting and encouraging this healthy differentiation.

The shifting balance as children grow to independence creates a symmetrical parent/child life-tie. Changing the life-tie without severing it, the renegotiation of the life-tie and the changes affecting it contribute to growth and development for the parent as well as the child. A balanced and reciprocal parent-child relationship will then act as a resource for positive self-esteem and continued growth in that parent.

Past research has characterized the vast differences that exist between mother love and father love. From Harlow to Bowlby (1969) the attachment between mother and child was thought to be special and better. Mothers are physically intimate with their babies, kissing, rocking, and cuddling them. A mother is food, warmth and safety. She and baby often seem like physical and emotional extensions of each other. Eventually this mother and child will have to learn to become separate beings.

A father's love has been characterized as remote and distant. A father's love, unlike a mother's love, presumably has to be earned or deserved. Fathering includes a system of punishments and rewards, setting limits, making demands, requiring obedience. Fathers have been the teachers and guides of the world that exists outside the home. Fathers expected their children to fulfill their expectations, to act with a sense of duty and, especially for boys, "be like them."

The NCWRR study found that the dichotomies between aspects of mothering and fathering are not quite as rigid as previously thought. Findings based on the NCWRR study show that being a parent contributed to feelings of high self-esteem in 50% of men and 43% of women and brought moderate self-esteem to 38% of women and 33% of men. This life-tie was, thus, a source of self-esteem for both women and men. However, there were individual differences in context, timing, and perception. The study found that more women below the age of thirty-five had satisfactory relationships with their children and that more men above the age of thirty-five had satisfactory relationships with children. Close to 50% of both women and men believed that being a parent was extremely difficult. However, both women (75%) and men (65%) perceived that their relationships with children improved when the children got older and were more independent.

The following sections will describe some of what has been documented regarding mothering and fathering as it relates to sense of self. The sections will also present the narratives of women and men as they share their various parenting experiences and the meanings they attach to those experiences.

MOTHERING A CHILD

The Paradox of Mothering

Throughout thousands of years of history, women, due to their extraordinary and mystical ability to give birth, have been both revered and feared. Women have been the object of great paintings, sculpture, sonnets and love songs and have been defended during times of war. They have also been marginalized, isolated, reduced to a form of property, been the object of witch hunts, taboos, and superstitions. Mothers have been accused of being either too overprotective or too cold, too suffocating or too distant, too neurotic or too selfish, too dull or too smart for her own good; too intrusive or too rejecting.

This paradox of mothering, shaped by society, often complicates and confuses a woman's sense of self, her identity and esteem during her adult years. Teachman and Polonko (1985) noted in their review of the parenting literature that the timing of the first birth affects a woman's career, the material assets of the household, risk of marital dissolution, and the number and timing of additional children. More important, the first birth (particularly if it occurs during the midlife years) may influence the mother's sense of self-worth.

The mother/child life-tie is intensified at the same time that it is often rendered powerless and impotent. For any choice a woman makes—to have a child or not to have a child, to be a stay-at-home mom or a working mom, to love or not to love too much —there always exists a negative aspect. Any positive encouragement will be followed by disapproval. A mother is open to both praise and criticism. All people need and seek love and approval, but women—in particular mothers—are in a double bind. If women elicit approval by being a stay-at-home mother, they lose status and self-esteem because traditional mothering roles are devalued. If women develop more autonomous selves in an attempt to combine mothering and work, they are judged as selfish by putting their own needs ahead of their children. Even though most women work for financial reasons, the understood message is, "Don't forget, your primary responsibility resides in the home with your family and children."

Thurer (1994) found that many of the mothers he treated harbored shameful ideas about how their behavior or feelings might have harmed their children. Mothers who lack confidence in their abilities, have romanticized notions of being the perfect mother that may only foster feelings of guilt regarding the reality of childrearing, and mothers often measure themselves against impossible external standards that they must be all-loving, patient, and selfless. A mother feels she has to be all things to her very young and helpless children. She eventually is held in final judgment by the society she lives in, measured against the standard of how her children have turned out. Often this judgment is not only passed by society, but by the children themselves. Even the NCWRR study found that more adult children held their mothers more responsible for their own feelings of low self-esteem and feelings of guilt than their fathers (see Chapter 2). The success or failure of one's children is often interpreted as a mirror of that mother's success or failure as a person. The cultural myth of perfect mothering haunts women's lives, always pointing out the personal inadequacies that often lead to confused, conflicted and guilt-ridden identities in adulthood.

Mothers have been given two opposing tasks in raising their children. One task is to create unity and bonding. They are then expected, piece by piece, to dissolve that unity and bond and to do it at prescribed times. Preservation and renunciation of the child life-tie development or it can tear down self-esteem and foster identity confusion. If she does not break that bond at the socially prescribed time, a mother is accused of being possessive and neurotic.

Somehow, it is thought that there is a switch to be thrown to sever that bond at just the right time—adolescence. Dispensing the right amount of mothering at the right time, however, does not come packaged like time-released cold capsules. Mothers and children do not come with instructions and time-honored warrantees. A very linear, one-size-fits-all mentality about proper mothering is harmful not only to the child, but to the mother's own development and feelings of self-worth. The model of good mothering that aligns with psychological age/stage theory does not accommodate and adjust for context, family interactions, social environment, family histories, and changing life events.

Positive Mother–Child Life-Ties

The love and connection between a mother and her child can be the most genuine and tender love there is. Nurturing a child makes that mother completely important and necessary in a child's life. The love and attachment a child gives back to the mother is a reinforcing pleasure that many never got from other adults. When children grow physically and emotionally strong, a mother will take enormous pride in her accomplishment. The small daily joys and close feelings that linger between a mother and her children can create a groundswell of maternal well-being.

For many women, including the study participants, mothering

represented renewal, a chance to start over, to relive their own childhood in a more satisfactory way. It is a developmental growth process that makes a woman more responsible. She no longer is a child; she becomes responsible for another person's care, teaching, and nurturance. A mother soon realizes that the way she acts and behaves will influence her child's development as well as her own.

When children ask questions, it makes a mother think, form new opinions and ideas. Her children's questions often lead a mother through her own growth process, seeing and viewing things she might have never considered before. Women often have to build new strengths, face tough situations that many would have run from before. In short, they have to cope. Raising a child creates a balance. Many women have described their own lives before children as being totally absorbed in their own pursuits. With children, women have found themselves to be more giving and have had to learn to share their time and lives with one or more small individuals.

Many women described the effects of motherhood in terms of expansion and tolerance. They also develop an understanding of their own mother's lives and attitudes while raising children. Patience, resourcefulness, and understanding are qualities that many women said they had not been born with, but slowly developed while raising their children. Mothering calls upon women to be less judgmental, to be more accepting, and to unearth qualities of empathy and love without holding back. Some describe the processes of learning to control their tempers, becoming more self-disciplined and growing from self-centered "child-women" to wiser and patient adults.

The more mothers view motherhood as a realistic challenge, the harder they work to meet that challenge and the more rewarding motherhood tends to be. Women who at times felt conflicted, overwhelmed, and constantly rushed—but who struggled to create time and who tried their best to provide a good environment—were women who grew into motherhood and saw it favorably. In this context, children and the process of raising children become a resource for personal growth and adult development, increasing positive feelings of self-worth.

The two narratives that follow represent many stories women told to us about how parenting was a source of high self-esteem and continued development in their personal lives.

Children As Catalyst for a Mother's Growth

Often it is a personal crisis coupled with a major responsibility to others that make an individual grow and change in positive ways. Jessica was a twenty-six-year-old woman who had gone through a tough divorce, its difficulties compounded by the fact that her husband had disappeared, had abandoned her two daughter's lives, and neglected his financial obligations of support. Jessica was married after high school to the boy she dated during her sophomore year. She was also four months pregnant when she and Bill decided to marry. Bill had a boatyard job and they lived in a garage apartment that belonged to her parents.

In those early years, Jessica explained, she remained at home, "playing house." Two years later she had her second daughter. Finances were tight—and the source of much arguing between the two. Her parents bailed them out financially whenever she told them that they were having money troubles. Jessica loved her children but spent most of her days at home watching game shows and soap operas and talking to girlfriends. She became more intrigued with the fantasy lives of TV characters than with her own personal development and that of her children. The marriage deteriorated over the years until Bill just told her he had had enough and was leaving. After the divorce, he left the state with a supposed friend of Jessica's. Her playhouse world had ended.

> I was devastated and just wanted to crawl back to my old bedroom in my parent's house and have my mother take care of me and the kids. That wasn't possible. Although the kids and I still lived in the garage apartment, my mother had had a stroke and my father had to take care of her. My two little girls missed their daddy and were scared as to what was going to happen to them. This was the first time that I had to take control of my life and grow up. Every time I looked at their faces I knew I could not let those two little people down, I was all they had.
>
> I sure didn't turn into a responsible dynamo over night, but after a lot of bad starts I got on track. My parents let me live rent-free in the garage apartment and I put my youngest in nursery school. My oldest was a second grader. After school I arranged with a girlfriend to have her sit with both girls. During this time I worked days as a salesclerk in one of the big discount department stores. Three nights

a week I went to night school at the community college. My days and nights off I spent doing things with the girls. I got real creative finding inexpensive things we could all do. We would go the beach collecting shells and stones; wc went to the park where we all got on swings; and they would run next to me while I jogged along beach roads. At home we all cooked, cleaned, and helped each other. They cut coupons and went yard sale hunting with me. I had to budget moncy, deal with medical crisis, study, work and be both a mom and a dad to my girls.

Most of the time I am exhausted, but the responsibility of raising my girls has made me grow into a responsible adult. Taking on so many responsibilities has made me grow. Knowing that my daughters depend on me has created a self-knowledge and a confidence that I never had before this challenge. Anytime you have a challenge you grow.

Jessica's self-esteem and growth in adulthood was a result of meeting the responsibilities of being a mother to her daughters. Before her divorce, she was little more than a child herself, but knowing she was the only thing standing between her children and disaster, she rose to the occasion. Parenting became a tool and resource for her growth in adulthood. Jessica, in order to be a good mother, had to take on enormous responsibilities in many different areas: household management, work, school, and coping with everyday crises that affected their lives.

Single Career Mom and Children

More women are putting off having children until they are established in their careers and have defined and carved out their own lives and personal identities. The age at which a woman can have and is expected to have children has changed and expanded. Motherhood is no longer a one-size-fits-all option. Many women assume that by spending their early years building careers and personal pursuits, their self-images are well-formed and shaped. They assume that having a child will have little impact on their very strong, capable, and highly developed identity. Neither assumption is well supported. The particular psychological, social, and economic issues faced by single mothers are well-documented in the literature (Children's Defense Fund, 1990; Greif, 1986; Hanson & Sporakowski, 1986).

Marla was single and thirty-eight when she became pregnant. The pregnancy was planned with the knowledge that she would be raising the child alone. Marla went about organizing her pregnancy as though she were organizing one of her ad campaigns for the advertising agency that employed her. She was financially secure, in good health, and had lined up good child care when she had to return to work after a six-week leave. The arrival of the baby went according to her timetable, but her feelings, behavior, and sense of self were changed by the arrival of her daughter Sara.

I had it all planned. My pregnancy and vision of raising a baby was organized around something that resembled a business daily planner. By the time I was thirty-five I was firmly established in my career, had financial security. I had no prospects of marriage, yet I wanted to have a baby. I gave this a lot of thought and spent two years weighing this decision carefully. I had been going with a man for about six months. We had a good relationship but also realized that marriage was out of the question. He was a freelance journalist, had been married once before, and did not want to get married for a long time. A "long time" for me meant the chance I might never have a child. I became pregnant. I told him that I was pregnant, but was going to be totally responsible. If he wanted to be part of my life, he could. If he wanted to distance himself from my decision that was fine also. He chose to distance himself.

I worked right up to my last month. I took the last month off from work, and busily decorated the nursery, bought baby clothes, finalized the nanny's schedule and got all my friends both male and female involved. My immediate family and my extended friends would be part of Sara's new family. I knew it was a girl based on my amniocentesis test, so I prepared for Sara's arrival.

I was not as prepared as I thought. Oh yes, the nursery was ready; my pantry was stocked with food, formula, diapers; and doctors numbers were all in place. What I was not prepared for was the overwhelming joy, love, and intensity of feelings that washed over me at her birth. I always knew I would be responsible and disciplined as a parent, but I never knew the intensity and depth of feelings I could have for this baby. At first I thought it was just my hormones going haywire, but my attachment and love for Sara just grew.

Sitting alone on my couch, all quiet, with Sara feeding in the middle of the night was an experience I never before imagined. I hated to put her back in the bassinet. I wanted to keep that physical attachment in place. This certainly was not the image I had of myself previously. I knew myself to be a methodical, no-nonsense, professional, and unemotional woman. I now had feelings of love, sadness, warmth, joy and a real nurturing feeling. This whole new side of myself brought out by Sara amazed me and my family and friends. As it got closer to the time when I had to return to work, I dreaded leaving Sara. My responsible side said I was silly, my emotional side said what I was feeling was natural.

I had a dilemma. I had a conference with upper management about my work schedule. At least for a year, I would work 2 days at home and 3 in the office. I was an art director and could do much of my work in my home office with the help of computers, fax machines, and telephones. I would be on call for special meetings and troubleshooting crisis accounts. I had an impeccable work record and respect from my colleagues; everybody believed it would work. It has worked. I am luckier than many women in that I can combine the best of both worlds. Beyond my professional life, I have discovered another side to my self that I feel makes me a more whole person. Sara has added to my life in ways that I could never have imagined. As she grows, so do I.

Marla represents the opposite to many women, who had their identities firmly entrenched in motherhood only to discover new aspects of their lives in the world of work. Marla had her identity firmly established within the confines of her career before tackling the challenge of motherhood. Having Sara expanded Marla's identity and self-worth in ways that she hadn't even considered or thought she was incapable of achieving. Her child became a resource and source of personal growth. Marla certainly doesn't fit the traditional image of a twenty-something young mother with a bread-winning husband, which has been the standard image of all of motherhood. New, positive images of mothering have to take into consideration the many options women have now, as well as their changing lifestyles and challenges to traditional timing of childbearing. The idea that adult development and self-esteem can be enhanced through an integration of both achievement and motherhood is an idea that should be embraced.

Problems in Mother–Child Life-Ties

As we stated earlier, 38% of women in the NCWRR study said children contributed to moderate self-esteem. However, 14% of women were not sure of how children contributed to self-esteem and 5% believed that their children contributed to low self-esteem. The paradox of mothering can produce feelings of ambivalence, insecurity and low self-esteem in a woman's perception of herself. It may not be the act of mothering or the children themselves that produce these feelings. Rather, it may be society's expectations and contradictions that cause women to doubt their ability to mother. The societal paradox that presents mothering as something to be both feared and revered, can confuse and distort the self-images of women. Women who try to be all things to all people end up pleasing no one, least of all themselves.

The mother/child relationship is taken as the model for a strong relational orientation and connectedness. In glorifying women's embeddedness in relationships as a virtue, one fails to consider the fallout for women who become totally embedded in childrearing. By following a strictly relational pathway, serving the needs of others—in particular, children—women may lose identity and self-esteem. Girls are taught early that their identity and self-esteem rest on their ability to maintain and develop relationships. However, a society that values individuality contradictorily leads females to develop a greater sense of themselves as embedded in social relationships.

Dilemma and confusion inevitably exist in a choice that, on one hand is encouraged by society as good, even Madonna-like, but at the same time is dismissed as lower in status to that of individuality and the self-pursuits of career and personal creativity. If a woman combines a career with motherhood, she is attacked as being unnurturing and inattentive to her children's needs. Anxiety, ambivalence, self-doubt and low self-esteem can sprout from the contradictions our society dispenses to women who mother.

Often it may be the illusion of motherhood and the impact of reality that lead to identity confusion and low self-esteem in women. Many women discussed themes centering around perfection. They wanted to be the perfect mother, to have the perfect children, and if they work, to combine the two roles perfectly. Expressions included such themes as "Best mommies have best children" or "My children will be different, better than the rest." Many women who want perfect children come from less-than-perfect families. A mother may remember the child she was, that she was not the prettiest, the brightest, or the most loved. She may try to integrate and change her own image in adulthood by trying to create perfect children and families. When her less-than-picture-perfect children and family strike a chord with reality and don't measure up to her internal image, a woman may often integrate these imperfections into her own self-concept.

If a woman is at home with children, and would rather be working, her self-esteem and personal satisfaction will be much lower than that of a woman who wants to combine both and does so or a woman who wants to stay home with the children and can do so. If a woman feels stifled, restricted, or feels she has missed opportunities and lacks choices in her life, childrearing may be viewed as a negative experience. The demands, stress, exhaustion, and sacrifice of self related to childrearing often contribute to a loss of self-esteem and feelings of well-being.

A woman may have serious doubts as to whether she wants to have children. If a woman has a child to please a husband, family members, or has a child because other couple friends are having children, negative feelings related to the pressure and self-doubts about the decision can often lead to undercurrents of tension, anger, and depression. A decision to have children induced by the pressures of external factors may lead a woman to view that decision as being forced upon her and out of her control. Losing control of this life-tie decision will affect her self-esteem in a negative way. Instead of the mother/children life-tie being interpreted as a resource, it will be seen as a source of external control—hence lowering self-esteem and potentially limiting its influence as a positive developmental experience in adulthood.

Mother-Blaming and Its Consequence

The paradox of mothering can be best described with the narrative of a survey respondent we call Gloria, whose self-esteem and identity were affected by accusations by her husband and family of overprotecting and coddling her son. The recriminations she endured made her doubt her ability to mother. She felt inadequate and resentful of her own son, to the point that she wanted to withdraw from her son's life.

My husband was so ecstatic when I gave birth to a son. My self-esteem was high, because I had produced a son for my football-loving husband, as if I had any control over whether it was a girl or boy. But that's how I felt at the time. My proud feelings were short-lived. I went back to work after Jeremy was two years old and put him in a nursery school. When I wasn't working I spent a lot of time with Jeremy. He helped me bake, he followed me around when I vacuumed and cleaned, imitating what I was doing. We listened to music together. I read to him all the time, things like that.

My husband started getting upset when Jeremy, who was about five, didn't like throwing around a football with him. Jeremy liked to swim and do gymnastics, but didn't like baseball or football. Ted, my husband, began blaming me for making his son soft and turning him into a mama's boy. If he didn't like contact sports, he wasn't going to be a man. His family also got on my case about being too overprotective, and they encouraged me to let Ted spend more time with Jeremy. By now Jeremy was old enough for Little League, but he didn't like to play and complained to me that his father was forcing him. I supported my husband and insisted that Jeremy play. I used to get angry and upset with Jeremy for not acting the way his father wanted him to act. Every time Jeremy cried, I felt I was a failure of a mother trying to raise a son. I became hard and didn't listen to his fears, I wasn't going to be accused of softening my son so I distanced myself from our relationship.

I was so confused. On one hand, my feelings were telling me to stop this insanity of my husband's—forcing Jeremy into sports and other macho activities; but by then I was very aware of what society expects of men and how women can damage a boy by having him spend too much time around women and activities related to women. When Jeremy hit his teen years, we had a lot of problems. He was angry all the time at both myself and my husband. His grades dropped; he dropped all sports; and he was developing a real attitude. I didn't like being around Jeremy. My husband still blamed me for not being a good mother. I was at an all-time low point with my marriage in trouble and with my son on the brink of all-out revolt.

The best thing that happened to all of us was therapy. All three of us went, my husband at first reluctantly. The main thing we found out was that a large part of Jeremy's anger was directed at the way his father and I both behaved. He was angry with his father for trying to turn him into an athlete, when he wanted no part of contact sports. He was mad at me for withdrawing from his life. He thought I was siding with his father and deliberately ignoring his real concerns and who he was. I began to reenter Jeremy's life in a different way. I no longer considered myself to be a poisonous influence on his life. When I feel my husband is wrong I tell him so and we discuss it. Jeremy and I spend more time together, just talking or doing yard work together. I like being his mother again, and I like myself. I realize that this relationship will undergo many new changes, especially when Jeremy leaves home, but I am confident I will be able to change and grow along as a result.

Gloria's negative outlook on mothering was not a result of Jeremy's behavior or of having a child. Her diminished feelings were a result of being accused of overprotecting and damaging her son, creating a soft and less manly image of masculinity. A contraction of the relationship occurred, which not only reinforced low self-esteem but also hurt Jeremy by creating his confusion as to why his mother had withdrawn.

Only when Gloria finally realized that she was not manipulating her son, but had only been in tune with and listened to what her son was saying about his need to do things with his life other than being an athlete, did she begin to have confidence about mothering. Her husband was the one who had never listened to what his son had been telling him. Only Gloria paid attention and respected that. Jeremy's identity came from other interests than sports, such as art and music. After therapy, Gloria no longer let outside influences and stereotypes regarding images of masculinity dictate how to relate to Jeremy. She respected herself and her son again and began to enjoy new aspects of a changing relationship.

Home with the Kids When You'd Rather Be Working

There has been a not-so-silent war between stay-at-home mothers and mothers who work outside the house. There is no one right way to mother. What is good is an individual decision that should be made within the context of the needs and issues of the mother and the family. As previously stated, when women enjoy and choose staying home with their children, the mother and children will thrive. If a mother wants to work outside the home, and cannot work outside the home, she may not feel that she is thriving.

Leah is a thirty-one-year-old mother of preschool twin girls who was a legal secretary before she married Glen. Glen's job as a computer salesman required the family to move to the West Coast. Leah did not make many friends and found the restrictions of being constantly in the company of two small children very stressful and demanding. She loved her girls but felt guilty about being so resentful of staying home. Leah felt that she was being selfish in wanting to go back to work and thought she was abandoning her kids. Her feelings of self-worth, as they pertained to being a mother, were low as a result of this conflict.

> Even during high school I had a job after school working for an accountant. I loved earning my own money and felt independent. I went to secretarial school after high school and took courses that prepared me to be a legal secretary. I found a job right after graduation. My computer and organizational skills were excellent. I loved being in a busy office, I made many friends and felt I was doing important work. I took pride in my job.
>
> Three years later I met Glen. Within a year we were married and both busy with our jobs. We both had pretty good salaries and could furnish our apartment, go out to restaurants, and take a trip occasionally. Glen wanted kids right away, I wanted to build up our savings account and, quite frankly, I didn't want to stop working. Things happen, and I found myself pregnant. Not only was I pregnant, I was carrying twins. Both families and especially Glen were ecstatic, and during my pregnancy I was treated like a queen.
>
> The queen part ended abruptly when I came home from the hospital. My mother helped for 3 weeks, but then I was on my own. Most new mothers have a difficult enough time dealing with one newborn, with the sleep and feeding schedules. Well, I had two with two different sleep and feeding schedules. The first 2 years are a complete blur as to how I coped and survived. I was too exhausted and stressed out to enjoy my adorable babies. When I look back at pictures I barely recognize myself.

When the girls were about 4 years old, Glen announced he was being relocated to the West Coast to supervise a sales office. I was angry and resentful at him and the girls for being locked into a situation that I had no control over. My life was ruled by my husband's job and the demands of the twins. We moved to a suburb in northern California where I knew no one and had no support. Both families were back East. My resentment grew at my family and at myself for feeling this way. I felt like a trapped animal. Glen would come home and find me either angry or in tears.

I was not a good mother during this time. I knew it and it certainly made me feel pretty worthless. Mothers are supposed to be all-giving, I wasn't. I felt like a total failure. Glen suggested I talk to somebody, because he didn't know what to do with me. Through our church, I went to a mothers' support group that had a peer counselor who helped. Since the girls were just about to enter kindergarten, it was suggested that I try to go back to work part time. This was the first time people were looking at my needs and not just my children's needs.

I brushed up over the summer on my computer skills and updated my resume and sent it around to some local law offices. I found a job with a law firm that needed a part-time girl. They were willing to work around the girls' school schedule, and what work I couldn't finish at the office I could take home. It was like a giant cloud lifted. My life and my children's lives are much better. When I am with the girls, I am totally theirs with a smile on my face. It's like both parts of myself have come together. I can be a good mother and I can also be the person I am.

There is no one kind of mother. Leah, by trying to fit the stereotype of stay-at-home mom, found that the image didn't fit the person she was. She loved her kids but needed and wanted more in her life. By existing only in relation to her children, she lost her identity and sense of self. She found herself resenting her children, family and herself for having these conflicting feelings. She was guilt-ridden because she was not a totally self-sacrificing mother who put her children's lives before her own needs at all times.

Each mother's story is different and unique. What is a good fit for one mother may not be comfortable for another. Blame, guilt, and mythic stereotypes of good mothering have no place in the real world of daily mothering. If a mother is comfortable with her own choices and life decisions, she in all probability will be comfortable with her mothering decisions; and so will her children. In order to be a good mother, a woman must be confident about her own self-image and identity as person. She must relate not only within this life-tie, but must also accommodate an identity that exists beyond being someone's mother.

Special Topic: Working Mothers

The majority of the NCWRR survey respondents had been working mothers (60%). In follow-up to the last narrative, and due to the predominance of mothers in the workforce, it is important to look at this phenomenon separately, as an area that impacts significantly on female adult development. Mothers are working, and for the vast majority it is a necessity. Society accepts working mothers as a new fact of life. However, the contradictions and paradoxes that abound with motherhood generally only heighten and expand within the context of work and mothering.

A mother is expected to be the primary caregiver to her children, to work at a job outside the home from nine to five, and then to come home and put in another five to six hours on domestic work. As author Arlie Hochschild described in her book, *Second Shift* (1989), women average a 70-hour or longer work week. The burden is great, with little support from employers regarding child-care considerations and with little help from husbands or partners who are unwilling to share child-care responsibilities. In fact, the NCWRR study found that 78% of women respondents strongly to moderately agree that their partners/husbands do not share childrearing responsibilities equally.

The majority of women who were interviewed enjoyed working outside the home and enjoyed being mothers. However, most women with partners wanted their partners to share more of the responsibilities of child care. The women also carried burdens of guilt about leaving their children, especially small children, in the care of others while they worked. Working mothers are experiencing internal conflict. On the one hand, they enjoy work, but, on the other hand, they hear a subtle societal message that states: "Don't enjoy your work too much or don't be too good at it."

Recently, a single mother in the midwest who planned to go back to college temporarily lost custody of her child to her ex-husband, who said he could provide a better environment for the child, since his mother was willing to stay home and care for the baby. He claimed the child's mother was unfit to parent, since she was going to place the baby in day care. Marcia Clark, lead prosecutor in the O.J. Simpson trial, similarly struggled for custody with her ex-husband, who stated that she could not adequately care for their two boys while working long hours on the trial. Working mothers have been blamed for the rise in the divorce rates, the recession, unemployed males, and delinquent and maladjusted kids. The effect on a woman's self-esteem and identity can be—at best confusing— worse, it can also make a woman feel she is a bad and selfish person.

It is interesting to note that, before the 20th century, childrearing was never a full-time maternal job. Extended family members gave help to women who worked the farms alongside husbands. Servants, nannies, and wet nurses took care of children for the wealthy. After World War II, psychologist John Bowlby (1969) developed his *attachment theory,* discussed earlier in this chapter. He concluded, after studying war orphans, that a young child who does not experience a continuous relationship with his or her mother may be damaged for life. Preceding his attachment theory in 1951 Bowlby stated that full-time employment by mothers outside the home constituted maternal deprivation. It may be relevant to take note that Bowlby himself was raised by a nanny.

On the heels of Bowlby's work, there were numerous baby books written for mothers on how they should care for their children. Most of these books were written by males, the majority of whom did not care for their own children on a daily basis. Dr. Spock (1954) was the leader of the baby-book authors and believed that a child's best interest was served if the mother stayed home and did not work. Even today, Brazelton (1989) and Fraiberg (1977) still portray full-time mothering as the desired norm.

Women's identity and self-esteem are shaped by the manner in which they negotiate an often paradoxical dilemma. If women are content working outside the home, their children most often will thrive (Long & Porter, 1994). If women have clarity about the choices they have made regarding combining work with motherhood, most likely self-esteem will remain positive. Women's development in adulthood will likely take even more diverse forms as they attempt in a variety of ways to reconcile the conflict between work and domestic responsibilities. (The topic of work and achievement will be examined thoroughly in the next chapter.)

The mother-child life-tie is never static. For both mother and child to develop, change is a necessary component of this relationship. Over the span of motherhood, the maternal bond changes. At its beginning it is emotionally and physically close. In its mature role, this life-tie will encompass an acceptance of differentiation and an acceptance of a necessary distance. Its ability to contract and expand will enable the continued development of a woman during her adult years.

FATHERING A CHILD

The Paradox of Fathering

The father–child life-tie is no less important than the mother-child life-tie. Children affect the development and self-image of both genders, albeit in different ways. Altogether, 83% of men in our study associated improved self-esteem with being fathers. A notable difference between men and women is that men tended to report more satisfactory relationships with their children as they got older (past age 35). While women's relationships with their children seem to be best below age 35.

As was reported earlier in Chapter 2, men's identification with children had been significant by its emotional and physical absence. Most bodies of research document the development of women in relation to children. Due to all the social changes that have occurred in women's and men's lives over the last thirty years, it is important to include the impact of fathering into the developmental picture of male adulthood. A father's presence or absence and changing social expectations not only make a large impact on the lives of his children but on a man's own development in adulthood.

The last two decades have witnessed more frequent and varied portrayals of father-child relationships and increased professional recognition of fathers' roles in young children's development (e.g., Bozett & Hanson, 1991; Lamb, 1981). In 1982 Biller stated that fatherhood could make a major contribution to a man's self-concept and personality. Fathering children is an important source of self-examination and psychological growth. Keen (1991) believed that to love, nurture and enjoy one's children is to honor one's self. Men can learn to heal old wounds by becoming the fathers they wanted, but didn't have. Fathers are able to reframe their own childhood memories in the context of parenting. Reframing events by putting them under a different light permits the participants to maintain their dignity or feel loved by others with whom they interact.

Men have also had to learn to live with the paradox of what it means to be a father in today's society. The context of the paradox is different for men and women, but both sexes have to juggle often opposing demands and expectations. Men are uncomfortable with old images of Ward Cleaver, the button-down character in the 1950s TV show, "Leave It to Beaver" and are confused by new identities of fathering that resemble the "dad-in-drag" image of a Mrs. Doubtfire.

The once-stable image of the American father has not remained consistent or predictable. At one time in history a man's family and children were considered his property, his physical assets. The more children a man had, the more control and the more status he acquired. Old images of the tireless provider—whether he be a farmer, industrialist, war hero, respected professional, entrepreneur, factory worker, or self-made man—have undergone considerable change.

Earlier, a father expected to be revered and honored by his community, friends, wife and children. His identity as a "family man" brought strength, discipline, and predictability to his life. Much of his identity came from control that was challenged by no one, except his male peers. Men no longer have a unified identity, especially when it comes to the image of a family man. A man must splice together his identity from an ever-changing menu of new attitudes, directions, and lifestyles. There is no one unifying theme of what it means to be a man or what it means to be a father today. Whereas in the past, a man's identity was imprinted by stereotypes of mythic heroes, history books full of male role models, and his own father's image, today there are few stable guiding principles, rules, or standards. This leaves many men lost in a wilderness of identity confusion. The "model father" has gone through many image changes, changes many cannot agree on even now.

The Fifties Father

Most men who are fathers today have a distant memory of their own fathers, many of whom were the last generation to symbolize control and dominance. The image of purity of fatherhood established in the fifties has been exploded by the social upheavals of the Sixties. The fallout continues into the nineties and will continue for years to come. The attitude that best signifies the era of the fifties father could be summarized as "Never cry, just provide." The vision of the middle-class fifties father was clear, precise, and socially sanctioned. A few stern words of discipline, fishing trips with sons, a few harsh warnings to would-be boyfriends of daughters, an allowance doled out once a week and the big umbrella of financial security summed up the role of father. The roles of mother, father and child were clearly defined. Everyone knew the script and made few editorial changes until the social revolution of the sixties.

The "Gentle" Man: Identity Confusion in the Seventies and Eighties

The social revolution of the sixties turned men's predictable and stable lives upside down. The identity of sole provider and family decision maker that a man previously relied on was either gone, diluted, or ridiculed. Men lost many of the benchmarks that symbolized their entry into the world of the adult male. Men's fears centered around the loss of familiar moorings that threatened their power and control. Women's control over reproduction, including access to birth control, abortion, artificial insemination, single parenting, and financial independence have lessened men's power. As a result, men's self-esteem may be low and their adult identity confused.

A movement to change the face of fatherhood and the concept of masculinity took root during the seventies and eighties. The old "fifties dad" was a relic of rigid gender roles, a remembrance of male dominance and financial control. This version of fathering and symbol of maleness was questioned by some American men. With the old image in dispute, there had to be something new to take its place. Feminists, joined by women across the country, decided that to be a good father a man must learn to be a good mother (Bartky, 1990; Friedman, 1990). If a man couldn't nurture like a woman, he couldn't possibly be good at fathering. If a man couldn't cry in front of his children, he was an insensitive father.

It was during this era that a man was encouraged to be emotionally expressive, noncompetitive, gentle, and quiet. He was there to please the women in and out of his life. This new image of masculinity and fathering mirrored women's nurturing and mothering characteristics. In a powerful backlash against the traditional image, it was believed that the qualities that were unique to men were of no value in the lives of their children, the implication being that to be a good parent, one must be female. So if a man wanted to parent, he had better take a crash course in mothering and develop his morally superior feminine side to succeed. It was made quite clear that women were the saints, and men were part of the problem and responsible for all the ills of the world.

Many men changed and broke away from traditional images of masculinity and fathering. Their self-images included a kinder, more caring, less aggressive aspect of masculinity. However, making these changes often creates identity problems. Men's power and control over women and children has declined. Few would deny that this more egalitarian arrangement is good for both women and men. However this new arrangement requires men to reshape an image that takes into account a loss of control.

During the fifties a father was essential to his children for financial support, status, and legitimacy. His wife and children were dependent on him, giving him a distorted and skewed image of his power and strength. Today the majority of women are in the workforce and contribute in a significant way to the financial maintenance of their families. Men have had to reassess their own lives and incorporate an image that takes into account the fact that their own status as men and fathers is less secure that ever before.

Just as women have had to contend with contradictions and paradoxes related to being female and mothers, men are being subjected to mixed messages and contradictions as to what it means to be a man and a father. New demands are placed on men to be sensitive, nurturing, empathetic, expressive, and peace-loving. However, at the same time that the warrior image is being mocked, sometimes contradictory demands are made on men to be strong, not wimpish, rugged, tough, able to provide financial security, and ready to fight.

The Nineties and Beyond: Joining the Best of Both Worlds

As was reported in the beginning of the fathering section, the NCWRR study reveals that men find parenting and find their children a positive source of self-esteem and identity. Men are trying to establish a balance that takes into consideration the positive aspects of a woman's style of nurturing, but retaining and cultivating many of the positive aspects of masculinity that can be reflected in their parenting style. By reflecting the positive aspects of masculinity, men can enhance their identity as fathers and develop new respect for themselves.

A variety of explanations can be provided as to why men's relationship with children becomes more satisfying with increased age. First, during midlife, men have a tendency to reappraise the importance of work-related accomplishments and redirect energy towards their children that might have been neglected due to career ambitions and pursuits. Second, when children become adolescents, more opportunities become available for fathers to share and participate in activities that are mutually pleasurable. Third, men may perceive a wife's return to work or devoting more time to career aspirations as a "window of opportunity" for him to enhance and foster a special relationship with their children. Finally, midlife introspection often leads to addressing one's relationships, including what has or has not transpired between father and child.

Without question, 'fathering' in the 1990s poses a variety of challenges that men are attempting to address. First and foremost, the dissolution of a marriage has often created strained relationships between ex-partners that often adversely affect the amount of time a noncustodial parent (often the father) has with the children. The media is rife with stories of "deadbeat dads" who abandon their financial and emotional responsibilities towards their children. There is a perception within society that men "wash their hands" of their paternal obligations once a divorce occurs. Divorced men throughout the country have expressed a great sense of anger and frustration concerning this gross overgeneralization.

Certainly, there are well-documented cases in which fathers who are clearly able to do so have not financially contributed to raising a child after a divorce. However, during the last five years, a variety of men's organizations have organized to advocate for a father's right to equal visitation, addressed bias in court decisions that grant custody only to the mother, and aired financial support concerns. This "father's rights movement" demonstrates that men do not want to be universally perceived as being uninvolved caregivers simply because they are divorced. It shows that men need to be recognized by society as being just as capable of childrearing as women and just as critical to the healthy development of their child. If midlife divorce rates increase, the foregoing issues will receive much greater scrutiny and attention.

Another area given scant attention in recent literature is what can be called *paternal questioning*. In prior generations, few men questioned their devotion and ability to be a good father—simply raising a child qualified one as a good dad. Fathers arising from the "baby boom" generation are the first to ask themselves questions that prior generations did not even consider in their stream of consciousness, such as: Am I devoting enough time to my children and family? Am I able to provide the same level of financial security to my children as my father provided to me? How can I play a role in developing a family environment that shelters my children from violence, teenage pregnancy, and drugs? Such questioning is not only healthy but demonstrates how far men have come in recognizing their responsibility in the parental caregiving equation. This is not to suggest that all men are practicing this introspection. There are still many young and midlife fathers of the "old school"; but there is an undeniable guilt (similar to maternal guilt) that many "new-school" fathers experience as to whether they are doing enough to be considered a good father in today's society.

The movement towards fathers being more involved in raising their children has also led to questioning whether men should be allowed to take paternal leave after the birth of a child. In the nineties, as more women are unable to take extended maternity leave due to restricted employee benefits, men will be increasingly called upon to fill the child care vacuum after a birth (or at least to share in staying at home for a certain period of time). Unfortunately, there have been many reports in the media of men feeling that their employers would not accept or understand their taking on such roles. It is ironic that men have been cast as uninvolved caregivers, but at the same time fathers are discriminated against when they want to take a more active paternal role. From a positive perspective, men are beginning to more fully appreciate how women have been treated when they must interrupt work and career responsibilities to address childbearing issues.

Society has long perceived men's roles in relationship to their "paid" work. Even in the era of two working parents, men are still expected to work. Being a father (and possibly taking paternity leave) is not viewed as acceptable work. However, much has been made of women staying home in the caregiving capacity as justifiable work. This paradox of perception must change if men are ever going to feel comfortable in fully participating and contributing to the responsibilities related to childbirth.

Men who establish rich ties with their children find that their own lives are fuller and more satisfying. Finding competence through discovering new abilities as fathers leads to a more positive sense of self and continued growth in adulthood. Fathers are trying to balance their public and private worlds, stay in touch with their inner feelings at the same time retain the essence of their masculinity.

The emphasis on blurring the roles of mother and father has only deceived people into believing that families and children can do very well without fathers. Nothing could be farther from the truth. There is a growing sense in this country that a mother and father do the same thing, that the roles are interchangeable. A father represents his gender and in doing so can bring the uniqueness of that experience to his children. Father-pride can only enhance his own growth and feelings of self-worth in adulthood.

There were many new types of fathering styles expressed by men in the NCWRR survey. More men are beginning to actively share child-care responsibilities with their partners; many men are struggling with being divorced dads who share custody; some are solo parents; some are gay fathers, stepdads, older second-family dads; and a growing number are teen fathers. Concepts of changing masculinity and fathering, the different types of fathering styles, as well as absence from the family and one's children all affect a man's development and self-worth throughout his adult years.

The following are stories from men who participated in the NCWRR study. They tell how being a father was a source of joy, pain, growth, change, confusion and pride. Children created new meaning to their adult lives, and broadened the concept of their male identity in positive ways.

Second-Time-Around Fathering

Often it is the second time around when a man discovers a new aspect to his identity through fathering a second family. Until recently most men were as locked into stereotypical roles as women were. The father role demanded that a man not involve himself with child care. He was expected to make all decisions, be the disciplinarian, and be emotionally distant and removed from the daily family activities. Fifty-six-year-old Martin, during his first marriage, was that type of traditional father. He married his college girlfriend, settled into a white-collar job in the city and started a family. The only role model for fathering Martin had was his father, who had been a auto factory worker. Martin's father was uninvolved, except when it came time to administer physical punishment and make threats. His father spent a great deal of his time at home listening to the radio and drinking bourbon.

> I was different from my father in that I was a professional, not a factory worker. I made more money, and didn't physically punish my kids. However, there were so many ways that I was like him when it came to being a father. I was distant and removed from my kids. I might not have been drinking bourbon or listening to the radio, but when I was home I was reading reports, practicing my golf strokes, or listening to television. I loved my kids, but I was constantly telling them to be quiet, not to disturb me and I viewed them from afar. I only wanted to interact with them on my terms, and then when they got older I felt like I was living with two strangers.
>
> I felt like an outsider to my kids and wife. They were close to her and seemed to view me as their own private bank. My marriage and

relationship with the kids just fell apart when they both hit their teens. It seemed like my wife and kids were the real family, I was on the outside looking in. I never quite understood, until much later, why my kids and wife were so angry with me. To them I was uncaring and cold, but I felt that I was a decent father doing the job he was supposed to be doing: that is, providing for my family's every need. When the kids started college my wife and I separated and within a year divorced.

I saw my kids occasionally on college breaks, but it usually was a forced visit and they always had an excuse as to why they had to leave. I was living alone for about three years when I started dating Laurel. I was about forty-nine at the time and she was thirty-eight. Laurel had been working as a book editor for about fifteen years with a big publishing house. We lived together for about a year and decided to get married. Laurel wanted to have a child; her clock had been ticking away and she was in a panic about waiting until it was too late. I had very mixed feelings about having children. I felt like I messed up with my own kids and that I just didn't have the right stuff to be a good father.

Laurel and I had many long discussions about fathering. She made me realize that I had to be involved right from the start. All through her pregnancy, I was involved with Lamaze classes, doctor's visits, sonograms, amniocentesis. I was right there helping her during labor and I was there for the delivery. When my first two kids were born, my role at the hospital was that of visitor and potential germ-carrier. I held Lilli right after she was born; I got goosebumps and started to cry from joy. I cried so hard I couldn't stop, I was so proud and happy. I felt like a father.

Being involved in the beginning made a big difference as to what it means to be a father. I felt part of my daughter's life, like I really mattered. She is now six years old, but when she was a baby I bathed her, fed her, changed her diapers. I carried her around in her little baby sack. I became physically and emotionally close to her. I've grown as a result of my involvement and love for Lilli. This caring and emotional side of myself gives me new meaning. I can love, cry, act silly, look at clouds in the sky, and little worms in the earth with Lilli. I am not angry or uptight, I have different priorities, I listen and have a better understanding of myself.

Lilli has made me come to terms with my father. After the divorce from my first wife, I thought I was as mean and cold as my father. I hated myself and blamed myself for being a failure in my marriage and children's lives. Through Lilli I know I am not my father, nor am I a cold and remote father. I have slowly been spending more time with my grown children, Meg and Bill. They see me with Lilli and can hardly recognize their father. They have come to love Lilli almost as much as I do. There are times when I go to the beach with Meg and Bill and Lilli, just the three of us. When not playing with Lilli; Meg, Bill, and I have had some really good talks. I have come to love being a father. I may be a little old in a lot of people's eyes, but I feel younger and more alive than I did in my twenties.

Martin learned that to love, care and enjoy his children was a way of honoring himself. This life-tie has gone through many expansions and contractions, contracting early in his life when he was a remote father and after his divorce, expanding with the arrival of his daughter Lilli. Martin's narrow concept of fatherhood and masculinity broadened to a much and fuller concept of what it means to be a father and a man in today's society. Becoming a father during his middle years has contributed to his self-esteem and has reframed his identity. This life-tie has become a resource for Martin's continued growth and development during his adult years.

Solo Parenting by a Father

Although they represent small numbers, more fathers are learning to be single parents. Sometimes through choice, by law or by accident, fathers must be both mother and father to their children. Facing this task brings a significant change to a man's lifestyle, his attitudes, and his self-concept. Lee was thirty-three when his wife was killed in an auto crash, leaving him the full responsibility of raising two-year-old Josh and five-year-old Kara. For the first three months his mother and sister helped out, but both had to return to their own families.

Lee had been an involved father, but relied on his wife for the daily running of the family and home. He had to develop new capabilities and strategies for coping with this vastly new and different role. The initial demands of trying to work, take care of his home and children were exhausting; and he found himself becoming depressed. He lost part of his salary when he had to stay home with sick children, had few social contacts with adults, and at times felt isolated. One of the biggest problems he encountered was from mothers who criticized his type of "mothering" behavior with his children.

> I didn't mind the salary loss, the long hours and demands or even being that exhausted. Sometimes being so tired made me less sad about missing of my wife. What made me feel really bad about myself, was the way some of the other mothers who had children Josh's and Kara's age behaved toward me. I got the feeling that in their eyes I couldn't do anything right. Sometimes Josh and Kara had more mud on them when playing than the other kids, or they thought that Kara shouldn't be rough-housed around like I did with Josh. They thought she might get hurt. At the beach I taught both Kara and Josh how to swim. Other mothers felt that Josh was too young and that I was taking a risk by teaching him to swim at such a young age. I dressed both Josh and Kara in a lot of overalls and T-shirts. Other mothers thought that Kara should wear a dress once in awhile, or they thought that I waited too long before taking them to the doctor.
>
> I had so much criticism heaped on my head. Some of it was well-intentioned, and I appreciate their efforts. For the most part, I felt like I was doing a lousy job as both a mom and a dad. I got so depressed that at one time I thought the kids would be better off with my sister. At that time I believed that maybe a child could have a mother and not a father, but that I had no business as a father trying to raise my own kids.
>
> This changed when I started going to a group for fathers. Most of the men were divorced and shared custody and were not in my situation, but I learned to value my style of parenting. I began to believe that although I may parent differently than a woman, that does not make my parenting less important than a woman's. The more confident I became about believing in myself as a good parent, the more my kids began to get real comfortable with me as their sole parent. I am even better at accepting advice from other mothers, but I also know that what I have to offer is just as good as what they offer their kids. I find myself being more relaxed and secure in my decisions and in my role as single parent. I love my kids and relish being close to them, I feel I am a good dad and a good role model for them.

Lee came to realize that his style of parenting, different from a woman's style, was no less important or valuable. Fathers who are active in raising their children should be given support and encouragement and should be valued for what they as men bring to the lives of their children. The interaction between a father and his children can only benefit both the children and the father. When Lee realized that as a man he had something irreplaceable and important to give to his children, he began feeling secure in his position as solo parent and began to see this very large life-tie as a source of growth and development in his own life, rather than as a barrier to development.

Absent-Without-Leave Fathers

The last two narratives have shown how men continue to grow and develop within the context of active parenting. However, a father can be affected and his development hindered by his absence from his children's lives. If a man has fathered a child, his self-image must include some perception of this role, whether it is perceived as being a financial provider, rule maker or by "hands-on" father engaged in the children's daily lives. The knowledge that one is a father, yet is removed and absent from that child's life, in many cases will have an effect on that man's life.

John was twenty-five when he found out that his girlfriend was pregnant. At that time he was out of work, a high school dropout; and the only thing he had ever nurtured was a 1988 Chevrolet Camaro. He tried to be there for Rickee while she was pregnant but was overwhelmed by and unprepared for arrival of his daughter. He had never had a father in his life, except the many "try-out dads" that were his mother's boyfriends while he was growing up. John fled and disappeared for three years not only from his girlfriend but from his own family.

> I just couldn't deal with everything I was feeling when Rickee gave birth. I felt like this kid was just going to show me up for what I was, pretty worthless. I never thought of myself as much, but when I was in my Camaro I felt like a cool dude. I was feeling real cool until this baby came along. It was something I couldn't handle; and I knew I wasn't up to this job, so I split. My father split when I was born, my mother always said he was useless and nothing but trouble anyway.

She said I was better off without him.

I just disappeared. I went down South to Florida for a time. I got a job busing tables in a restaurant and hung out with a new group of friends. I always tried to act cool and in control. I was good at that for a while, but I don't have any sense of what I'm all about. I am now over twenty-five and where I got respect three years ago is not what counts now. I can't seem to get a steady job. I don't have skills and an education to make it in this world. What do I have to offer some kid, when I can't give myself a break?

That kid is better off without me. But I'm not proud and don't feel good about this whole thing. I feel like a bum. I barely pay my rent and keep myself alive. I'm no father image. I'm just bad news for everybody. That baby is better off without ever knowing I exist. I've thought about going back. I'd like to see the kid, but I'm afraid of starting something I just can't finish. If the baby got to know me and I split again, that wouldn't be right for her. She's better just getting used to the fact that I just don't exist. Maybe her mother will make up a cool story about me.

John's story may be shorter than the other narratives, but it is important because John's child has an influence on his life even though he is not present in that baby's life. The baby seems to highlight all of John's feelings of inadequacy as not only a father, but as a man. The image of father, according to John, should signify control, strength, security, and protection. John cannot see himself representing any of those qualities. His self-image and self-esteem are both very low.

Recently John wrote to Rickee and asked about the baby. She wrote back and sent a picture. He does not want to be involved in their lives until he knows he can get his own life in order. He writes to Rickee and sends her a little money for the baby. He has taken steps to make his own life better. By enrolling in GED classes, he has structured his life so that he has a schedule and responsibilities to meet, as well as a goal. He takes his test in two months and has been working diligently. Previously, a long-term goal meant something that would occur at the end of the week, usually hanging out with buddies. Now John has the beginning of a small dream. He is afraid to talk about it too much, for fear that he won't make it happen. John has looked into the future far enough to see himself with a high school diploma and the possibility of enrolling in a vocational school in auto mechanics.

The child, who once magnified only his shortcomings and led him to believe he was worthless, now is a source of growth in his own life. His baby represents a small chance at hope for his own life. This life-tie has begun to turn from a source of fear and self-loathing to a source of potential strength for his own life.

A Very Rare Teen Father

Often what has been reported about teen fathers has shown neglect, incompetence, and irresponsibility. There are some male teens, however, who have taken responsibility along with the mother for the child that they both conceived. This responsibility has catapulted them into a maturity unusual for their age and has incorporated new meanings and interpretations into their own lives.

Chris was a young male who at the age of eighteen found his girlfriend pregnant with his child. At the time she found that she was pregnant, she had already broken up with Chris and had a new boyfriend. There was talk of an abortion, but both the girl and Chris wanted to have the baby. There was little hope of this relationship ever developing into a long-term commitment. Neither Chris nor his prior girlfriend were interested in each other, beyond sharing the responsibility of a child. However, the baby turned this short teen relationship into a long-term adult commitment. Chris, a rock guitarist with long black hair, had very strong ideas about responsibility and his role in his new son's life. Outside of music he had a job as a plumber's apprentice and was learning a viable trade.

My love is my son Eric and my music. My ex-girlfriend, Gena, and I will never be together. She is interested in dating other guys. She was eighteen when she became pregnant. I wanted to marry her, but she said she didn't want to. She felt marriage just to make everything legal was never going to work out long-term. She was right on that one. I guess what she never expected was my involvement in my son's life.

I was there when Eric was born. I held my son and was just so blown away by this experience. I was so happy. When he came home to my ex-girlfriend's, I spent that first month coming over when the baby was awake, feeding and changing him. I even went on the first doctor's visit. As the months went by, I took Eric to my house. At the time I was living with my mother, so I had some back-up if things got a little out of my league.

Eric was close to a year old when I wanted to increase my visitation from once during the week and on Sunday. My ex-girlfriend liked to go out a lot with her friends and new boyfriend and she often left the baby with other friends or her mother. We argued a lot about my visitation of Eric. I wanted to see him both Saturday and Sunday and two nights a week. I felt that if she wasn't home and going out, that it would be a good time for Eric to spend that time with me. We got lawyers involved, and it got pretty ugly for awhile. The visitation was settled by my spending a day and a half on the weekends and two nights during the week with Eric. However, we agreed to be flexible enough that the days might change depending on our individual schedules. It's worked so far, I also get a month in the summer and a week, either before or after Christmas.

Eric is now four and a big part of my life. I don't have a steady girlfriend, and I guess I'm not really looking for one at this time. People seem to think that I need a wife so that she can take care of Eric. They think I am burdened by Eric, nothing could be farther from the truth. He has helped me grow up, take on and deal with more responsibility, as well as making me feel good about who I am.

Chris may be a rare male teen who was mature enough to cope with the responsibility of fatherhood at an early age. He has met his emotional as well as financial obligations with concern and love. The responsibility for Eric has matured Chris and contributed to a positive identity as active father and provider. He may not nurture the way Eric's mother does, but Chris brings to his relationship with Eric a different type of nurture. Eric spends time beating on an old drum while Chris practices guitar with his band. Chris has taken him to his job site, and has had Eric watch him tinkering with his motorcycle. Eric rough-houses with his father and shares in the hoots and howls when Chris and his friends get together to watch TV basketball and football.

The important issue is not whether the care Eric is receiving is essentially feminized or masculinized nurturing. The important factor is that Chris is a father who expresses his unique and special type of care and love for Eric. Chris's relationship with Eric has contributed to Chris's growth and maturity and has enhanced his self-image and self-esteem. Eric is a resource for Chris's continued development in adulthood, and Chris is a resource for Eric's budding development as a new and powerful image of what it means to be male.

SUMMARY

Both women and men undergo change, development and a shift in self-esteem as a result of the parent-child life-tie. The relationship between parents and their children is one of movement, fluidity, contraction, and expansion as well as renegotiation of the life-tie experience. Dichotomies are not as rigid between the acts of mothering and fathering as myth presumes. Raising children—and sometimes declining to raise them—will affect both women and men. The effects may be different in context and timing for women and men, but differences are not always drawn along gender lines. Rather, they are more idiographic in nature.

Parenting a child is an experience that draws on not only adult experience, but also the experiences that adult had as a child. Each decision in parenting may evoke memories of a parent's own childhood. Through recognition of both pleasant and sad memories, adults can rework them with new meaning into their own lives. Martin was a father who had to renegotiate themes from his childhood experience with his distant, punishing father when he became a new and more involved father the second time around in a second marriage.

The pattern of growth and change within the context of this life-tie is one of contraction and expansion for both women and men. Both mothering and fathering demand going from states of embeddedness to differentiation, a process of holding and letting go. Development for an adult female or male demands that the parenting role remain flexible, a role that must acknowledge the life-tie changes without severing that life-tie. Jessica was the mother who went from being a woman-child into being a responsible and resourceful woman. Divorce and the new role of single parent created changes in this life-tie for Jessica, who underwent a transformation that clarified her identity and sense of self-esteem.

Both women and men have to challenge the paradoxes and double standards that often can influence the nature of the role of parent. Women are often placed in a cultural double bind: being revered and at the same time feared; blamed for being over-protective or too self-centered, too dull or too smart. They are pushed to live up to distorted images of perfect mothering to have perfect children. Gloria was accused of being an overprotecting mother, and consequently suffered feelings of low self-esteem. Leah was an at-home mother, who wanted to work. Although she loved her children, as long as she felt restricted and guilty, a confused identity and less-than-positive self-esteem was a result.

Men live with paradoxes and stereotypical images within the context of the father role. They are expected to be strong and secure providers, much as their own fathers were, but at the same time men are now required to be emotional, soft, and to nurturing like women. Lee was criticized for not nurturing his children as a woman would. The judgment leveled at Lee for not being a good-enough "mother" left him doubting his fathering abilities. Confusion and unrealistic expectations exist for both women and men and their roles as parents. There is no one unifying theme in good parenting unless, perhaps, unconditional love. It may require balance, flexibility and recognition of the idiosyncratic nature of the role of parent. That role, which must expand and contract when deemed in the best interest of child and parent, will lead to a positive sense of self and clear identity for both.

There are many new forms of parenting that have to be acknowledged as important to the change and development of individuals within families. The nuclear family and predictable early timetable that once governed the timing of marriage, and the duration of marriage, the roles that each parent played are not longer typical. Value-laden judgments about the different styles of parenting and or assessments that rank the skills of a woman higher than the parenting skills of a man no longer make sense. Both women and men bring their unique qualities and characteristics to their respective roles.

The NCWRR study surveyed and interviewed many single parents, divorced parents, late-in-life parents, second families and stepparents, working mothers, stay-at-home dads, shared-custody parents, as well as gay women and men who are defining different timeframes for parenting and new aspects of what it means to be a parent. Self-esteem and development in adulthood can be derived, in part, from the many different types of mothering and fathering styles.

- Marla, as we saw was a single, career-oriented woman who decided to be a mother in her late thirties. She had a plan for combining work and motherhood, but the plan was abandoned when she discovered new and untapped emotional feelings and love for her baby daughter. Her image of self now included not only that of successful career woman, but that of a loving and caring mother who was renegotiating and incorporating new aspects to her identity.
- Martin discovered a new meaning to fatherhood when he remarried and had a newchild, Lilli.
- Lee became a solo parent when his wife died, leaving him completely responsible for his two children.
- Chris was a teen who defied the stereotypical image of irresponsible male teenagers and becoming an active and caring father to his son, Eric.

The multidimensional aspects of this life-tie today reflect a change in women's and men's attitudes toward child-rearing, a change in their actual experience as parents, and a change in their psychological perspectives regarding their identities and self-worth. The changes and negotiations that occur within the context of this life-tie will continue to reshape the views women and men have regarding their self-images as parents well into later adulthood. Older fathers and mothers typically report strong feelings of affection for their sons and daughters—feelings that the adult children typically reciprocate (e.g., Aldous, 1987; Bengtson, Rosenthal & Burton, 1990; Treas & Bengtson, 1987).

The myths and biases that endure in a social and political climate must be tempered and altered with the knowledge that each individual mother and father bring their unique and valued qualities to the parent-child life-tie. Honoring their own experience and wisdom within this relationship, as well as adapting and remaining flexible when appropriate, will only enhance this very precious life-tie relationship. Part of an adult's identity can come from being a loving and caring parent. Love and nurturance of a child can bring continuity and feelings of worthiness, for this life-tie is the most permanent of all.

CHAPTER 7

Work

> "Work—it is about a search for daily meaning
> as well as daily bread, for recognition as well as cash,
> for astonishment rather than torpor; in short, for
> a sort of life rather than a Monday through
> Friday sort of dying."
>
> —*Studs Terkel*

Overwhelmingly, both women and men who participated in the NCWRR study identified their work experiences as one of their greatest sources of self-esteem and identity. This reaction was astonishingly uniform. Eighty-eight percent of women and 91% of men stated that work and task-related experiences contributed to positive self-esteem. Responses to open-ended questions reveal that, even among those individuals who did not hold traditional paid workplace jobs, personal accomplishments played a similar role in producing a sense of personal fulfillment and self-worth.

What emerges from the study is that both women and men, as a whole, have an important need to point to some tangible product as uniquely their own. It is also clear that the term *work* requires a broad definition, one that encompasses various kinds of productive endeavors producing a tangible result—its use should not be limited to those on a fast-paced career track. The work life-tie is not static; it involves the act of doing, of being actively engaged in some activity. Work/task orientations involve forming, shaping, molding, and cultivating something by means of physical and/or mental effort.

Our definition is reinforced by the data concerning the type of reward or satisfaction that the work experience produced. Ranked in order of importance, satisfaction came from the following:

*   the work or task itself and the opportunity to use their minds creatively (22%)
*   the rewards of pay and benefits from traditional workplace jobs (18%)
*   The people with whom women and men worked and with whom they came in contact (13%)
*   the ability of women and men to control events and aspects of their work and tasks (11%)

Of equal importance to our analysis is the fact that men and women respondents reacted identically. Not only were the various work-related rewards scaled in the same order, but the responses percentages were the same within a 1% variation.

The work life-tie is both an extension and reflection of oneself. When a carpenter builds a house, when a business executive closes a deal, when an amateur artist creates on canvas, or when an individual bakes a perfect loaf of bread or sews a beautiful quilt—that person can stand back, feel a surge of pride and self-esteem, and discover clarity in his or her identity. As Moore (1992) stated, "The flowering of life depends on finding a reflection of oneself in the world and one's work is an important place for that kind of reflection " (p. 66).

Work is central to the concept of self. It is a very important way in which a person crafts and constructs an identity and builds self-esteem. Work can excite, comfort, bring peace and wholeness to a life. Work can be full of imagination, conjure up memories and dreams that have special significance, perhaps related to family, traditions, and ideals. Ordinary tasks often can have a profound significance in a person's life, for work and daily tasks can be the raw material for a meaningful sense of self. To enhance self-esteem, work must be more than just keeping busy or a mindless activity. A person's behavior must be oriented toward some pragmatic end in order to have meaning. It may be that the more deeply one feels about his or her work, work that may inspire and stir the imagination, the more one is able to form a fulfilling identity.

PAST AND TRADITIONAL DEVELOPMENTAL THEORY ON WORK

Havighurst (1982) stated that there is an interaction among values, attitudes, and careers. An occupation has been described as a complex social role, which is made up of many behaviors, skills, and attitudes that society expects of a person in that role. When theory has examined the effect of work on adult development, it has focused primarily on men and their traditional—usually professional—workplace, that is, on paid jobs. Havighurst, like others, described a strict pattern linking timing and role of work in an adult's life. He described the first sequence of work periods as a time when young adults, usually aged 16 to 25, would engage in a process of trial and error. Following this sequence was the "stable work period," whereby adults between the age of 35 and 60 would normally be in a stable, consistent and permanent work role. This long work period was follow by retirement, the assumption being that productivity and useful accomplishment ended for adults in their later years.

Levinson et al. (1978) and Erikson (1959) both considered work to be an important task in adulthood, but like Havighurst's, their theories were related to men, careers and the particular stage and age when tasks and their resolutions were supposed to take place. These developmental stage theories identify certain tasks (or things an individual must learn) related to life itself. The completion of that task that leads to successful adaptation and life satisfaction for an individual during the adult years. An amalgam of what traditional theory has stated regarding adult development and work includes the following stages:

1. *Adolescence/early adulthood.* Preparing for an economic career organizes one's plans in such a way as to begin an orderly pattern, that is, a career in which a person can grow in responsibility and competence as well as income, can plan for the

future, and can invest time with certainty of future gain.

2. *Middle adulthood.* A time when men attain their highest status and income levels as a result of a successful choice and application of their energy to a work/career goal.

3. *Retirement.* The vast majority of individuals give up their jobs after age 65. For some, whose life was the job, this could be a time of great difficulty.

This model of adult development as it relates to work proposed by developmentalists and stage theorists must be reexamined in light of the social and economic forces that are reshaping the work experience during adulthood today. For example, the meaning of individual change, the perception of career change, longevity, gender perspectives, and the various meanings of work have been changing the career and employment landscape. Corporate downsizing, the development of secondary career skills, age discrimination, and other factors have modified our understanding of the work experience.

There are problems with this model of adult development as it relates to work proposed by theorists such as Erikson and Levinson. This model, still one of the main theories taught on academic campuses across the country, does not take into consideration many of the social changes and individual meanings and definitions of work in men's and women's lives. Their portrayal of an inevitable age/stage-linked series of transitions in the role of work in adult lives, aside from reflecting an unswerving developmental optimism, fails to explore the meaning of individual change, the perception of change, longevity, gender perspectives, or the various meanings of work.

Social change, longevity and new meanings associated with work have cast a different perspective on how work affects the development and self-esteem of adult women and men. As reported by many of the NCWRR survey respondents, work fills a large portion of their lives; but to be meaningful and enhancing to their sense of self, work must also be purposeful. Purposeful work takes an individual past particular age/stage criteria and past traditional definitions of classical 9-to-5 work to new areas. These new realms of work include women's experiences, work-related achievement in late life, unpaid work that enhances personal growth, creative expression, spiritual enhancement, the work that goes into overcoming obstacles and meeting challenges, as well as important development and growth that can occur with work that unfolds in one's own home.

Women and men are both affected by the work life-tie, although there are differences as to themes among individuals and between the genders. The themes are identified personal, idiosyncratic ways of experiencing and communicating the meaning of work in a person's life. The ways in which people interpret work experience so as to give continuity and structure to the self are unique. Work does not have the same meaning for all people, nor does it have the same meaning at a particular age or developmental stage for all men and women. At times, the work life-tie is a positive contributor to self-esteem and identity. At other times it can deter and detract from personal development. When work acts as a controlling influence it can hamper growth. When work acts as a resource it can become a source of self-esteem and identity direction.

WOMEN

A History of Barriers

Throughout history women were encouraged to follow the pattern laid down by Eve. A woman was to be maid, wife, mother, and widow. These aspects were thought to be enough to sustain her life. Life in relation to her mate and others was supposed to be enough to fulfill her feminine needs. However, women have actively worked within the home as well as outside the home in paid work during all historic periods. As Harris (1989) described, in the colonial northeast women routinely kept taverns, operated printing presses, worked as compositors, ran their husband's business affairs, ran mills, and served as apprentices. During the 1800s many women worked in factories while residing on their own in approved boarding houses.

There were at the same time, however, societal messages about western women and work which stated that women were only to pursue employment before marriage or if they were in dire financial trouble. Women who had qualities of piety, delicacy, and gentility became the standard of social mobility for both women and the men who chose them. Marrying a doll-like woman was the badge of success for many men.

Postindustrialization and American capitalism, as described by Kolbenschlag (1981), saw the "leisure woman" as a symbol of wealth and progress. Women assumed that the most important choice in life was entering a relationship wherein they could become "leisure ladies." The Victorian culture perpetuated the myth of the leisured lady as the ideal of all womanhood. This ideal created a myth that women needed more protection, more pedestal worship and more restriction. If a woman worked outside the home, it was seen as low class and degrading—a terrible misfortune. Female idleness, the cultivation of female inactivity, gave men prestige.

If a young, single woman had to work, her work was considered just an interim occupation until real life and adulthood began in and through marriage. For many years, a woman's life completely bypassed the world of work, the world of being valued for paid and unpaid work. Women never experienced the active world of work in the public realm as a factor in personal growth and enhanced self-esteem.

There were periods, usually during times of war, when women were expected to work. Harris (1989) described how women replaced men in jobs when they went off to war during the two world wars. During the war years, women could be seen flying and servicing airplanes, running lathes, cutting dies, reading blue prints, maintaining road beds, greasing locomotives, working as stevedores, blacksmiths, and drill press operators. However, when the men came back from war, women were told to go back to their kitchens. When the women weren't being laid off fast enough, many of the men went on strike until all the women were fired.

After World War II, women were actively encouraged to stay home. Campaigns were undertaken to persuade the government to bolster programs that encouraged women to have children and to help women develop their talents and skills in the active art of professional consumption. Simone De Beauvoir (1952) wrote that she was appalled by the notion that so many American women were living lives of inertia and would never know the capacity for growth that comes from work and active engagement. She believed that, without some type of work, the road to autonomy and self-worth would be blocked for most women.

Society for many years confined women to a narrow sphere of expectations and limited her hopes for creative work. This socialization limited women psychologically until the sixties' women's movement. Sweeping social changes insisted on equal rights for women, an end to sex-stereotyping of jobs, changes in family structures—including control over reproduction—that would free women who wanted to work outside the home and pursue personal goals and achievements. One of the most dramatic changes to occur was the lengthening of a woman's life span, coupled with the shortening of the time devoted to childrearing and childbearing. Motherhood and intimate relationships no longer occupied a lifetime (Williams, 1985).

Women have extricated themselves from the one-sided feminine roles which history prescribed. New concerns centering around work and mastery have opened up opportunities for gaining new aspects of identity fulfillment and created new resources of self-esteem. However, current political and social climates seem to be hindering women in the workforce by proposed changes in affirmative action, cutbacks in small business loans, little incentive to create day care and a perpetual "glass-ceiling" effect in corporate America.

Women, Work, and Self-Esteem

A little-known study as early as 1949 by Merton suggested that meeting the many challenges of a goal, activity or job contributes to self-esteem in women. An early study done by Baruch and Barnett (1979) also reported that multiple roles, such as work, enhance self-esteem in women by offering the potential to draw upon various sources for self-worth. The NCWRR's initial "Self-Esteem Poll" disseminated through its newsletter in 1990, to which close to 1,000 women responded, found that over 90% of women's main source of self-esteem was a work activity, placing work ahead of relationships with partners, and children.

Following that poll, the NCWRR designed the in-depth survey

that explored the sources of self-esteem and development in adult women and men. The findings from the survey that related to women's sources of self-esteem closely matched the findings from the poll. Work and work-related activities were a main source of self-esteem for 88% of the women surveyed, ahead of relationships with other people. From the open-ended questions, women listed 505 experiences in the areas of work/task activities that contributed to positive self-esteem over time. Men listed 357 work/task experiences that contributed to self-esteem.

Tavris (1986) reported on the effect of paid employment on women's well-being. She stated that employment is associated with feelings of competence among women. Women who work outside the home have higher self-esteem than other women, and they evaluate their abilities more positively. Paid work enhances feelings of competence in an arena that can produce tangible and explicit rewards.

Women have extricated themselves from the one-sided feminine role which history prescribed for them. They have learned self-respect and the means to be independent. Women in the NCWRR study discussed not only the paid aspects of work as a reward but revealed that other types of recognition, such as awards, honors, praise, a simple thank-you, a smile, a pat on the back and—most importantly—self-praise and self-recognition were just as important as salary. Beyond praise and other accolades, achievement itself symbolized a milestone of completion, the accomplishment of hands-on hard work, sweat, and the creative stretch of one's mind. To many, work represented a very personal, one-on-one experience. Women spoke of the overwhelming sense of personal accomplishment and giddy sense of fulfillment from the time and patience spent to get to that very special place called self-worth. Work represented a tangible outline of personal identity, something that set them apart from others. It had boundaries and involved active engagement on the part of many women.

There is no one timetable, particular stage, or special level for achievement and self-esteem that has been derived by women from the work life-tie. Some women from the NCWRR study reported on finding self-esteem through work in midlife, some in their later years of adulthood, and many early in adulthood. Many found clarity of identity from paid work. Others found a profound sense of self from work done in their own backyards, or from work done to overcome a life obstacle or challenge such as alcoholism or drug dependency. The important point to consider is that the individual, not a particular theory, defines the area, the level and the satisfaction of the life-tie experience.

However, there are many new mixed messages about being female and being a female of accomplishment. Women can be smart and can contribute to their own and their families' needs, but there remains a not-so-hidden message of, "Thou shalt not take thyself so seriously." Women can achieve, contribute and get paid, but they had better take care of their "real" work, which is still nurturing and caring for their primary relationships. Women are still held accountable for the maintenance of families and other important relationships.

The New Female Psychology
New research in female psychology has stated that developmental traditionalists such as Erikson and Levinson did not study or understand female development. New female psychology describes female psychological development, particularly in the area of identity and self-esteem, as being different from that of men. Josselson (1987) and Gilligan (1982) have declared that a woman's sense of self is derived primarily through relationships that are built around care and concern for others. If a woman is engaged in an activity or work pursuit, it is the skill and success of the relationship within the work arena that is the cornerstone of her identity, not the mastery derived from the job itself. Josselson believes that women do not make a clear separation between relating and work, further stating that as women recount their lives and the meaning of their lives, it is the relational history that provides them with their identity.

Josselson further argues that work is not a central anchor of women's identities. Relatedness is the core for inner psychological functioning of women. She also writes that women's self-esteem is based primarily on relationships and that work is tangential to their lives, stating, "Hopes and dreams are built around areas of relationship—work does not claim their spirit." Thus, female psychology does not adhere to the traditional developmental perspective that believes identity development is constructed through characteristics of autonomy, self-reliance and self-actualization.

Miller (1976) also stresses the relational pathway to identity development, proposing that self-esteem is related to the degree of emotional sharing and openness as well as a shared sense of understanding with others. According to Miller, competence and agency are developed for women within the sphere of relationships at all life stages; relationships are primary and are the motivating force that propels female development.

Recently Jordan, Kaplan, Miller, Stiver, and Surrey (1991) wrote that caretaking was the basis of all female psychological growth and that female self-esteem was based on the feeling that a part of a relationship and believing that she is maintaining and taking care of her relationships. They also stated that women feel a sense of effectiveness arising out of connection and participation in a feedback process.

Challenge to relational theory.   It is interesting that female psychology has stated that theories developed by age/stage psychologists have no understanding of female development. Many female psychologists, such as Miller and Josselsen, seem to be aligned with Erikson when it comes to development through relationships. Erikson wrote about women's and men's sense of generativity as a developmental task, stating that women's generativity unfolds primarily through her intimate relationships with others, and that it becomes focused in motherhood and in the invisible maintenance work of love. Female psychologists have been, in essence, agreeing with some of the theorists that they have been trying to challenge.

The NCWRR findings show, however, that a strong sense of self and independent identity for women requires something beyond developing oneself only through relationships. As Hancock (1989) found that women need a sense of purpose, goals, work, and achievements to nurture an adult identity that goes beyond an identity based on relationships. Nurturing is an important characteristic for both women and men to have, but nurturing can be valuable to the self as well as to others. There can be something very nurturing about the incremental growth that occurs through purposeful work.

Relationships are important to a woman's life, but a separate identity cannot be found nor personal worth built through another person or persons. This is also, of course, true for men. The journey that women take to create self-worth through the many different expressions of the work life-tie is not always smooth; it is often filled with frustration and risk taking. When the work life-tic becomes a resource, it can contribute to a woman's development in great ways.

Narratives of Women's Work

The following narratives illustrate how purposeful work, achievement, and accomplishment can be expressed in different ways, can occur at any time, and can be used as a resource of self-esteem for women. The NCWRR findings support the idea that work, in its many forms, is important for self-validation in women's lives.

Making a Labor of Love into Work

Sometimes a person can be engaged in a work activity that may not at first be appreciated and can be viewed as more of a source of entrapment than a source of self-esteem.

Helen was a divorced woman who had turned her talent as a good cook into a successful money-making business that rewarded her not only with financial security, but with a new sense of personal worth that contributed to a strong identity in her middle years. She had been married for 16 years. Early in her marriage she enjoyed baking and cooking for her family. She never worked outside the home but spent a lot of her time poring through cookbooks and experimenting in her kitchen. Family and friends always praised her great meals and were constantly asking for more recipes. However, toward the end of her marriage, cooking became a form of entrapment for Helen. Her husband stayed away from home, and missed her elaborately cooked meals. Her children were in their early teens and preferred the local McDonald's to her home-cooked meals.

After the divorce, she rarely cooked meals and dreaded food shopping. Helen and the children lived on pizza and fast food for a few months during this turbulent time in Helen's life. She associated cooking with being a failure at marriage; she expressed feeling stupid for staying home instead of working like other women.

At first I never wanted to look at a stove or pantry again. After the divorce from Bob I felt like a big fool in an apron. I had been so naive to think that trying to be a good homemaker and good cook would keep my marriage together. Well my marriage and what little self-esteem I had sank like a bad soufflé. The kids and I for a few months lived on Chinese takeout, flame-broiled burgers, and soggy French fries.

I dragged myself around to job interviews and only became depressed. I had no marketable skills and couldn't even type. I was feeling pretty low, when I got asked to make some food for the local hospital benefit. I agreed to this, because the hospital and staff had been terrific when they treated my son with a burst appendix. After the benefit I got so many phone calls from people wanting me to make special dishes for their parties. The real kicker was that they wanted to pay me. Now I have never been a person who needed to have a lot of money or spend a lot. Suddenly I felt something very different, it was the association of money with personal value.

I kept the first check I received from catering a small party for a doctor's wife. I never knew how good I could feel about myself. I was full of pride and practically giddy. It was like I was a real person, valued and respected for what I could create and do. I was happy and felt strong. That one small check for one small party made the difference and gave me confidence to try to do this professionally. I left flyers around on the local bulletin boards, put a small ad in the local papers and started taking orders for catering. I worked out of my kitchen for about a year a half. I worked 7 days a week, catering small parties, business lunches, local benefits and doing boxed picnic lunches in the summer. I was exhausted, but it was not a depressing exhaustion, it was a "good" tired.

I took a risk, and eventually moved to a small store and hired a couple of college kids to work in the kitchen and make deliveries. I have a thriving business that has been written up in the local papers and, outside of a few disasters like the four-tiered birthday cake that slipped off the plate due to heat, it's been a success. I should say I am a success and feel like such a different person. I am proud of my accomplishment and have a lot of self-esteem due in large part to my work.

Helen developed early talents as an unappreciated cook in her own home and turned them into a successful business that not only provided her with money but also contributed to feelings of self-worth. Cooking was something she had to do as part of being a homemaker, but it was something she did not feel valued for.

It wasn't until she turned these talents into a business, into work that she could feel was an achievement and an accomplishment, did she see cooking as a source of self-esteem, as opposed to being a control in her life. When Helen perceived her cooking skills to be a negative influence, she contracted, retreating to fast foods. When she perceived this work as a source of pride and value she expanded within the context of this life-tie. Helen's identity and self-esteem developed through the work life-tie when it became a resource of personal accomplishment.

Traditional Career Track

Many women who have joined the workforce have discovered personal satisfaction and rewards in careers and jobs that were once the province of men only. Levinson et al. (1978) elaborated on the importance of a man's dream in the construction of his adult life. A vision and dream of unlimited potential can generate excitement and vitality in women as well as men.

Twenty-nine-year-old Tina grew up in a large Italian family, with four brothers and one other sister. Her mother remained in the home to take care of the family while her father worked as a brick mason. She had a dream about becoming a veterinarian; she grew up taking care of the wounded and lame pets of her childhood friends and offered a home to stray cats, wild birds, and an occasional mallard duck. Making her dream a reality was complex and sometimes full of guilt and mixed emotions. One of her brothers was in college, and she knew the financial drain, even with scholarships added, would prove burdensome to her parents.

> I had this dream of being a vet since I was a kid. I love animals and love taking care of them. As a teen I worked most summers in a dog-grooming place, just so I could earn some money being around animals. My senior year in high school I worked for the local vet as an assistant and I also worked for him summers when I came home from college. The vet doctor really encouraged me to pursue my goal. He really focused my attention, especially when I started to drift and get cold feet. I was smart and got good grades, but I knew that getting into a good veterinary school would be tough. Some said

it would be tougher than trying to get into medical school.

My parents were proud that I was in school, but were dubious about me going beyond college and into veterinary medicine. They thought I would work, but this type of work, they thought, would absorb all my time. It was a heavy-duty career, a major commitment. I guess they feared I would be so involved that I wouldn't have time to meet some nice guy and get married. I got into Cornell College of Veterinary Medicine. It's one of the best, I worked hard to keep my grades up and had a sound recommendation from my local vet, who went to Cornell also.

Those years at Cornell were some of the toughest and the best years of my life. When I graduated, I made it. I felt so good about accomplishing my dream. I felt like I could do anything. I had such a powerful sense of who I was and what I had achieved. I went into practice with a veterinary group about fifty miles from my home town, close to home but still far enough to maintain my own life. I love the work I do. It's hard to believe the dream I had as a little girl has come true. But this dream didn't happen because of some fairy godmother waving a wand. It happened because I made it happen.

Tina was actively engaged in making her dream a reality. Work was important to Tina's sense of self, but, more important, it was the type of work that gave purpose and direction to Tina's life. She had always loved working with animals, and this passion coupled with drive, discipline and determination made the dream possible. She created a life that was realistic, fulfilling, and worthy of her special talents. The fabric of her positive self-image is woven together by the work she has chosen to do and what she has done to accomplish her goals.

The Greenhouse Builder

Even among women who did not hold traditional paid jobs outside the home, task-related accomplishments played an important part in producing a sense of personal fulfillment and self-worth.

Fifty-eight-year-old Martha has been married to her husband for over 30 years and has three children. Her family has always been a great source of joy and happiness. She has a good marriage and has maintained a close relationship with her children. However, Martha always felt a part of herself was missing and couldn't understand why she felt so lacking, that is until she met the challenge of the greenhouse.

I've always considered myself very lucky to have such a wonderful family. I enjoyed being home with my children while they were growing up. To me it was important that I be there. I know a lot of feminists would disagree, but for me my place was at home. My husband Dick and I have had a close and sharing relationship, although his schedule as a doctor made it difficult to make plans. I spent many late nights alone while he was on call at the hospital.

I've always been an avid gardener. Over the years my once-simple vegetable garden has turned into a showplace of flower annuals, perennials, and exotic herbs and vegetables. I've taken courses on gardening and my knowledge has expanded. The one thing I always wanted was a greenhouse so I could start my flowers and vegetables from seeds and nurture them early in the season. I knew enough not to ask my husband to build one for me. He's all thumbs. My son is handy, but was either away at college or working at a resort near his college town. Dick said to hire a carpenter. I refused.

I got this crazy idea in my head that I was the only one who could put the dream that was in my head on paper and build it myself. Dick thought I was crazy and too out of shape to do that kind of physical labor, plus I didn't know anything about construction. I was stubborn enough to think I could do this thing, so at the end of summer I signed up for a fall course at the local high school in carpentry. I found a blueprint of the garden greenhouse I wanted and with some custom additions I knew what I wanted to build. I became quite skilled at handling tools and reading blueprints and grew knowledgeable about building materials.

We live in a warm climate all year round, so by December I was ready to tackle this project. For Christmas, instead of the usual nightgown and perfume, I got a good set of tools, including a power saw from my family. I hired a high-school boy to help with some of the heavy lifting, but for the most part this was my project. The first few weeks, I ached and hurt and would spend most evenings sitting in a bathtub with Epsom salts in it. I got discouraged and at times thought I was crazy to take on this project. I broke many glass panes; I got numerous cuts and bruises and made some wrong cutting angles with the saw.

By March I had the most beautiful greenhouse. It was such an accomplishment. I can't even begin to express the feelings I had about what I did and what I could do. Every time I look out my kitchen window I feel such pride and feel so good about myself. It was the part that was lacking inside. My family shares my pride, but there is something so special and so uniquely mine that can only be celebrated deep inside myself.

What emerges from Martha's story is the message that women have a great need to point to some tangible product that is uniquely their own. Martha's relationships with family filled her with love and joy, but she needed to clarify her self-definition and find that missing part through the life-tie of work. She was able to say to herself that the work that was a product of her hands and mind was a large part of who she was and how she felt about herself.

Volunteering
Volunteerism has been considered the poor stepsister of paid work. However, just because a person has a paid job, doesn't always mean that the paid work contributes to positive self-esteem. Sometimes it is through volunteer work that an individual can find clarity of identity and strong feeling of self-worth.

Hope was a forty-five-year-old woman who had worked in the cosmetics industry during her twenties and thirties. The job became less satisfactory to her as she got older. It was very demanding, full of pretentious people that made her feel shallow and empty. Her unhappiness was masked by alcohol; the problem got out of hand and Hope had to enter a rehab center. She successfully met the challenge and did the hard work it took to stay clean and sober. Hope considered achieving sobriety a very important marker in her life, a turning point at which to consider a new way of living.

I was lucky I had a husband who stood by me. We both realized that we had to make changes in our lives. One change was moving to the country. This was a major change for me. I had lived so long in the city and worked in a very sophisticated and fast-paced world. We also had no children, so here I was in the suburbs with an old house to restore and five acres of land. Maybe because I don't have children, animals became very important to me. I have two beagles and three cats who have brought me a great deal of pleasure and joy. It was because of this pleasure and joy in having pets that I began to think others might experience these same feelings.

I found a school that trained dogs to become therapy pets. The beagles and I went through training. They graduated and got their degrees. I am probably one of the few people who has the distinct honor of having pets with more degrees than their owner. They spent months training to be well-behaved and patient around elderly people, small children, and groups in different surroundings. With their certificates that proclaimed them pet therapists, we were in business.

I have spent the last 4 years taking Henry and Tillie (my beagles) to nursing homes, prisons, and facilities that have children with emotional and behavior problems. I am not paid for this work, but I consider it the most rewarding and meaningful work I have ever done.

To see the old people's eyes light up when Tillie and Henry visit them in a nursing home, to witness the gentle handling of them by a prisoner or to hear the squeals of laughter and big smiles that appear on a lost child's face, these are things that a fat paycheck was never able to give me. To me my old job was shallow and meaningless. I believe it contributed to my experience with alcohol. The work I do with Tillie and Henry is important to how I feel about myself. I am doing something of value, I feel good about me.

Hope was able to draw important meaning from this life-tie experience through her volunteer efforts with her therapy dogs, Henry and Tillie. The work she did in nursing homes, prisons, and with children contributed to self-esteem and a positive identity, aspects of herself that were lacking when she was working in a traditional nine-to-five paid job. Hope's previous work in the consmetics field acted as a souce of control and a souce of low self-esteem. However, when she changed her work life-tie to one that brought personal meaning and reward, this life-tie became a resource and a source of positive self-esteem. Hope's work in battling alcoholism was also an important task and achievement that she was able to integrate into her sense of self as a worthy and valued person.

Expanding Sources for Self-Esteem

Before concluding this section on women and the work life-tie, it is important to understand that although the NCWRR findings report that a main source of self-esteem in women is work and task-related activity, that does not diminish the relevance and importance of relationships to a woman's life. What has to be taken into consideration in view of female psychology is that relationships do bring women contentment, happiness and fulfillment. However, the NCWRR findings point to the relevance of work/achievement to women's identity and to their self-esteem. Sources of self-esteem may be different from sources of well-being and contentment. What may be very relevant is that the more sources an individual has to draw from for self-esteem, the chances become better for the individual to gain self-esteem. This is particularly true since women have more freedom to choose work opportunities and more choices for their lives; hence they have more sources for gaining self-esteem and more sources for personal growth in adulthood.

MEN

Just as women have been encouraged and socialized to seek self-definition through one main area—relationships—men have also been socialized to define themselves through the narrow concept of paid work roles. Not only was this male definition of self to take place through traditional paid work, but the concept of a work-related identity was to be solidified during the period of early adulthood. Definition of self was to come from traditional masculine roles and behavior, through competition, acquiring wealth, power, conquest and control.

The NCWRR study found that work is a vital component of self-esteem. The study reports that 91% of men perceive that work contributes to self-esteem, 40% saying work contributes to high self-esteem. However, the interviews reveal that when men tie their self-images strictly to traditional paid work, self-esteem can be affected in a negative way if that work is lost. The study also demonstrates that many men are trying to redefine themselves within a broader definition of work and achievement. Men may find themselves entering and exiting a number of traditional jobs at various times throughout adulthood, so that identity and self-esteem through the work life-tie may be achieved later than early adulthood.

Similar to women, men have had to live with cultural stereotypes. Women have been pigeonholed into self-definition through the maintenance of intimate connections and relationships. Men have had to seek self-definition within the confines of paid work and strict career pathways. Both genders have had to move beyond cultural stereotypes and barriers that limit sources, meanings, and interpretations of self-esteem and identity.

An Historical Perspective

Male definition through the traditions of particular work pathways has been established throughout time. However, as Keen (1991) described, there were earlier periods in time when men worked long, hard, and joyless hours at work out of necessity and survival. Meaning in their lives came from their free time. In Greek civilization, slaves and women were associated with a life of work, while free and wealthy men indulged themselves in thoughtful contemplation and the pursuit of leisure activities.

It was the Protestant Reformation that declared men had a calling and obligation to secular work. After the Industrial Revolution, work dominated the lives of men, pulling them away from home and family. The world of acquiring, spending, and power occupied the greatest importance in western men's lives and became their definition. The financial bottom line, the Dow Jones, a secure paycheck and the threat of a "pink slip" became the factors that controlled a man's sense of himself. The traditional aspect of the work life-tie, as imposed by society, can be restrictive, confining and controlling, all of which can reduce a man's self-image, shrink his self-esteem, and limit development and personal growth.

Maybe little girls were never asked the question by adults, "What do you want to be when you grow up?" Little boys were not only asked that question before they even entered school, they were supposed to envision and develop a life plan of work, all before they left school. Boys learned from family that the world of work was going to be a large part of their life. The school system reinforced parental admonitions, and began the process of preparing men for their life's work. The standards that men measured themselves against were the restrictive standards of being a winner or loser, a success or failure. By the time a boy left school, he knew that to be a successful male he must be a successful wage earner and provider.

It is in this setting that men can be imprisoned by the economic needs of work and the societal expectations that govern this attitude. They can be imprisoned by work they are not suited for work they do not like, or work that has lost relevance and meaning in their lives. Men can be caught up in economic traps that keep them in work just to stay financially afloat. They can be swept up by cutthroat competition and spend 80% of their days at the job; or mindless activity that doesn't do justice to their talents or ideas can envelop them. It is in cases like these that the work life-tie can be a controlling influence in a man's life and a source of low self-esteem and confused identity. When men live to work, rather than work to live, the work life-tie can become an end rather than a means to growth.

Developmental Theory on Men and Work

Erikson (1968) addressed the developmental task of work through his developmental stage of *identity versus role confusion*. He believed that identity is established when the adolescent (male implied) discerns in himself his true capabilities, interests, and desires. Through this process the adolescent can make a life plan that encompasses his interests and capabilities and that will propel him into a long-term commitment to work. Erikson believed that an unsatisfactory resolution of this process during adolescence can impair later stage development.

Vaillant (1977) agreed with Erikson's developmental task theory, but added another sequence which he described as "career consolidation." Young men in their twenties and early thirties struggle to achieve security through work stability and work success. The result is a precarious balance between settling down in a relationship and trying to climb the ladder of career success.

Levinson et al. (1978) revised Erikson's stages into four major life stages: infancy through adolescence, early adulthood, middle adulthood, and late adulthood. Each transition was marked by stability and change. His theory was based on the study of forty men, predominantly career professionals. Levinson's developmental theme of growth in adulthood centered around a man's career trajectory.

Levinson believed that work/career was a major part of a man's life and his social structure. A man's job was the primary factor that determined his financial status, prestige, and place in society. Traditional work influenced a man's options, choices, and opportunities. He believed that a job or career had an important function in establishing a self and the consequences for that self. Choice of one's work can create fulfillment of values and goals, or it can be an oppressive and large disappointment.

In Levinson's early adult phase, men explore the adult world's interests and, values in a process of making choices, form an adult identity. During his twenties a man spends his time shaping an occupation and establishing himself at a junior level; then he advances up the career ladder through his forties. But it was during late adolescence and early adulthood that the core of Levinson's theory resides.

The cornerstone of his theory was built around what he labeled the "dream." This male dream represented a vague sense of self in the adult world. It had the quality of a vision, an imagined possibility that generates excitement and vitality whether it be the dream of war hero, artist, tycoon, athlete, intellectual, or excellent craftsman. The task for young men was to give the vision concrete definition and find a way to live out the dream.

Levinson also believed that the middle years could be a process of gradual or rapid stagnation, of alienation from the world and from the self. He described age forty as the turning point, the culmination of either success or failure. Forty seemed to Levinson the age when promotions or failures at work occur and major life difficulties or satisfactions are found. Like Erikson's, the theory was linear and age regulated. Levinson's stages of forming an occupation, linked to identity development and self-worth, were direct and predictable, progressing in a straight line without gross conflicts or shifts in direction until the magical age of forty.

Challenge to Traditional Theory on Men and Work

A dream can and should animate a man's life, as well as a woman's life. Many men have been able to implement an early career dream; and that dream can be the right choice and can lead to success and fulfillment. Problems occur for many men, however, when this vision of what one will become has to be made a long-term reality in late adolescence and early adulthood, according to formula.

Based on this model, a young adolescent is encouraged by family and educators to make choices concerning education and work that should make the vision a reality. Sometimes this dream is not the adolescent's dream, but rather the dream of a parent or family member. Projecting oneself into the future is a awesome task and is a risk for any adolescent or young adult, considering the volatility and changing nature of today's economic, political, and social world, as well as the prospect of living a much longer life than one's parents or grandparents.

Dreams are not the province of young men only. Men and women can have many dreams at many different times and ages during adulthood. Fulfillment or failure can occur some of the time or part of the time, or many times. Allowing for only one dream per person in early adulthood may lead a man to disappointment, confusion, and job-imposed limitations. That one dream may not hold the dreamer's interest or have potential for fulfillment and further growth. Loss of that dream may have devastating effects on a man's identity and self-esteem. When men define themselves within the confines of paid work, they become what they do. When a man loses his work, he often loses his purpose and sense of self.

There is significant literature in the fields of career development, retirement planning, and gerontology that indicates that a loss of paid employment negatively impacts on a man's sense of identity (Weiss, 1990). As reported by Gradman (1994), unemployed men feel worthless and reduced to marginal social standing, regardless of previous status. In a similar vein, the termination of work at retirement is equally painful. Close to the retirement transmission, a significant number of men become anxious once they sense a lack of familiar masculine anchors (Ochberg, 1987; Weiss, 1990).

Kupers (1993) found that many of the men he studied reported feeling a lack of power, vitality in their jobs. Lack of vitality in work, Kupers stated, is often subtle to the point of being invisible, when a man is perceived as working competently and complaining little about dissatisfactions his state of mind goes unnoticed. Only when problems are extremely visible—such as layoffs, business failures, stress-related illness and bankruptcy—do men reveal the true nature and depth of their discontents. Kupers believes that unemployment, underemployment and demeaning conditions are the biggest cause of feelings of inadequacy in American men today, further stating that the gap is widening between rich and poor; working class and minority men are the most strongly affected.

Often, as Keen (1991) wrote, men put aside real dreams—distinct from mere occupational dreams—and settle for the economic and marketing dream of paid work. A corporate or job personality is foisted on men as a substitute for personal dreams, ideals and pursuits. The world of paid work rewards men for a corporate identity, rather than valuing the personal identity. That personal identity often remains buried under layers of societal expectations surrounding men and traditional work.

Women who spend much time within this corporate work culture may also find themselves governed by the corporate/business "group think" and lose aspects of themselves that are vital to personal identity and self-esteem. A man or woman who is controlled by work is neither masculinized or feminized; rather, that person becomes neutralized (Keen, 1991). The overemphasis on the economics of work devalues the identities of both women and men. Work in this type of environment is often a control and can be a source of low self-esteem, rather than a resource for positive self-esteem. Even Levinson (1978) believed that one's work can create fulfillment or be a source of disappointment, yet he still adhered to the pessimistic view that paid work or careers were the main source of self-definition for men.

Work is a central component of male identity and self-esteem, as the NCWRR reports. However, interviews and further study show that work has taken on a broader meaning and context for some men, in much the same way that it can and has for women.

The work dream is important in men's lives, but a dilemma unfolds when a male is expected to make the dream a reality very early in life. Levinson and Erikson both feel that the work dream must bear fruit in early adulthood. A dream without maturity and self-understanding is just that—a simple dream, perhaps one of many that might be followed.

Men can be trapped by early expectations and identifications with narrowly defined aspects of work/career in much the same way women have been narrowly defined through their relationship capabilities and ability to nurture others. Without denying the value and wonder of an individual's dream we must acknowledge that men may have many dreams that will fulfill and inspire them, dreams may bear fruit later in life, dreams can be delayed, and dreams can be changed. The dreams surrounding work have to be broad enough to include new meanings and definitions that are also unrelated to age or particular stages of development. Although traditional careers and pride in economic work will always be important to many men's identity and self-esteem, men are creating new self-definitions that center on the broader meaning of the work life-tie that may be volunteer and unpaid, work that is a hobby, but central to personal meaning, new careers that blossom after midlife. White-collar men can trade a computer for a power saw, or young males locked into blue-collar jobs can turn in their tool boxes for briefcases.

Stories of Men and Work

Men have been locked into cultural stereotypes that are associated with what it means to be male. The following narratives reveal the importance of work to men's self-esteem and identity, but also expand the meaning, timing and context of the work life-tie for men.

A Midlife Career Beginning

The career dream and its realization sometimes don't happen during the prescribed time in early adulthood, but can happen at any time during adulthood. Late adolescence and early adulthood can be a time of confusion, unawareness, and deficient self-knowledge about long-term commitments and work goals. Sometimes a man finds his career and vocation in midlife, after numerous struggles, wrong turns, and disappointments.

Victor, now fifty, tells a story of unhappiness with who he thought he was during college. The Vietnam War took him down a path that altered his self-views and stalled any attempt at formulating a life dream. It was only after many years that he found his direction and found work that became central to his identity and self-esteem.

There are different reasons why I left my Ivy League college to join the Marines. I had never been happy at college back in '67. I was not happy with who I thought I was, or with what I was doing. I wanted to pay some dues, get some real life experience. I had also seen a lot of World War II movies, so I had a lot of romantic notions about war. I got myself tossed out of college deliberately. I guess that way it was someone else's decision rather than mine. I enlisted in the Marine Corps. It was just a matter of time before I was shipped to Da Nang. All romantic notions about war were gone in eight months of Vietnam. I did my tour, left Vietnam behind, and entered a world vastly changed from when I had left.

I still had no direction, so I headed to Colorado and worked in construction for a while and ended up in a vocational school: From Ivy League to shop class. I ended up working in auto body out in Denver. I needed that time to work off a lot of frustration, without a lot of thinking. I placed a great deal of value on working in that auto body place. Life seemed more real there; sometimes it still does. People were real and I felt the simple pleasure of doing and completing a piece of work. There were no gray areas.

Years later, I went back to that Ivy League college I got thrown out of. It finally came together for me, perhaps at a different time than my friends got it together back in '67. Over the years I have worked through many levels of self-understanding, acceptance, forgiveness and have found meaning and value in my career as a federal prosecutor. I care about it and I work hard at it. I don't think I would have had this kind of understanding about myself and my work if I had made this decision back in the Sixties. It would have been a hollow decision, and I probably would have been burned out by now if I had chosen my career then, rather than years later.

War is a tragedy no matter what the cause. However, war can create a situation for young males that permits critical decisions affecting life choices to be forestalled for a while. This "break-away" period allows for experience, maturity and self-knowledge to develop in a young adult. It allows some space and time before the world expects him to make a career/job choice. It would be beneficial to many young adults to have a peacetime time-out period so that some personal seasoning and relevant self-knowledge could begin to develop before career/job decisions are made.

For Victor, the war, experience at other types of work, and enough time away from decisions he wasn't ready to pursue, made the choice of a career all that much more meaningful to his life. He has incorporated many levels of self-awareness and knowledge into his work life that are complementary to his ideals and sense of self. His work life-tie acts as a resource, rather than as a controlling, mindless activity; and it formed at midlife, not young adulthood. The journey has taken Victor over many slow, bumpy roads. The landscape along the way has been scenic and sometimes horrific, but the winding path has made his destination and career choice more satisfying and meaningful to his life. Identity and feelings of self-worth through the work life-tie have occurred later in life then most theorists would have deemed appropriate. Nevertheless, a richer meaning of self and purpose seems to have been the result of delayed timing of the work life-tie.

Tie by Day, Volunteering by Night
Sometimes a man will accept the economic and work responsibilities of his life but derive small satisfaction from his effort. Often well-paid jobs are full of frustration, office politics, and corporate uncertainty. Michael had a well-paying job in a big city financial brokerage house. With a wife in a similar career track, he had the trappings of a man who could be perceived as having it all, and having it all by age twenty-seven. However, Michael did not feel as though he had it all, for there were aspects of himself that he felt were missing. He always enjoyed being around children and felt that there might be something he could do to help kids in need.

> I had been putting in very long hours in the brokerage house where I work. I'm good at what I do and have been successful in making my clients and myself financially comfortable. But along with the money came a lot of frustration, exhaustion, and emptiness. Looking at my escalating bank balance did not seem to satisfy me. I was doing important work, but it wasn't something I valued or believed in. I had this feeling for quite a while, then one night on my way home from work I walked by a local school with kids playing basketball by themselves. There were no coaches, parents, or adults around, just a few kids trying to get a game together. The next thing I knew I walked into the school and started talking to a teacher who put me in touch with someone in the Physical Education Department. I had volunteered my time after the office to play basketball with these

kids and organize some kind of a team.

Most of the kids are without family support and are close to being dropouts; some are trying to stay clear of drugs. They are a tough group. At first they were suspicious of me and my motives and reject-ed my being involved. That was a year ago. I've played basketball with these guys three nights a week. They have come together as a team, and they trust who I am and what I say to them. As well as play-ing ball, I try to listen to their problems and fears. I'm not a social worker, don't have that kind of training, but I am there, and I listen. It seems to help, especially building a trust with them. I never promise anything I can't deliver on.

I may be helping those guys, but this whole thing is a lot more than being a volunteer and a simple basketball game. This is proba-bly the most important work I can do. This is important to me. I feel good about doing it, I feel that by giving something to these kids I am also giving something to myself. This is work that fits my spirit, not my bank account. It seems to have spilled over on my personal life. My wife seems to think I am happier, more patient and less stressed out. I even tackle my office job with a better attitude. I guess some would say that my real work is the office because I get paid. I don't believe that anymore. The work that is real to me is the work I do off-hours on a basketball court.

Michael has found self-definition and self-worth from his unpaid volunteer work with kids on a basketball court. Too often men have been defined and judged by their paid work. The more impressive the paycheck the more likely that a man is looked upon with high regard. This old standard of measuring success by paid work alone is changing for men like Michael. Work is important and vital to self-esteem, but the definition of work has to be broad enough to include new meanings. Work, like Michael's work with kids, has to be purposeful and mindful in order to contribute to feelings of self-worth and identity in adulthood.

From Truck Driver to Ambulance Driver

Sometimes skills that an individual has in one job can be trans-ferred to another line of work, acquiring new and rewarding meaning. Thirty-year-old George had been driving a truck route for about 9 years, hauling fresh produce from country markets to a large midwestern city. He enjoyed driving a truck, liked the freedom of being on the road, but he felt there had to be a little more to his life than driving around fruits and vegetables. Being newly divorced, George began to take stock of his life situation and felt it time to make changes. Having no children, he had the freedom to move and was not mired in support payments.

At one point earlier in his life he had been a volunteer ambulance driver and had very much liked the work. George began forming a vague dream about finding a job similar to the one he had had as an ambulance driver, a job that would make him feel more useful. The dream became a reality when he began training for a job as an emergency medical technician.

> I was so tired from driving that produce truck. I was on "autopilot" most of the time, not a good practice when driving a vehicle. I had gotten divorced. My life was a mess. I didn't have a relationship, and I didn't have a job that I liked. I was feeling very low and dissatisfied with myself. I guess when you get divorced, you start thinking about your life and past things that had made you happy. I started remembering working as a volunteer ambulance driver and how I loved that work and being on call. I thought to myself, Wouldn't it be great if I could get paid and do something like that for a living!
>
> Well, my dream became real when I moved to the city and started training to become an emergency medical worker. This would lead to a possible job driving an emergency vehicle and assisting in a medical crisis. The training was hard. I had gone for two years to a community college years ago. That helped, but I really had to use my mind in ways that were new and tough. I didn't give up, I had a dream that this was what I wanted to do with my life.
>
> I got through training and moved permanently from the suburbs to the city. I found a small apartment and started to rebuild my life. I was hired as an emergency medical driver and worked with a team of other technicians. I am not paid as much as I was when I drove that produce truck; but right now I don't have a wife or kids to support, so the pay cut doesn't matter. Besides, I have a new lease on life. My work is an important part of what makes me feel good about getting up in the morning.

George developed a new vision, a dream regarding work. Divorce was the catalyst that opened the door to examining his life and sorting through past choices. Many choices he had made, he decided to change. The biggest change occurred when he decided to give up an unrewarding job and find another, taking advantage of his driving skills, that would open the door to a more rewarding life. He was bold enough to change course, not to stay with a job decision that was made early in life and that offered little satisfaction. George was able to formulate a new dream that later blossomed into work that contributed to a new sense of self.

New Meanings from Hobby and Vocation

It is a fortunate man who can find a vocation and challenging hobbies to bring a purpose and meaning to his life, when a career does not touch the vitality and spirit of that man. Elliot had followed his father into the family law practice, had tried to make his father's dream his dream. But dreams by their very nature are personal and can only be authored and signed by one person.

Elliot had excelled in law school, loved the mental challenge, the legal history and the broad areas of conflict and debate, but found the day-to-day business of running a small law practice stifling, predictable, routine, and often beyond control. He not only had to practice law, but be a business manager, accountant, public relations person, and amateur social worker. His law practice, not unlike many other practices, had more to do with skill, care, and detail than original thought and creativity. It was lucrative and he did it well, but Elliot needed more to fill in his life and make it meaningful than a sharp knowledge of the law and a waiting room full of clients. He found two areas that contributed to personal meaning, a fuller identity and self-worth. His vocation of teaching a paralegal course and his hobbies of model airplane building and ham radio and radio electronics became his avenues for control, complex thinking, creative expression and tangible results.

> I enjoy thinking, solving problems, reflection, and writing. The day-to-day life of practicing law certainly is active and busy, what with phones ringing, walk-in clients, and under-the-gun deadlines. It sometimes resembles a firehouse and I am the fireman putting out the client's fire of the moment. Days are unpredictable, unstable and often out of my control. What I set about to do at 9 a.m. on a

Monday morning is often shoved on the back burner until Thursday by some client emergency. I have found that I have little control over my work environment. My life is shaped by events, rather than me being able to shape the circumstances around me.

For instance, during the summer I love to take a swim after work in the ocean. The people have left the beach for the day, and I look forward to some quiet time by myself. It was near sunset. The water was calm. The only voice was a seagull looking for dinner. However, as I started to float and look skyward, I heard another voice, unmistakably human. I was startled, looked up to see a man waving frantically in the air yelling, "Elliot, Elliot, I have to talk to you." As he started wading out in my direction I recognized him as a client. He was about 50 feet away with waves slapping against his side when he started a monologue about some problem that he thought needed my urgent attention. Luckily, he didn't like to swim in the ocean. He finally gave up and yelled he would make an appointment at my office to talk to me further. After he disappeared over the horizon I came out of the water.

I guess the lack of control, the unpredictability plus personal demands have made me seek other areas that give me pleasure, control and a sense of what my life is all about. I have found solace, contentment, self-esteem in two other areas of my life. One area is teaching a night course to paralegals at a local college. The other area of importance is my hobbies: building scale-model airplanes and radio, electronics, and computers.

My teaching at a local college has given me meaning, pleasure and fulfillment. My students appreciate me—something I don't often hear from my clients. I also feel I can make a difference in their lives—in contrast to my office life, which seems to be just so much paper pushing. Teaching is also a controlled environment. The hours are regular. There is a beginning and an end, as well as definite expectations and behaviors on the part of myself and my students. Teaching is creative and can be open to debate and new areas of thought. Based on my teaching, I am writing a textbook on what paralegals and teachers need to know and cover in the fast-growth world of paralegals. If a student remembers what I taught a few years down the road that's important to me. I remember now, 25 years out of law school, the great teachers I had. I hope a few of my students remember me.

The other work area that has been important is my hobbies. They are an important expression of myself. I build scale-model airplanes and I'm a ham radio operator as well as a radio builder. I've lately taken up computer programming. These are areas where I can creatively think and solve problems. The work is tangible with a beginning and an end. It is result oriented, and the only person I have to please is myself. With a well-made airplane I can reward myself, not have to worry about the approval of others. My airplane building has led to a broadening of thought in other areas. I have delved into military history, let my imagination take flight. My mind becomes a rich place, a wonderful playground of thought and expression. My radio electronics hobby has satisfied the frustrated engineer inside me. I can use physics and math that I had in college and see practical results. I like the challenge of finding solutions to problems. It doesn't depend on chance or human fallibility. The electronic design works or it doesn't, it's rational and predictable. I can be innovative and experiment, stretch my mind and my capabilities.

Teaching and my hobbies have rounded out my life. It makes me a better lawyer. I feel good about myself when I am doing work that I feel is relevant, can be seen, and is important to me. I often think to myself of other lawyers who had vocations and interests outside the law. Edgar Lee Masters, Clarence Darrow's partner, gained much pleasure from being a poet; so did Wallace Stevens, who was an insurance company attorney and executive in Hartford, but who also expressed himself through poetry. Their avocations gave them an opportunity to do what they enjoyed and to express themselves in a new and different way.

Elliot is a man who could seek identity and self-worth beyond his traditional career choice. Teaching and his hobbies helped him cope with his day-to-day law practice, renewed and added to his sense of self. He found work that was able to fit and invigorate his spirit. Traditional careers and jobs can make men great, but sometimes they threaten to capture the soul and stifle the spirit.

There are many men who find identity and self-worth through a career or traditional nine-to-five job. If men can find a positive sense of self and identity this way, so much the better. However, men also must realize that identity and self-esteem through the work life-tie can come from more than work based on early adult decisions, work that is paid, and work that is narrowly defined. The work life-tie contributes to self-esteem and identity in adulthood for men in new and important ways that may be untraditional, off-time, and not socially unrecognized.

SUMMARY

This chapter has tried to demonstrate that the work life-tie is an important part of self-esteem and identity development in adulthood. It contributes to a positive and strong sense of self for both women and men in many ways. Work can represent a resource for problem solving, a chance for interaction with others, a source of pride, a means of making a difference, a source of structure in daily life. Work can enhance feelings of competence and achievement, can act as an outlet for creativity or a source for tangible results. Work can provide the basic pride in earning money, enhance independence and a sense of personal control over one's life, and serve many other personal needs and goals.

White (1959) wrote over 30 years ago that individuals have a drive to behave competently, to encounter problems and solve them, in much the same way that people have a drive for sex. White believed that to thwart the drive for competence would result in unhappiness, bitterness, frustration and self-defeating behavior. The ability to point to something of achievement, a task completed, or other types of accomplishments and work are important not only to feeling good and alive, but also to a sense of wholeness and integration in the lives of adults. Work that affords a man, woman, or child a sense of accomplishment promotes psychological strength and clarity of self.

The NCWRR study found that for both women and men, meaningful work/task accomplishments contribute in a very large way to positive self-esteem. The work life-tie is a reflection of oneself. However, the word work requires a broad definition, one that goes beyond, yet includes, traditional paid work and careers. Work is any purposeful physical or mental effort that engages an individual in doing, making, or performing by means of either skill, exertion, perseverance, or practice. *Work* is really best used, not as a noun, but as an active verb, for work is the act of doing.

Past developmental theory on work has emphasized it as a route for identity and development for men only, leaving out women's work experience. Past theory, even when it has pertained to men, has narrowly defined work to mean a nine-to-five professional career, and has insisted on strict timing of this developmental event to occur in early adulthood, with an orderly and predictable series of stages. Those linear stages begin in early adulthood, peak in intensity at age forty, and decline until retirement.

This very restrictive way of looking at work does not take into consideration individual change, gender experience, longevity, or the broad meanings and individual values placed on work. When the developmental aspect of work is narrowly defined and restricted based on gender, timing and social expectations, this important life-tie can hinder personal growth, become a controlling influence, and lower feelings of self-worth. When the developmental aspects of work are gender free, defined broadly (and not age/stage defined), and can encompass personal themes and values, this life-tie can enhance self-esteem and positive identity throughout adulthood.

Women have been narrowly defined through their nurturing and relationship abilities. However, a main source of self-esteem and positive identity for women, as the NCWRR study has found, is based on achievement and work themes. Relationships are important to women as a source of joy and happiness, but work-related activities are even more significant as a source of personal worth.

- Helen went from viewing her cooking abilities as a control, something that went unappreciated in her family, to developing her ability into a resource of self-esteem when she created a business from her talents.
- Tina had a dream, much like the dream described by Levinson for men, of being a veterinarian. She achieved her dream, proving that dreams are not for men only.
- Martha had a loving relationship with her husband and children, but found a sense of soaring pride and accomplishment in building her greenhouse.
- Hope went from a traditional career to finding personal worth in volunteering with her therapy dogs and in overcoming a long-

term addiction. The work life-tie, when it is purposeful, is important to women's continued growth and development in adulthood.

Perhaps, just as women have been socialized to find a sense of self through relationships, men have been just as socialized to find identity through the narrowly defined theme of paid work—particularly highly paid and highly professional careers. A work goal, or dream, is important to men. However, when that dream has to be formed and crystallized at one particular stage or limited to social and culturally approved definitions of work, problems may arise for men. If they become controlled by the narrow definition of work, yet the task itself holds little meaning or purpose, growth will be hampered and self-esteem will not develop in a positive way.

Men can have many dreams related to achievement, and may dream at different times during adulthood. There are midlife dreams, late life dreams, delayed dreams, unpaid dreams, and dreams that lack social prestige. These more unconventional dreams are nonetheless vital and important to the dreamer's self-knowledge and personal growth.

- Victor started out in life on a prescribed Ivy League college road. He discovered it wasn't for him, and his life journeyed in other nonlinear, circular directions. When he finally found out where he wanted to be, he went back to school, and formed a meaningful career at an untraditional time.
- Michael had a traditional career by day, but found meaning and pride in the volunteer work he did with kids on a basketball court.
- George was able to turn his truck-driving skills into skills that provided him with meaning and a sense of purpose as an emergency medical service worker.
- Elliot, a lawyer by day, found growth and a strong sense of self through his avocation as a paralegal teacher at night and found pride and a strong sense of accomplishment through hobbies that produced tangible results.

The work life-tie can be a resource for continued growth for both men and women. There may be great differences between the genders regarding personal meaning, value and timing; however the life-tie of meaningful and purposeful work nourishes a sense of competence and strong sense of self for both genders throughout adulthood.

CHAPTER 8

Conclusion

T he life-tie theme that has been presented as a framework for the NCWRR study findings represents another way to organize and understand adulthood in the nineties and beyond. They are broad enough to allow for an understanding of adult development that is not bound to gender or age-stage and that can encompass the richness of individual differences as well as similarities. Past developmental theories based upon gender, particular age, or linear stage have been too restrictive and judgmental; they failed take into consideration the complexities of modern-day life for most women and men. The life-tie approach to adult development includes the experiences of both genders, independent of age or stage, at the same time highlighting the individualized processes of change and growth that occur in every individual's life throughout adulthood.

We found that women's and men's lives were similar to a patchwork quilt so full of color and textures that with a quick glance and a close look at only one small patch, it is not easy to discern or understand the overall theme or pattern. However, when one looks at the quilt from a distance, with perspective, the complexity of the pattern reveals a richness and depth that is uniquely each person's own. Men and women of the study seemed to derive this depth from their numerous meaningful life-tie experiences.

As the findings reveal, for both genders, a strong sense of self depended on change and continuity. Identity commitments made early in life often changed during the adult years. Flux and change occurred many times within the context of the life-tie. Of course, increased longevity does not make for a smooth, predictable, and stable journey. This very long life journey can no longer be mapped through particular sequences, predictable cycles, or become a divided road based on gender.

Family arrangements, intimate relationships, children, friendships, work roles, educational pursuits, and retirement can no longer be tied to social clocks, specific age patterns, or divisive gender roles. Adult life is a process of adapting to change that unfolds within individuals as a result of ongoing interaction with people, contexts, and other aspects of their environment—their life-tie—which, in turn affect self-esteem and identity development. This book has attempted to describe how adult women and men from this study sometimes created anew, rearranged, repeated, and often reinvented their life themes and self-views within the context of family, work, education, intimate relationships, children, friends, and mentors. Life-tie themes persist, evolve, contract, expand, and are renewed from childhood throughout adulthood—often with no particular pattern or sequence.

Most past research has failed to consider the changing nature of the experience of life itself. Boxing life experience and adult development into sequential and divisive categories may be more a reflection of the social sciences' necessity for predictable order and need for an easy and concrete way to catalogue adult experience than of reality. However, changes in life contexts, the presence idiosyncratic meanings, extended longevity, and changing relationships across the adult life course are significance of observable behavior. We need another way of interpreting and organizing development, life events and their impact on identity development and self-esteem.

The findings from the NCWRR study were organized around the principles of the life-tie theme. Major elements of these principles, which attempt to demonstrate a less exclusive and more inclusive way of understanding adult development are:

- The life-tie principle can embrace gender similarities as well as account for differences. Similarities between men and women seem to be that both genders are affected by the same life-tie. Many differences among women and men may occur within the life-tie due to context, timing, and personal meaning.

- The life-tie principle is a paradigm of fluid adult development. Growth and change during adulthood depend on a process of contraction and expansion within the life-tie framework. This movement may occur at any time or within any context during the life course.

- Finally, positive feelings of self-worth and identity development were found to occur in individuals in this study when the life-tie ceased to be an influence (control) and began to be a resource for those individuals throughout adulthood. However, low self-esteem could be the result when the life-tie interaction remained a control and an undue influence in a person's life.

- Both genders settled and resettled life-tie issues. To understand the way these individuals created meaning in their lives, it was necessary to understand the interaction between them and their life-tie. The study found that the life-tie interaction sometimes supported and encouraged development and self-esteem; and at other times hindered or slowed individual growth and self-esteem.

The core of this framework acted as a large "umbrella" that was able to house and shelter the experiences, development and self-definition of both women and men. The life-tie framework and findings did not rely on sequencing of events, chronological age, or stages. This framework's essence lies in its capacity to enlighten a process of personal meaning-making through the use of the universal life-tie experience that provides the context for self-esteem and identity development in both genders.

HIGHLIGHTS OF FINDINGS
FROM THE NCWRR STUDY

- The cornerstone for self-worth for both women and men is achievement/work-related activities.
- Education is a critical component of self-esteem for both women and men.
- Among women, intimate relationships (spouses, partners and marriage) are much less important than work as a source of positive self-worth. This is not to say that relationships are not valued, and do not bring joy, or do not complement positive self-esteem. However, relationships do not seem to be a primary source of self-esteem and self-definition.
- Among men studied, personal relationships, although not the primary source of self-esteem, are much more important than previously believed.
- Among both women and men studied, parenting and self-selected friendships are important to feelings of self-worth. The ability to raise and nurture children is strong with both genders. However, the family workload still rests primarily with women. Friendship, by their very nature, allow for reflected appraisal and can be so structured that one can choose to expand or withdraw from the relationship. Mentoring is just as important to women as for men as a source of encouragement and direction.
- The influence of one's own parents (both positive and negative) continues to have an impact on people well into adulthood. Data reveal that women seem more susceptible to this lasting parental influence.

This study found that women's and men's self-esteem and identity development changed in adulthood as a result of how they framed their self-views within the context of their life-tie connections. A sense of self did not seem to be influenced by factors such as whether they were male or female, aged thirty or seventy, or whether they were in early adulthood or their middle years. Women and men did not travel down totally different roads nor did they take the same road in life; rather they crisscrossed, backtracked, circled, stopped, and then started again along their life paths, forging very idiosyncratic courses that provided richness of experience, personal growth, and self-knowledge, along with loss, sorrow, and setbacks. Each man and woman was an interpreter of his or her own experience. Individual identity and self-esteem were related to the patterns of symbolic and idiosyncratic meaning that characterized a woman's or man's unique interpretation of their life-tie experiences.

It is hoped that this book presents a new way to interpret, inform, and organize the way individuals think, evaluate, and describe the development of adult women and men. If women and men can develop and grow and gain self-esteem as individuals throughout their adult years without being stereotyped, categorized, and evaluated on the basis of gender or age, then the understanding of human adult development will represent a more humanistic and inclusive way of describing adulthood now and in the future.

Afterword

As authors of *Gender, Identity, and Self-Esteem* we have come to realize that, like many of the survey respondents, we have woven life-tie experiences into the fabric of our present life, identity, and self-esteem—and in particular the life of this study. Our personal stories are retold so that the reader understands the impetus of this book.

DR. ANDERSON'S STORY

I had a personal experience that put me on a collision course very early with traditional linear age-stage developmental theory, as well as theories that divide women and men. Of course, at the age of twenty-two I knew nothing about developmental theory, social clocks, on-time normative events, theories surrounding the predictable sequencing of life events, theories that address women and men's lives differently. However, my becoming a mother at the age of twenty-two, and then becoming a widow at that same age within a period of six weeks made my social clock and predictable life story stop. The clock got thrown out and the story was re-edited and revised many times during my adult life.

I found myself in a developmental limbo. I came home from California, accompanied by my parents, who had flown West to be with me during this critical, dual life-transition phase. I found myself not only a new mother and a new widow, but also a daughter again. I had virtually no moorings, no familiar places in my life: This was not supposed to have happened. I was supposed to have left home, which I did; embark on a new career life, which I did; then marry, have kids, have fond memories, grow old and then— much later on—perhaps become a widow. Someone rewrote my script, without giving me any cues as to how to deal with the changes.

My identity and self-esteem were at best confused, at worst nonexistent. Friends and family were well-meaning, but somehow they didn't have the script, either, as to the best way to behave and act toward a twenty-two-year-old woman who had just become a widow, as well as a new mother. There was nothing predictable, linear, or sequential about these events. When people don't know how to behave in a given situation, they sometimes ignore or avoid it, and often pretend that what has happened did not happen. I frequently found this to be the case. They might know how to console their grandmother if she became widowed, but no one knew how to approach me and my situation. Other people's avoidance of the situation and their pretending nothing was wrong only made me feel as though I were the one at fault.

It didn't help when I had to apply for survivor's benefits at the Social Security office and was surrounded by old people. I felt like I had entered a time-warp. This was a place I wasn't supposed to have to enter for many years. I sat next to widows who had spent a lifetime with their partners, women who had shared memories, both good and bad, that spanned a lifetime, women who had children and grandchildren, and who had experienced many other life events. This was a club that I had joined prematurely, and I was not really welcome. I made people feel uncomfortable, for I had arrived at this destination long ahead of schedule.

Comfort and understanding came to me by way of seeing the pain and confusion of another person who was going through a similar life event. This was not a widow, divorcee, or other female who had suffered the loss of a partner or loved one; rather it was a Vietnam vet who had also arrived at a destination before it should have been his turn to do so. Alex and I had played together as children during the summers when he visited his grandparents. We lost touch after high school: I went away to New York; he went farther away—to Vietnam.

When he later found out that I had lost my husband, he came by to visit. He was the first visitor I had who understood what I was going through. He, too, was experiencing untimely death and loss. Twenty-three-year-old males were supposed to be realizing dreams of the future and making long-term commitments, not facing the ends of their lives. He was mourning the loss of many new and good friendships, while I was mourning the loss of a young relationship. We were both angry at being deprived of many years of memories that come with long-term relationships and friendships.

He felt as out of place in the world as I did, for this was not the way young women and men were supposed to begin adulthood. Our self-esteem and identity had been shaken due to life events that were unexpected and out of developmental sequence. However, both of us went on with our lives, eventually reworking and weaving the loss related to those life-tie into the present.

I had also crossed the gender bridge very early in life, realizing that women and men do share many common experiences, feelings, and interpretations about events that happen to them. This realization became further clarified when I began work on the NCWRR study. Through the questionnaires, open-ended questions, and in particular the personal interviews, I began to see how age, gender, and linear stages of development are not crucially important to development, to identity development and self-esteem. Most of the basic concepts, such as age patterns and gender, that have been used to measure identity and self-esteem seem to be losing relevance and can even be detrimental to positive development in adulthood.

DR. HAYES' STORY

My interest in the field of gerontology began when I started working as an orderly in a nursing home at the age of sixteen. After completing my graduate studies, I was committed to starting a

counseling program for older adults in Southern California entitled Psychological Alternative Counseling for Elders (PACE). At the
age of twenty-four, after I had formed a nonprofit organization to
provide in-home counseling services, I quickly learned that my
youthful appearance was a severe detriment to fulfilling my career
dreams. Many of my colleagues in the field, and older adults themselves, often disregarded my professional expertise and commitment to the field because of my age. After much reflection, I realized that my age had become a serious problem and that if I wanted to stay in the field of my choice I would have to look older. For
this reason, I grew a beard in the hope that this would camouflage
the youthfulness of my appearance.

The theme of not fitting in followed me as I moved into acade-
mia. As a result of my experiences with PACE working with many
older women who sought support due to impoverishment, widowhood, divorce, and late-life chronic health problems, I wanted to
develop a program that would alert younger and midlife women to
the importance of pre-retirement planning. In 1986, I developed
Pre-Retirement Education Planning for Women (PREP), a national preretirement planning program that was funded by the
Administration on Aging. At the completion of PREP's two-year
grant, I wanted to continue to maintain the program's work and
establish a national nonprofit organization dedicated to research,
education, and training on the financial, social, and emotional
needs of midlife women. Thus, in 1988, I established the first academic research center in the country targeting midlife women, entitled the National Center for Women and Retirement Research
(NCWRR).

My experiences of being a male running a national organization
for women was a primary impetus for assisting in the work of this
research study. In the last ten years, I have arrived at the painful
realization that gender plays a critical role in how one is perceived,
respected, and evaluated. Although NCWRR has completed a variety of ground-breaking studies on midlife women and has received
tremendous media recognition for its work, it has come with a
price. Since PREP's and NCWRR's inception, I have received many
letters, telephone calls, and personal communications to the effect
that a man is not adequately suited to be an advocate for the needs
of women . . . and is particularly not in a position to direct a

woman's organization! Due to my gender alone, my motives have been questioned and the Center's research has been disregarded or ignored by a variety of national, state, and local organizations and within certain quarters of the academic community. The "Divorce Over Forty" project that resulted in the book *Our Turn: Women Who Triumph in the Face of Divorce* was a particularly challenging experience in that certain media outlets and organizations questioned the value of the work because a man was the principal author.

The above has made me realize that society has a tendency to like neat-fitting boxes. Men are not "supposed" to run organizations for women, understand their needs, or advocate for them. From a positive perspective, these experiences gave me a fresh insight into gender discrimination and the issues that women have faced for hundreds of years. In any speech I give these days on my work I often state, "The day that a man can advocate for a woman, and a woman can advocate for a man is the day when we have reached true gender equality in the United States." In addition, age cannot be used as a benchmark to evaluate whether an individual can understand, negotiate, or address individuals in other life phases or transitions.

The Gender, Identity, and Self-Esteem Study has validated our need to foster a "gender bridge" between the sexes. What is needed is to turn the divisiveness that marked the sexual wars of the eighties and create bridges of understanding between the sexes in the nineties. The results of our study, chronicled in this book, indicate that men and women have much in common and that, through communication and mutual understanding, the gulf that supposedly separates men and women can be bridged.

Long Island University: The National Center for Women and Retirement Research Self-Esteem Survey

Please CIRCLE the box in front of the answer that best describes your feelings. Some questions may be answered with more than one response.

Part I The First Part of the survey is intended to provide some general factual information about your present status

1. Your approximate age:
[1] 13–15; [2] 16–19; [3] 20–25; [4] 26–30; [5] 31–35; [6] 36–45; [7] 46–55; [8] over 56.

2. Are you:
[1]Never married; [2] divorced; [3] separated; [4] married; [5] widowed.

3. If divorced, separated, or widowed, for how many years:
[1] Less than 1 year; [2] 1 or 2 years; [3] 3–5 years; [4] or more years.

4. Approximate income of your entire household last year:
[1] under $10,000; [2] $10,000–$14,999; [3] $15,000–19,999;
[4]$20,000–$24,999; [5] $25,000–$34,999; [6] $35,000–$49,999;
[7] $50,000–$74,999; [8] above $75,000.

5. Your personal income last year:
[1] none; [2] under $10,000; [3] $10,000–$14,999; [4] $15,000–$19,999;
[5] $20,000–$24,999; [6] $25,000–$34,999; [7] $35,000–$49,999;
[8] $50,000–$74,999; [9] above $75,000.

6. Do you consider yourself financially independent at present?
[1] Yes; [2] No.

7. Racial/ethnic background:
[1] White; [2] Afro-American; [3] Native American; [4] Hispanic; [5] Asian;
[6] Other.

8. Sex: [1] Female; [2] Male.

9. Sexual preference:
[1] heterosexual; [2] homosexual/lesbian; [3] bisexual; [4] celibate.

**Part II The second part of this survey deals with events and activities in
your life, relationships you have formed with other people, and how these
affect your view of yourself. Some of these questions relate to the present
time. Others ask you to describe past events.**

Parents, brothers and sisters. (You may CIRCLE more than one box, if applicable.)

10. Is your mother now living? If not, how old were you when she died?
[1] My mother is living.
My mother died when I was: [2] younger than 5; [3] 5–12 years old; [4] 13–15
years old; [5] 16–19 years old; [6] 20–25 years old; [7] 26–35 years old; [8] 36–45
years old; [9] 46–55 years old; [10] over 55.

11. Is your father now living? If not, how old were you when he died?
[1] My father is living.
My father died when I was: [2] younger than 5; [3] 5–12 years old; [4] 13–15
years old; [5] 16–19 years old; [6] 20–25 years old; [7] 26–35 years old; [8] 36–45
years old; [9] 46–55 years old; [10] over 55.

12. Were your parents divorced? If so, how old were you at the time of the divorce?
[1] My parents were never divorced.
My parents were divorced when I was: [2] younger than 5; [3] 5–12 years old;
[4] 13–15 years old; [5] 16–19 years old; [6] 20–25 years old; [7] 26–35 years old;
[8] 36–45 years old.

13. Do you have brothers or sisters?
[1] I am an only child; [2] I have (had) one or more older brother; [3] I have
(had) one or more older sister; [4] I have (had) one or more younger brother;
[5] I have (had) one or more younger sister.

14. At what age did you *first* leave home?

[1] 15–19 years old; [2] 20–25 years old; [3] 26–30 years old; [4] 31–35 years old;

[5] I continue to live at home.

15. At what age did your mother cease to be a strong influence on your life?

[1] I never felt my mother was a strong influence on my life; [2] 13–15 years old;

[3] 16–19 years old; [4] 20–25 years old; [5] 26–30 years old; [6] 31–35 years old;

[7] My mother continues to be a strong influence on my life.

16. At what age did your father cease to a strong influence on your life?

[1] I never felt my father was a strong influence on my life; [2] 13–15 years old;

[3] 16–19 years old; [4] 20–25 years old; [5] 26–30 years old; [6] 31–35 years old;

[7] My father continues to be a strong influence on my life.

17. At what ages did you have your most difficult relationship with your mother?

[1] 5–12 years old; [2] 13–15 years old; [3] 16–19 years old; [4] 20–25 years old;

[5] 26–30 years old; [6] 31–35 years old; [7] 36–45 years old; [8] 46–55 years old;

[9] old than 56.

18. At what ages did you have your most difficult relationship with your father?

[1] 5–12 years old; [2] 13–15 years old; [3] 16–19 years old; [4] 20–25 years old;

[5] 26–30 years old; [6] 31–35 years old; [7] 36–45 years old; [8] 46–55 years old;

[9] old than 56.

Here is a series of statements describing various feelings that people have about their relationship with parents, brothers and sisters. Some of these may apply to you, some of them will not. Read each statement. Then CIRCLE *one* box to indicated whether you, yourself, feel this way about your parents and their influence.

19. When I was growing up I felt my mother loved a brother or sister more than she loved me.

[1] Strongly agree; [2] Somewhat agree; [3] Not sure; [4] Somewhat disagree;

[5] Strongly disagree.

20. When I was growing up I felt my father loved a brother or sister more than he loved me.

[1] Strongly agree; [2] Somewhat agree; [3] Not sure; [4] Somewhat disagree;

[5] Strongly disagree.

21. I felt my loved me more for what I accomplished than for who I was.

[1] Strongly agree; [2] Somewhat agree; [3] Not sure; [4] Somewhat disagree;

[5] Strongly disagree.

22. I felt my father loved me more for what I accomplished than for who I was.
[1] Strongly agree; [2] Somewhat agree; [3] Not sure; [4] Somewhat disagree;
[5] Strongly disagree.

23. When I was a child, my mother often made me feel guilty.
[1] Strongly agree; [2] Somewhat agree; [3] Not sure; [4] Somewhat disagree;
[5] Strongly disagree.

24. When I was a child, my father often made me feel guilty.
[1] Strongly agree; [2] Somewhat agree; [3] Not sure; [4] Somewhat disagree;
[5] Strongly disagree.

25. My parents encouraged my brother's or sister's goals, not mine.
[1] Strongly agree; [2] Somewhat agree; [3] Not sure; [4] Somewhat disagree;
[5] Strongly disagree.

26. My mother often made me feel insignificant.
[1] Strongly agree; [2] Somewhat agree; [3] Not sure; [4] Somewhat disagree;
[5] Strongly disagree.

27. My father often made me feel insignificant.
[1] Strongly agree; [2] Somewhat agree; [3] Not sure; [4] Somewhat disagree;
[5] Strongly disagree.

28. My mother considered me rebellious.
[1] Strongly agree; [2] Somewhat agree; [3] Not sure; [4] Somewhat disagree;
[5] Strongly disagree.

29. My father considered me rebellious.
[1] Strongly agree; [2] Somewhat agree; [3] Not sure; [4] Somewhat disagree;
[5] Strongly disagree.

30. I have grown closer to my parents as I got older.
[1] Strongly agree; [2] Somewhat agree; [3] Not sure; [4] Somewhat disagree;
[5] Strongly disagree.

31. My mother contributed to my feelings of:
[1] High self-esteem; [2] Moderate self-esteem; [3] Not sure; [4] Low self-esteem.

32. My father contributed to my feelings of:
[1] High self-esteem; [2] Moderate self-esteem; [3] Not sure; [4] Low self-esteem.

33. Looking back, during my childhood and teen years, I feel that my mother's self-esteem was very high.
[1] Strongly agree; [2] Somewhat agree; [3] Not sure; [4] Somewhat disagree;
[5] Strongly disagree.

34. Looking back, during my childhood and teen years, I feel that my father's self-esteem was very high.
[1] Strongly agree; [2] Somewhat agree; [3] Not sure; [4] Somewhat disagree;
[5] Strongly disagree.

35. I feel that my parent's self-esteem influenced my own feeling of self-worth.
[1] Strongly agree; [2] Somewhat agree; [3] Not sure; [4] Somewhat disagree;
[5] Strongly disagree.

Education. (You may CIRCLE more than one box, if applicable)

36. Please indicate the highest education level you completed:
[1] Did not complete high school; [2] high school graduate; [3] technical/vocational; [4] some college; [5] college graduate; [6] post college.

37. Did you ever return to school or college as a adult? If so, how old were you when you returned?
[1] No, my studies were never interrupted.
I returned to school when I was: [2] 20–25 years old; [3] 26–30 years old;
[4] 31–35 years old; [5] 36–45 years old; [6] 46–55 years old; [7] older than 56.

38. What did you like most about school or college?
[1] The chance to get away from home; [2] the chance to meet new people;
[3] Sports; [4] Extracurricular activities other than sports; [5] The advantages it gave me in getting a job; [6] New learning experience.

39. Did you ever feel that teachers discriminated against you or expected less of you because of some factor you could not help? If so, what? (You may check more than one box.)
[1] I never felt discriminated against.
I felt teachers discriminated against me or expected less of me because of:
[2] my race; [3] my sex; [4] my religion; [5] my nationality; [6] difficulties with English; [7] a physical or emotional handicap; [8] family economic or cultural background; [9] a physical characteristic, such as weight or appearance;
[10] Other—please identify _____.

40. At what ages did you have your most positive educational experience?
[1] younger than 5; [2] 5–12 years old; [3] 13–15 years old; [4] 16–19 years old;
[5] 20–25 years old; [6] 26–30 years old; [7] 31–35 years old; [8] 36–45 years old;
[9] 46–55 years old; [10] older than 56.

41. At what ages did you have your most negative educational experience?
[1] younger than 5; [2] 5–12 years old; [3] 13–15 years old; [4] 16–19 years old;
[5] 20–25 years old; [6] 26–30 years old; [7] 31–35 years old; [8] 36–45 years old;
[9] 46–55 years old; [10] older than 56.

Here is a series of statements describing various feelings that people have about their educational experience. Some of these may apply to you. Probably many of them will not. Read each statement. Then CIRCLE *one* box to indicate whether you feel this way about your education and its influence.

42. Education has contributed to my feelings of:
[1] High self-esteem; [2] Moderate self-esteem; [3] Not sure; [4] Low self-esteem.

43. I always felt that other students were smarter than I was.
[1] Strongly agree; [2] Somewhat agree; [3] Not sure; [4] Somewhat disagree;
[5] Strongly disagree.

44. During high school I would rather have been known as popular than as being smart.
[1] Strongly agree; [2] Somewhat agree; [3] Not sure, [4] Somewhat disagree;
[5] Strongly disagree.

45. A teacher or teachers I had at school strongly supported my goals in life and helped me to achieve them.
[1] Strongly agree; [2] Somewhat agree; [3] Not sure; [4] Somewhat disagree;
[5] Strongly disagree.

Employment (You may CIRCLE more than one response, if applicable)

46. During your entire life, how many years have you worked outside the home:
[1] Never; [2] Less than 5; [3] 5–10; [4] 10–20; [5] More than 20.

47. Present employment:
[1] Full-time; [2] Part-time; [3] Seeking work; [4] Unable to find work;
[5] Disabled; [6] Retired; [7] None of the above.

48. How old were you when you got your *first* full-time job? (over 35 hrs.)
[1] 13–15 years old; [2] 16–19 years old; [3] 20–25 years old; [4] 26–30 years old;
[5] 31–35 years old; [6] 36–45 years old; [7] 46–55 years old; [8] older than 56.

49. Have you ever been fired or laid off from a job?
[1] I have never been fired; [2] I have never been laid off.[3] Poor performance;
[4] Problems with alcohol or drugs; [5] Problems at home; [6] A boss or co-workers who disliked me; [7] The company closed down or relocated; [8] Inability to get along with co-workers.

50. What do you like most about your job?
[1] The work itself; [2] The pay and other benefits; [3] The fact that I have control over events and the people I work with; [4] The status that goes along with

the position; [5] The opportunity to use my mind creatively; [6] The people I work with; [7] There really isn't much about my job that I like.

51. Have you ever been the victim of job discrimination in hiring or promotion? If so, what was the discrimination based on?
[1] I was never the victim of job discrimination. I was the victim of job discrimination based on [2] race; [3] sex; [4] nationality; [5] religion; [6] age; [7] my sexual preference; [8] marital status; [9] physical or mental handicap; [10] Other—please identify _____.

52. If you have been the victim of job discrimination, what was your reaction?
[1] I was never the victim of job discrimination: [2] I made no complaint and continued to work for the same employer; [3] I complained within the company but continued to work; [4] I complained within the company and was fired or disciplined; [5] I complained outside the company (to a union or government agency) but continued to work; [6] I complained outside the company (to a union or government agency) and was fired or disciplined; [7] I resigned or sought work elsewhere.

53. At what age did you have your most positive experience in working?
[1] I never worked outside the home; [2] 16–19 years old; [3] 20–25 years old; [4] 26–30 years old; [5] 31–35 years old; [6] 36–45 years old; [7] 46–55 years old; [8] older than 56; [9] Working has been positive throughout my life; [10] I never had a positive work experience.

Here is a series of statements describing various feelings that people have about their work experience. Some of these may apply to you. Probably many of them will not. Read each statement. Then CIRCLE *one* box to indicated whether you feel this way about your job and its influence on you.

54. My work has given me a lot of financial rewards.
[1] Strongly agree; [2] Somewhat agree; [3] Not sure; [4] Somewhat disagree; [5] Strongly disagree.

55. My work/career has contributed to my feelings of:
[1] High self-esteem; [2] Moderate self-esteem; [3] Not sure; [4] Low self-esteem.

56. Success in the work world requires taking many risks.
[1] Strongly agree; [2] Somewhat agree; [3] Not sure; [4] Somewhat disagree; [5] Strongly disagree.

Married or Unmarried Partners (You may CIRCLE more than one box, if applicable)

57. How many times have you been married?

[1] never; [2] once; [3] twice; [4] three times; [5] more than three times.

58. How old were you when you married for the first time or had your first long-term relationship?

[1] 16–19 years old; [2] 20–25 years old; [3] 26–30 years old; [4] 31–35 years old; [5] 36–45 years old; [6] 46–55 years old; [7] older than 56.

59. How did your first marriage or long-term relationship end?

[1] I am still married to my original partner or in the same relationship; [2] Death of my spouse or partner; [3] My spouse or partner left me or divorced me; [4] I divorced or left my spouse or partner.

60. Have you been financially independent of your spouse or partner? Include not only wages buy also savings, inheritances, benefits and the like. If so, at what ages or periods of your life?

[1] I have never been financially independent; [2] 16–19 years old; [3] 20–25 years old; [4] 26–30 years old; [5] 31–35 years old; [6] 36–45 years old; [7] 46–55 years old; [8] older than 56; [9] I have always been independent.

61. Do you earn more than your spouse or partner?

[1] I earn more; [2] My spouse earns more; [3] We earn the same amount; [4] I have no earnings; [5] My spouse or partner has no earnings; [6] Neither of us has earnings.

Please consider the following statements about your spouse or other person with whom you have had the *longest* relationship. Some of these may apply to you; many of them will not. Read each statement. Then CIRCLE a box to indicate whether you, yourself, feel this way about your spouse or partner and his or her influence on your life.

62. My partner/spouse contributed to my feelings of:

[1] High self-esteem; [2] Moderate self-esteem; [3] Not sure; [4] Low self-esteem.

63. Marriage/living together contributed to my feelings of:

[1] High self-esteem; [2] Moderate self-esteem; [3] Not sure; [4] Low self-esteem.

64. Many of the relationships I have formed over the years have proved to be destructive.

[1] Strongly agree; [2] Somewhat agree; [3] Not sure; [4] Somewhat disagree; [5] Strongly disagree.

65. Being economically dependent on my spouse or partner would make or has made me doubt my self-worth.

[1] Strongly agree; [2] Somewhat agree; [3] Not sure; [4] Somewhat disagree;
[5] Strongly disagree.

Children

Please answer the following questions about your children and your relationship with them. If you have no children, please answer *only the first question* **and then** *skip the rest of the questions in this section.*

66. How many children have you had?
[1] none; [2] one; [3] two; [4] three; [5] four; [6] five; [7] six; [8] more than six.

67. If you are a woman, have you ever had an abortion? If so, how old were you when this occurred? (You may CIRCLE more than one box.)
[1] I never had an abortion. I had an abortion when I was: [2] 13–15; [3] 16–19; [4] 20–25; [5] 26–30; [6] 31–35; [7] 36–45.

68. How old were *you* when you had your most satisfying relationship with your children?
[1] 20–25 years old; [2] 26–30 years old; [3] 31–35 years old; [4] 36–45 years old;
[5] 46–55 years old; [6] older than 56; [7] my relationship with my children has been satisfying regardless of age.

Here is a series of statements describing various feelings that people have about their experience as parents. Some of these may apply to you, many of them will not. Read each statement. Then CIRCLE *one* **box to indicate whether you, yourself, feel this way about a parent, and its influence on you.**

69. Being a parent contributed to my feelings of:
[1] High self-esteem; [2] Moderate self-esteem; [3] Not sure; [4] Low self-esteem.

70. My relationship with my children has improved as they have grown older and more independent.
[1] Strongly agree; [2] Somewhat agree; [3] Not sure; [4] Somewhat disagree;
[5] Strongly disagree.

71. Being a parent made it impossible for me to pursue the career I wanted.

[1] Strongly agree; [2] Somewhat agree; [3] Not sure; [4] Somewhat disagree;
[5] Strongly disagree.

72. Being a parent was extremely difficult.
[1] Strongly agree; [2] Somewhat agree; [3] Not sure; [4] Somewhat disagree;
[5] Strongly disagree.

73. Although my spouse or partner believes that we equally share in the responsibility of child-rearing, I know this is not accurate.
[1] Strongly agree; [2] Somewhat agree; [3] Not sure; [4] Somewhat disagree;
[5] Strongly disagree.

Friendships/Relationships

Please answer the following questions about the friendships and relationships you have formed over the years with people outside your immediate family. (You may CIRCLE more than one box, if applicable.)

74. Do you now belong or have you recently belonged to any of the following groups or organizations? (Please CIRCLE as many as apply.)
[1] Veterans organization; [2] Sports team, bowling league, etc., [3] Hobby club or group; [4] Political committee, public interest group; [5] Church group or campaign; [6] Country club or athletic club; [7] Parents group; [8] Bridge, chess or card club; [9] Fraternal order (Masons, K of C, etc.); [10] Civic organization that meets regularly; [11] Business organization that meets regularly; [12] Alcoholics Anonymous or drug rehabilitation group.

75. Most of my friends are:
[1] People of the same sex; [2] People of the opposite sex; [3] Couples.

76. Check the statement that best describes your friendships.
[1] I have difficulty making friends; [2] I have a few very close friends; [3] There are a lot of people I am friendly with but few I am really close to; [4] I have many close friends.

77. At what ages were close friendships most important to you?
[1] Close friendships have never been particularly important to me; [2] 13–15 years old; [3] 16–19 years old; [4] 20–25 years old; [5] 26–30 years old;
[6] 31–35 years old; [7] 36–45 years old; [8] 46–55 years old; [9] over 56;
[10] Close friendships have always been important to me.

A "Mentor" is a trusted friend, counselor, teacher or guardian—someone who offers guidance and encouragement to another person's growth and development. Please answer the following questions about people who may have been a "Mentor" to you.

78. Did you ever have a person who acted as a Mentor to you? If so, how old were you when that person had the greatest positive effect on your life?

[1] 5–12 years old; [2] 13–15 years old; [3] 16–19 years old; [4] 20–25 years old; [5] 26–30 years old; [6] 31–35 years old; [7] 36–45 years old; [8] 46–55 years old; [9] over 56; [10] Close friendships have always been important to me.

79. Was that person male or female?

[1] I had no Mentor; [2] Male; [3] Female.

80. In what areas did your Mentor encourage and aid in your personal growth?

[1] I had no Mentor; [2] Education; [3] Spirituality; [4] Employment; [5] Sexuality; [6] Creative expression; [7] Emotional development; [8] Personal Empowerment; [9] Other—please identify _____ .

81. My Mentor greatly influenced the direction of my life.

[1] Strongly agree; [2] Somewhat agree; [3] Not sure; [4] Somewhat disagree; [5] Strongly disagree; [6] I had no Mentor.

Here is a series of statements describing various feelings that people have about their friendships. Some of these may apply to you. Probably many of them will not. Read each statement. Then CIRCLE *one* box to indicate whether you, yourself, feel this way about the influence of friendships on your life.

82. I often feel inadequate next to my friends.

[1] Strongly agree; [2] Somewhat agree; [3] Not sure; [4] Somewhat disagree; [5] Strongly disagree.

83. I often feel extreme loneliness.

[1] Strongly agree; [2] Somewhat agree; [3] Not sure; [4] Somewhat disagree; [5] Strongly disagree.

84. Having good friends has contributed to my feelings of:

[1] High self-esteem; [2] Moderate self-esteem; [3] Not sure; [4] Low self-esteem.

85. Many of the friendships that I formed have proved to be destructive.

[1] Strongly agree; [2] Somewhat agree; [3] Not sure; [4] Somewhat disagree; [5] Strongly disagree.

Financial (You may CIRCLE more than one box, if applicable)

86. During what periods of your life did you feel financially secure?
[1] I have never felt secure; [2] 5–12 years old; [3] 13–15 years old; [4] 16–19
years old; [5] 20–25 years old; [6] 26–30 years old; [7] 31–35 years old;
[8] 36–45 years old; [9] 46–55 years old; [10] older than 56.

87. The main source of my financial security has been money:
[1] That I earned; [2] That I inherited; [3] Provided by my parents; [4]
Provided by my spouse or partner.

88. During what periods of your life did you feel financially insecure or suffer
financial hardship?
[1] 5–12 years old; [2] 13–15 years old; [3] 16–19 years old; [4] 20–25 years old;
[5] 26–30 years old; [6] 31–35 years old; [7] 36–45 years old; [8] 46–55 years
old; [9] older than 56; [10] Have always been secure.

89. Money has contributed to my feelings of: (Circle only *one* box)
[1] High self-esteem; [2] Moderate self-esteem; [3] Not sure; [4] Low self-esteem.

90. I am happiest when I:
[1] Earn money; [2] Save/invest money; [3] Spend money; [4] Money doesn't
mean that much to me.

Physical/Emotional Abuse and Health (You may CIRCLE more than one box, if
applicable)

91. Have you ever been sexually abused? If so, by whom?
[1] I was never sexually abused.
I was sexually abused by: [2] a parent, step-parent or other older family member;
[3] a brother or sister; [4] a teacher, principal or someone else in authority at
school; [5] a spouse or partner in an established relationship; [6] a boss or
someone in authority at work; [7] a date or acquaintance; [8] a stranger.

92. How old were you when the sexual abuse occurred?
[1] I was never sexually abused; [2] younger than 5; [3] 5–12 years old;
[4] 13–15 years old; [5] 16–19 years old; [6] 20–25 years old; [7] 26–30 years
old; [8] 31–35 years old; [9] 36–45 years old; [10] 46–55 years old; [11] older
than 56.

93. How long did the sexual abuse continue?
[1] I was never sexually abused; [2] There was a single instance; [3] It continued
for weeks; [4] It continued for months; [5] It continued for years.

94. Have you ever been physically abused? If so, by whom?
[1] I was never physically abused.

I was physically abused by: [2] a parent, step-parent or other older family member; [3] a brother or sister; [4] a teacher, principal or someone else in authority at school; [5] a spouse or partner in an established relationship; [6] a boss or someone in authority at work; [7] a date or acquaintance; [8] a stranger.

95. How old were you when the physical abuse occurred?
[1] I was never physically abused; [2] younger than 5; [3] 5–12 years old; [4] 13–15 years old; [5] 16–19 years old; [6] 20–25 years old; [7] 26–30 years old; [8] 31–35 years old; [9] 36–45 years old; [10] 46–55 years old; [11] older than 56.

96. How long did the physical abuse continue?
[1] I was never physically abused; [2] There was a single instance; [3] It continued for weeks; [4] It continued for months; [5] It continued for years.

97. Have you ever been emotionally abused? If so, by whom?
[1] I was never emotionally abused.
I was emotionally abused by: [2] a parent, step-parent or other older family member; [3] a brother or sister; [4] a teacher, principal or someone else in authority at school; [5] a spouse or partner in an established relationship; [6] a boss or someone in authority at work; [7] a date or acquaintance; [8] a stranger.

98. How old were you when the emotional abuse occurred?
[1] I was never emotionally abused; [2] younger than 5; [3] 5–12 years old; [4] 13–15 years old; [5] 16–19 years old; [6] 20–25 years old; [7] 26–30 years old; [8] 31–35 years old; [9] 36–45 years old; [10] 46–55 years old; [11] older than 56.

99. How long did the emotional abuse continued?
[1] I was never emotionally abused; [2] There was a single instance; [3] It continued for weeks; [4] It continued for months; [5] It continued for years.

100. Have you ever tried to kill yourself or thought seriously about it? If so, how old were you when this occurred? (You may CIRCLE more than one box.)
[1] I never tried to kill myself and never thought seriously of doing so.
I tried to kill myself or thought seriously of killing myself when I was: [2] 13–15 years old; [3] 16–19 years old; [4] 20–25 years old; [5] 26–30 years old; [6] 31–35 years old; [7] 36–45 years old; [8] 46–55 years old; [9] older than 56.

101. Have you ever been seriously involved with drugs or alcohol or sought treatment for drug or alcohol dependence? If so, how old were you when this occurred? (You may CIRCLE more than one box.)
[1] I've never been seriously involved with drugs or alcohol, and I never sought treatment for drug or alcohol dependence.

I was seriously involved with drugs or alcohol when I was: [2] 13–15 years old; [3] 16–19 years old; [4] 20–25 years old; [5] 26–30 years old; [6] 31–35 years old; [7] 36–45 years old; [8] 46–55 years old; [9] older than 56.

102. Have you ever had a serious injury, illness or physical disability that has required long-term treatment? If so, how old were you when this occurred? (You may CIRCLE more than one box.)
[1] I have never had a serious injury, illness or physical disability that has required long-term treatment. I had a serious injury, illness or physical disability that has required long-term treatment when I was: [2] 5–12 years old; [3] 13–15 years old; [4] 16–19 years old; [5] 20–25 years old; [6] 26–30 years old; [7] 31–35 years old; [8] 36–45 years old; [9] 46–55 years old; [10] older than 56; [11] I have had a lifelong illness or physical disability.

103. Have you ever had professional counseling? If so, how old were you when this occurred?
[1] I never had professional counseling. I had professional counseling when I was: [2] 5–12 years old; [3] 13–15 years old; [4] 16–19 years old; [5] 20–25 years old; [6] 26–30 years old; [7] 31–35 years old; [8] 36–45 years old; [9] 46–55 years old; [10] older than 56; [11] Professional counseling was not helpful; [12] Professional counseling was helpful.

104. Have you ever been diagnosed as having clinical depression? If so, how old were you when this occurred? (You may CIRCLE more than one box.)
[1] I have never been diagnosed as having clinical depression. I was diagnosed as having clinical depression when I was: [2] 5–12 years old; [3] 13–15 years old; [4] 16–19 years old; [5] 20–25 years old; [6] 26–30 years old; [7] 31–35 years old; [8] 36–45 years old; [9] 46–55 years old; [10] older than 56.

Sexuality/Body Image

105. During what periods of your life did you feel you were most physically attractive? (You may CIRCLE more than one box.)
[1] I never felt physically attractive. [2] I always felt physically attractive. I felt most physically attractive when I was: [3] 5–12 years old; [4] 13–15 years old; [5] 16–19 years old; [6] 20–25 years old; [7] 26–30 years old; [8] 31–35 years old; [9] 36–45 years old; [10] 46–55 years old; [11] older than 56.

106. During what period of your life did you feel you were most physically unattractive? (You may CIRCLE more than one box.)
[1] I never felt physically unattractive; [2] I was felt physically unattractive. I felt most physically unattractive when I was: [3] 13–15 years old; [4] 16–19 years old; [5] 20–25 years old; [6] 26–30 years old; [7] 31–35 years old; [8] 36–45 years old; [9] 46–55 years old; [10] older than 56.

107. How old were you when you had your *first* sexual experience?

[1] I have never been sexually active.

My first sexual experience happened when I was: [2] 13–15 years old; [3] 16–19 years old; [4] 20–25 years old; [5] 26–30 years old; [6] 31–35 years old; [7] 36–45 years old.

108. How old were you when you had your *first* positive sexual experience?
[1] I have never had a positive sexual experience.
I had my first positive sexual experience when I was: [2] 13–15 years old; [3] 16–19 years old; [4] 20–25 years old; [5] 26–30 years old; [6] 31–35 years old; [7] 36–45 years old; [8] 46–55 years old; [9] over 56 years old.

109. During what times of your life has sexual fulfillment been important to you?
[1] Sexual fulfillment has never been important to me; [2] Sexual fulfillment has been important throughout my life.
Sexual fulfillment was most important to me when I was: [3] 3–15 years old; [4] 16–19 years old; [5] 20–25 years old; [6] 26–30 years old; [7] 31–35 years old; [8] 36–45 years old; [9] 46–55 years old; [10] older than 56 years old.

Here is a series of statements describing various feelings that people have about their sexual experiences. Some of them may apply to you. Probably many of them will not. Read each statement. Then CIRCLE *one* box to indicate whether you, yourself, feel this way about your sexual experiences and their influence on you.

110. Most of the time I feel sexually inadequate.
[1] Strongly agree; [2] Somewhat agree; [3] Not sure; [4] Somewhat disagree; [5] Strongly disagree.

111. I often have (had) sex just to please my partner.
[1] Strongly agree; [2] Somewhat agree; [3] Not sure; [4] Somewhat disagree; [5] Strongly disagree.

112. I often have (had) sex just to please myself.
[1] Strongly agree; [2] Somewhat agree; [3] Not sure; [4] Somewhat disagree; [5] Strongly disagree.

113. My sexual performance is extremely important to my self-esteem.
[1] Strongly agree; [2] Somewhat agree; [3] Not sure; [4] Somewhat disagree; [5] Strongly disagree.

114. Emotional intimacy is just as important as sex.
[1] Strongly agree; [2] Somewhat agree; [3] Not sure; [4] Somewhat disagree; [5] Strongly disagree.

115. Making a sexual conquest is important for my self-esteem.
[1] Strongly agree; [2] Somewhat agree; [3] Not sure; [4] Somewhat disagree;
[5] Strongly disagree.

116. Fantasy is necessary for my sexual pleasure.
[1] Strongly agree; [2] Somewhat agree; [3] Not sure; [4] Somewhat disagree;
[5] Strongly disagree.

Needs and Feelings (You may CIRCLE more than one box.)

117. How old were you when someone you respected, other than a parent, *first* told you they loved you?
[1] 5–12 years old; [2] 13–15 years old; [3] 16–19 years old; [4] 20–25 years old;
[5] 26–30 years old; [6] 31–35 years old; [7] 36–45 years old; [8] 46–55 years old;
[9] older than 56; [10] I was never told.

118. How old were you when someone you respected, other than a parent, *first* told you you were a caring and sensitive person?
[1] 5–12 years old; [2] 13–15 years old; [3] 16–19 years old; [4] 20–25 years old;
[5] 26–30 years old; [6] 31–35 years old; [7] 36–45 years old; [8] 46–55 years old;
[9] older than 56; [10] I was never told.

119. How old were you when someone you respected, other than a parent, first told you you were talented or creative?
[1] 5–12 years old; [2] 13–15 years old; [3] 16–19 years old; [4] 20–25 years old;
[5] 26–30 years old; [6] 31–35 years old; [7] 36–45 years old; [8] 46–55 years old;
[9] older than 56; [10] I was never told.

120. How old were you when someone you respected, other than a parent, *first* told you you were a bright person?
[1] 5–12 years old; [2] 13–15 years old; [3] 16–19 years old; [4] 20–25 years old;
[5] 26–30 years old; [6] 31–35 years old; [7] 36–45 years old; [8] 46–55 years old;
[9] older than 56; [10] I was never told.

121. How old were you when you *first* felt that your opinion mattered?
[1] I have never felt that my opinion mattered; [2] I have always felt that my opinion mattered; [3] 5–12 years old; [4] 13–15 years old; [5] 16–19 years old; [6] 20–25 years old; [7] 26–30 years old; [8] 31–35 years old; [9] 36–45 years old; [10] 46–55 years old; [11] older than 56.

122. How old were you when you *first* felt that you were in control of your own life?
[1] I have never felt that I was in control of my life: [2] I have always felt that I was in control of my life; [3] 5–12 years old; [4] 13–15 years old; [5] 16–19 years old; [6] 20–25 years old; [7] 26–30 years old; [8] 31–35 years old; [9] 36–45 years old; [10] 46–55 years old; [11] older than 56.

Here is a series of statements describing various personal needs and feelings that people have. Some of these may apply to you. Probably many of them will not. Read each statement. Then CIRCLE *one* box to indicate whether you, yourself, feel this way.

123. Religion and/or Spirituality is an important source of my self-esteem.
[1] Strongly agree; [2] Somewhat agree; [3] Not sure; [4] Somewhat disagree;
[5] Strongly disagree.

124. You can't accomplish anything worthwhile without taking risks.
[1] Strongly agree; [2] Somewhat agree; [3] Not sure; [4] Somewhat disagree;
[5] Strongly disagree.

125. Winning has always been very important to me.
[1] Strongly agree; [2] Somewhat agree; [3] Not sure; [4] Somewhat disagree;
[5] Strongly disagree.

126. I sacrificed too many of my own needs for others.
[1] Strongly agree; [2] Somewhat agree; [3] Not sure; [4] Somewhat disagree;
[5] Strongly disagree.

127. I often look back on the things I've failed to accomplish.
[1] Strongly agree; [2] Somewhat agree; [3] Not sure; [4] Somewhat disagree;
[5] Strongly disagree.

128. Beating a competitor, in love, business, or sports, etc., increases my self-esteem significantly.
[1] Strongly agree; [2] Somewhat agree; [3] Not sure; [4] Somewhat disagree;
[5] Strongly disagree.

129. I was unable to do many of the things I wanted to do because of:
[1] parents; [2] finances; [3] opposition of others; [4] children;
[5] ethnic/racial reasons; [6] sex; [7] lack of education; [8] physical appearance/
handicap; [9] I have always been able to do the things I want to do; Other, _____
_____.

Self-Esteem

Rate the following periods of your life according to your level of self-esteem, or how good you felt about yourself.

130. My self-esteem was at a very high level when I was:
[1] 5–12 years old; [2] 13–15 years old; [3] 16–19 years old; [4] 20–25 years old;
[5] 26–30 years old; [6] 31–35 years old; [7] 36–45 years old; [8] 46–55 years
old; [9] older than 56; [10] It was never high.

131. My self-esteem was at a very low level when I was:
[1] 5–12 years old; [2] 13–15 years old; [3] 16–19 years old; [4] 20–25 years old;
[5] 26–30 years old; [6] 31–35 years old; [7] 36–45 years old; [8] 46–55 years old;
[9] older than 56; [10] It was never low.

132. My source of positive self esteem comes from being: (Please CIRCLE no more
than five characteristics)

[1] Intelligent	[7] Caring
[2] In Control of My Life	[8] Financially Successful
[3] Assertive	[9] Loved
[4] Moral	[10] Creative
[5] Competitive	[11] Courageous
[6] Attractive	[12] Physically Fit

133. Name 5 experiences in your life that you feel contributed to a positive sense
of self-esteem, and give the approximate "Age Stage" in your life that this experience occurred: "Age Stages" include: [1] (5–12 years old); [2] (13–15 years old);
[3] (16–19 years old); [4] (20–25 years old); [5] (26–30 years old); [6] (31–35
years old); [7] (36–45 years old); [8] (46–55 years old); [9] (older than 56).

Experience	Age Stage #
1. _____	_____
2. _____	_____
3. _____	_____
4. _____	_____
5. _____	_____

134. Name 5 experiences in your life that you feel contributed to feelings of low
self-esteem and give the approximate "Age Stage" in your life that this experience
occurred: "Age Stages" include: [1] (5–12 years old); [2] (13–15 years old); [3]
(16–19 years old); [4] (20–25 years old); [5] (26–30 years old); [6] (31–35 years
old); [7] (36–45 years old); [8] (46–55 years old); [9] (older than 56).

Experience	Age Stage #
1. _____	_____
2. _____	_____
3. _____	_____
4. _____	_____
5. _____	_____

Part III Please complete the following statements. Make your responses as long or short as you wish.

135. How have your feelings of self-esteem changed over time? What experiences and/or people have influenced these changes?

_____

_____

_____

_____

136. A personal crisis such as a loss of job, loss of relationship, or remaining in an abusive situation, etc., can undermine a person's self-esteem. If you have experienced a personal crisis of any nature, how did you maintain or regain a positive sense of self-worth in the face of your tragedy or crisis? What personal strengths did you draw on to help you? _____

_____

_____

_____

137. Define what it means to you to be a man or a woman. Include the negative as well as positive aspect _____

_____

_____

138. If you have ever had a person who acted as a mentor to you or in some way encouraged your personal goals and influenced your self-esteem, please tell us about the experience and at what age in your life this experience happened.

_____

_____

_____

_____

Would you be willing to discuss some of your experiences further with an interviewer from the NCWRR Research Center?

[ ] Yes [ ] No

If so
In person (give phone number and area code): _____
By telephone (give phone number and area code): _____
If you have a MALE family member, friend, or colleague who would like to participate in this study, please write in their name and address so we can send them a survey, or have them call 1-800-426-7386 to receive a survey form.
Name: _____

Address:_____ State: _____ Zip: _____

Methodology of Gender, Identity, and Self-Esteem Study

In the present study the following steps were implemented to explore self-esteem and identity development in adulthood:

1. SELF-ESTEEM POLL

Through the use of the NCWRR newsletter, a self-esteem poll was distributed to over 10,000 women. The poll contained questions on how women perceived their relationships with parents, intimate partners, and children. Questions relating to body image, employment, friendship, and age, etc. were also included. More than 900 women completed it, giving a rich foundation for the development of an in-depth study.

2. DEVELOPMENT OF QUESTIONNAIRE

Based on the findings of the poll, an in-depth, 11-page questionnaire was developed containing over 120 questions. A unique aspect of the questionnaire is that topics and sources of self-esteem and identity are covered over the entire life course of an individual. The questionnaire covered the following broad areas: demographic

background; major events and activities and their impact on relationships; the impact of education, employment, marital relationships, children, financial security, and mentors on self-esteem; and
life events and personal characteristics that shaped identity formation, such as physical/emotional abuse, health status, sexuality and
body image; and the changing nature of personal needs and
sources of self-worth at various points of an individual's life.

3. PILOT TESTING THE QUESTIONNAIRE

The questionnaire was pilot tested utilizing approximately 50 women
and men, spanning the entire age range from college students to
the elderly. Adjustments and changes based on the pilot test were
incorporated into the final instrument. Participating organizations
and individuals included the following:

- Women from the NCWRR mailing list
- Women who responded to an ad placed in the Women's Record,
  a Long Island newspaper
- United States Coast Guard (Suffolk County, NY)
- Suffolk County Police Dept.
- Riverhead, NY Senior Citizen Services
- Male and female college students from Long Island University

4. IN-DEPTH INTERVIEWS

An interview guideline was developed for follow-up interviews. The
interviews were used as the basis for narratives to personalize the
study findings and to describe individual feelings of self-esteem as
experienced by women and men. A total of 60 women and men (38
women and 22 men) were interviewed.   Forty individuals were
interviewed by telephone and 20 were interviewed in person. The
average length of the interviews was 3 hours. When necessary, a follow-up interview was conducted for clarification.

5. ACCESSING ORGANIZATIONS TO PARTICIPATE IN NATIONAL STUDY

Below is a list of organizations which were contacted and agreed to disseminate and notify potential respondents of the survey through notations in organizational newsletters, bulletin boards, mailing lists and during workshops and classes:

- University of Minnesota's Men's Group
- National Medical Association
- American Association of University Women
- American Medical Association
- Delta Kappa Gamma Society
- United Auto Workers
- National Association of Colored Women's Clubs
- National Parent-Teacher Association
- American Business Women's Association
- National Young Men's Christian Association
- Association for Asian Studies
- Hispanic Women's Council
- American Legion Auxiliary
- Clearinghouse on Women's Issues
- National Assembly of Religious Women
- Older Women's League
- Junior League of America
- International Ladies Garment Workers Union

In order to acquire more male respondents, a request was made at the end of the questionnaire, asking women to write the name and address of a male friend, colleague, or family member who would like to be sent a questionnaire.

6. DATA ANALYSIS

Primary data analysis was done through the use of cross-tabulations, using frequencies to compare answers to the survey questions based on gender. Comparison tables were produced to illustrate how the

215 females and 60 males answered each of the 134 survey questions. Data was also cut by age and education to compare responses to specific questions in the survey. Column means, standard deviations, standard errors, and chi squares were used when producing cross-tabulation data. Part III of the survey consisted of four open-ended questions. These responses were compared according to gender through content analysis of all responses.

The National Center for Women and Retirement Research

BACKGROUND

The National Center for Women and Retirement Research (NCWRR), based at Southampton College of Long Island University, is the first academic entity in the country to focus on the preretirement planning needs of midlife women. Established in 1988, by Dr. Christopher L. Hayes, the center addresses three broad mandates:

1. *Research.* Undertake applied studies that uncover and articulate the economic, psychological, and social needs of midlife women prior to retirement.
2. *Education.* Foster an increased awareness of the need for women to plan for retirement during the middle adult years in order to avoid impoverishment later in life.
3. *Training.* Sensitize community, public, and corporate leaders regarding the needs of midlife women.

Since it's inception, NCWRR has conducted a variety of landmark studies that have gained international recognition. These projects have included *The Divorce After 40* (1989), *Money Matters in the 90's* (1993), *The Money Knowledge Survey* (1993), and *The Women Cents Study* (1995), *The Baby Boom Retirement Preparation Survey* (1996), and *The Gender Comparison Study* (1996).

Beginning in 1993, NCWRR began to focus on adult development issues that addressed both sexes. This book is the first product of this shift in orientation of NCWRR.

THE PREP PROGRAM

A major activity of the center, the Pre-Retirement Education Planning for Women (PREP) Program was launched in 1986 with a $300,000 grant from the Administration on Aging, Department of Health and Human Services. The purpose of PREP was to provide women with the information and skills needed to create a secure and independent future. The overall goal of PREP is to ensure that we don't produce another generation of impoverished older women in our country.

By attending PREP seminars and using specially designed handbooks, women are provided the tools to gain financial knowledge and confidence in building their own financial resources. Along with addressing the financial needs of women, PREP focuses on other life-planning skills for women, such as health and fitness, knowledge about employment, long-term care, and the emotional issues associated with the aging process.

Since 1986, more than 200,000 women have contacted PREP and participated in life-planning seminars nationwide. Professional facilitators help women build a strong foundation in understanding how to navigate through the variety of transitions that mark the middle years of life. Special attention has been given to organizing seminars within business, union, university, and community settings.

The PREP program has been featured on such programs as *Good Morning America*, the *Today Show*, and in hundreds of magazines and newspaper stories.

ADDITIONAL NCWRR RESOURCES

A major commitment of NCWRR is to produce educational materials based on its research studies. The following handbooks and audiovisual materials are produced by the center:

* *Looking Ahead to Your Financial Future* (handbook)
* *The Psychology of Women and Money* (book)
* *Social and Emotional Issues for Mid-life Women* (handbook)
* *Employment and Retirement Issues for Women* (handbook)
* *Taking Control of Your Health and Fitness* (handbook)
* *Long-Term Care Issues for Women* (handbook)
* *Mid-Life Women and Divorce* (book)
* *Women and Money* (videotape)
* *Women and Divorce* (videotape)
* *Mid-Life Women: Planning for Tomorrow* (book)

ADDITIONAL INFORMATION

For additional information on NCWRR and it's programs and materials, individuals can call 1-800-426-7386 or write:

National Center for Women and Retirement Research
Long Island University
Southampton College
Southampton, NY 11968

References

Abbott, F. (Ed.). (1990). *Men and intimacy*. Freedom, CA: Crossing.

Ackerman, D. (1994). *A Natural history of love*. New York: Random House.

Adams, R. G. (1984). Secondary friendship networks and psychological well-being among the elderly. *Activities, Adaptation and Aging, 8,* 59–72.

Adams, R. G., & Blieszner, R. (1994). An integrative conceptual framework for friendship research. *Journal of Social and Personal Relationships.*

Adams, R. G., & Blieszner, R. (Eds.). (1989). *Older adult friendship: Structure and process.* Newbury Park, CA: Sage.

Adams, R. G., & Markstrom, C. A., & Abraham, K. G. (1987). The relations among identity development, self-consciousness, self-focusing during middle and late adolescence. *Developmental Psychology. 23,* 292–297.

Adelson, J. (Ed.). (1980). *Handbook of adolescent psychology.* New York: Wiley.

Aldous, J. (1987). New views on the family life of the elderly and the near-elderly. *Journal of Marriage and the Family, 49,* 227–234.

Alexander, C. N., & Langer, E. J. (Eds.). (1989). *Higher stages of human development: Perspectives on adult growth.* Oxford: Oxford University Press.

American Association of University Women. (1992). *How schools shortchange girls.* American Association of University Women's Report. Researched by the Wellesley College Center for Research on Women. Washington, DC: AAUW Educational Foundation.

Apter, T. (1991). *Altered loves: Mothers and daughters during adolescence.* New York: St. Martins.

Argyle, M. (1987). *The psychology of happiness.* London: Methuen.

Arling, G. (1976). The elderly widow and her family, neighbors and friends.

Journal of Marriage and the Family, 38, 757–768.

Bakan, D. (1979). *And they took themselves wives.* San Francisco: Harper & Row.

Baldwin, A. L. (1980). *Theories of child development* (2nd ed.). New York: Wiley.

Baltes, P. B. (1968). Longitudinal and cross-sectional sequences in the study of age and generation effects. *Human Development. 11,* 1145–1171.

Baltes, M. M., & Bartor, E. M. (1977). New approaches toward aging: A review of the aperant model. *Educational Gorontology, An International Quarterly, 2,* 383–405.

Baltes, P. B., Featherman, D. L., & Lerner, R. M. (Eds.). (1987). *Life-span development and behavior.* Hillsdale, NJ: Erlbaum.

Bancroft, J. (1989). *Motherless daughters,* New York: Knopf.

Barnett, R., & Baruch, G. K. (1987). Role quality, multiple role involvement, and psychological well-being in mid-life women. *Journal of Personality and Social Psychology, 51,* 578–585.

Bartky, S. L. (1990). *Femininity and domination: Studies in the prenomenology of Oppression.* New York: Routlodge.

Baruch, G. K., & Barnett, R. C. (1979). *Multiple roles and well-being: A study of mothers of preschool age children (Working paper No. 3).* Wellesley, MA: Wellesley College.

Baruch, G., Barnett, R., & Rivers, C. (1983). *Lifeprints: New patterns of love and work for today's women.* New York: McGraw-Hill.

Baruch, G. K. & Brooks-Gunn, J. (Eds.). (1984). *Women in mid-life.* New York: Plenum.

Basseches, M. (1984). *Dialectical thinking and adult development.* Nowood, NJ: Ablex.

Bassoff, E. (1988). *Mothers and daughters: Loving and letting go.* New York: Plume.

Baumgardner, A. H. (1990). To know oneself is to like oneself: Self-certainity and self-affect. *Journal of Personality and Social Psychology, 58,* 1062–1072.

Baumrind, D. (1989). The permanence of change and the impermanence of sta bility. *Human Development, 32,* 187–195.

Beckman, L. J. (1981). Effects of social interaction and children's relative inputs on older women's psychological well-being. *Journal of Personality and Social Psychology, 41,* 1075–1086.

Belenky, M. F., Clinchy, B. M., Goldberger, N. R., & Tarule, J. M. (1986). *Women's ways of knowing.* New York: BasicBooks.

Bell, R. R. (1981). Friendships of women and of men. *Psychology of Women Quarterly, 5,* 402–417.

Bengston, F. L., Rosenthal, C., & Burton, L. (1990). Families and aging: Diversity and heterogeneity. In R. H. Binstock & L. K. George (Eds.), *Handbook of aging and the social sciences* (3rd ed., pp. 263–287). San Diego, CA: Academic Press.

Benjamin, J. (1988). *The bonds of love: Psychoanalysis, feminism, and the problem of domination.* New York: Pantheon.

Bepko, C. & Krestan, J., (1990). *Too good for her own good: Searching for self and intimacy in important relationships.* New York: Harper & Row.

Bergmann, B. (1986). *The economic emergence of women.* New York: BasicBooks.

Bernard, J. (1981). *The female world.* New York: Free Press.

Betcher, W., & Pollack, W. (1994). *Fallen heroes.* New York: Atheneum.

Biller, H. B. (1982). Fatherhood: Implications for child development. In B. Wollman (Ed.), *The Developmental Handbook* (pp. 702–725). New Jersey: Prentice Hall.

Binstock, R. H., & Shanas, E. (Eds.). (1985). *Handbook of aging and social sciences.*

New York: Van Nostrand Reinhold.

Birren, J. E. & Schaie, K. W. (1985). *Handbook of the psychology of aging* (2nd ed.). New York: Van Nostrand Reinhold.

Bleier, R. (1988). Sex differences research: Science or belief? In R. Bleier (Ed.), *Feminist approaches to science.* (pp. 147–164). New York: Pergamon.

Blieszner, R., & Adams, R.G. (1992). *Adult friendship.* Newbury Park, CA: Sage.

Block, J. D. (1980). *Friendship.* New York: MacMillan.

Block, J. (1983). Differential premises arising from differential socialization of the sexes: Some conjectures. *Child Development, 54,* 1335–1354.

Block, J. (1990). Ego resilience through time: Antecedents and ramifications. In *Resilience and psychological health.* Boston: Symposium of the Boston Psychoanalytical Society.

Block, J. H. (1982). Psychological development of female children and adolescents. In P. Berman & E. Rainey (Eds.), *Women: A developmental perspective* (DHHS Pub. #82–2298.) Bethesda, MD: National Institutes of Health.

Bloom, A. (1987). *The Closing of the American mind.* New York: Simon & Schuster.

Bloom, M. (1980). *Life-span development.* New York: MacMillan.

Blos, P. (1962). *On adolescence.* New York: Free Press.

Bly, R. (1990). *Iron John.* New York: Addison Wesley.

Bolen, J. S. (1985). *Goddesses in everywoman: A new psychology of women.* New York: Harper Colophon.

Bowlby, J. (1969). *Attachment and loss* (Vol. 1). London: Hogarth.

Bowlby, J. (1988). *A Secure Base.* New York: BasicBooks.

Bozett, F. W., & Hanson, S. M. H. (1991). *Fatherhood and families in cultural context.* New York: Springer.

Brazelton, T. B. (1989, February 13). Working parents. *Newsweek.* pp. 66–72.

Brecher, E. M. (1984). *Love, sex, and aging.* Boston: Little, Brown.

Brecher, E. M. (1984). *Love, sex, and aging.* Mount Vernon, NY: Consumers Union.

Brim, O., & Ryff, C. (1980). On the properties of life events in life-span development and behavior. In P. B. Baltes & O. G. Briar (Eds.), *Life-Span Development and Behavior* (Vol. 3, pp. 368–388). New York: Academic Press.

Broofensrenrer, V. (1979). Contents of Childreasing. Problems and prospects. *American Psychologist, 34,* 844–850.

Burke, R. J., McKeen, C. A., & McKenna, C. (1990). Sex differences and cross-sex effects on mentoring. *Psychological Reports. 67,* 1011–1023.

Buscaglia, L. F. (1978). *Personhood and the art of being human.* New York: Faucelt Columbine.

Buscaglia, L. F. (1991). *The act of feeling human.* New York: Viking.

Campbell, J. D. (1990). Self-esteem and clarity of self-concept. *Journal of Personality and Social Psychology. 59,* 538–549.

Campos, J. J., Campos, R. G., & Barett, K. C. (1989). Emergent themes in the study of emotional development and emotion regulation. *Developmental Psychology, 25,* 394–402.

Cancian, F. M. (1987). *Love in America: Gender and self-development.* Cambridge, England: Cambridge University Press.

Carroll, B. A. (1976). *Liberating women's history.* Urbana, IL: University of Illinois Press.

Castillejo, I. C. (1974). *Knowing woman: A feminine psychology*. New York: Harper & Row.

Cernic, D. & Longmire, L. (Eds.). (1987). *Know thyself: Collected readings on identity*. New York: Paulist Press.

Children's Defense Fund (1990). *A vision for America's future*. Washington, DC: Children's Defense Fund.

Chira, S. (1994, June 19). War over the role of American fathers. *The New York Times*.

Chodorow. N. (1974). Family structure and feminine personality. In M. Z. Rosado & L. Lamphere (Eds.), *Woman, culture and society* (pp.43–66).

Chodorow, N. (1978). *The reproduction of mothering*. Berkeley, CA: University of California Press.

Chodorow, N. (1989). Women's development. *Research and Human Development, 9*, 356–371.

Chodorow, N. (1991). *Feminism and psychoanalytic theory*. New Haven, CT: Yale University Press.

Chodorow, N., & Gilligan, C. (1982). *In a different voice: Psychological theory and women's development*. Cambridge, MA: Harvard University Press.

Cockrum, J., & White, P. (1985). Influences on the life satisfaction of never-married men and women. *Family relations, 34*, 401–409.

Cohen, M., (1988). *The sisterhood*. New York: Fawcett/Columbine.

Cohler, B., & Grunnebaum, H. (1981). *Mothers, grandmothers, and daughters*. New York: Wiley.

Cohn, L. D. (1991). Sex differences in the course of personality development: A meta-analysis. *Psychological Bulletin, 109*, 252–266.

Colby, A., & Damon, W. (1987). Listening to a different voice: A review of Gilligan's *In a different voice*. In M.R. Walsh (Ed.), *The psychology of women: Ongoing debates*. New Haven, CT: Yale University Press.

Cole, J. B. (1986). *All American women: Lines that divide, ties that bind*. New York: Free Press.

Cole, M., Gay, J., Glick, J., & Sharp, D. (1971). *The cultural context of learning and thinking*. New York: BasicBooks.

Coleman, L. M., Antonucci, T. C., & Adelman, P.K. (1987). Social roles in the lives of middle-aged and older black women. *Journal of Marriage and the Family, 49*, 761–771.

Coleman, L. M., & Antonucci, T. C. (1983). Impact of work on women at mid-life. *Developmental Psychology, 19*, 290–294.

Collins, P. (1991). *Black feminist thought: Knowledge, consciousness and the politics of empowerment*. New York: Routledge.

Connelly, F. M., & Clandinin, D. J. (1990). Stories of experience and narrative inquiry. *Educational Researcher, 19 (5)*, 2–14.

Contratto, S. (1984). Mother: social sculptor and trustee of the faith. In M. Lewin (Ed.), *The shadow of the past: Psychology portrays the sexes*. New York: Columbia University Press.

Coopersmith, S. (1967). *The antecedents of self-esteem*. San Francisco, CA: Freeman.

Cowan, R. S. (1987). Women's work, housework, and history: The historical roots of inequality in work-force participation. In N. Gerstel & H. E. Gross (Eds.),

Families and work (pp. 164–77). Philadelphia: Temple University Press.

Crawford, M., & Marecek, J. (1989). Psychology reconstructs the female: 1968–1988. *Psychology of Women Quarterly, 13,* 147–165.

Crouter, A. C., Perry-Jenkins, M., Huston, T. L., & McHale, S. M. (1987). Processes underlying father involvement in dual-earner and single-earner families. *Developmental Psychology, 23,* 431–440.

Cushman, P. (1990). Why the self is empty: Toward a historically situated psychology. *American Psychologist, 45,* 599–611.

Cytrynbaum, S., et al. (1980). Mid-life development: A personality and social systems perspective. In L.W. Poon (Ed.). *Aging in the 80s.* Washington, DC: American Psychological Association.

Dacey, J. S., & Travers, M. S. (1994). *Where the world is.* Glenview, IL: Scott, Foresman.

Daly, M. (1985). *Beyond god the father: Toward a philosophy of women's liberation.* Boston, MA: Beacon.

Deaux, K., & Major, B. (1990). A social-psychological model of gender. In D.L. Rhode (Ed.), *Theoretical perspectives on sexual difference* (pp.81–125). New Haven, CT: Yale University Press.

de Beauvior, S. (1952). *The second sex.* New York: Alfred A. Knopf.

Dinnerstein, D. (1977). *The mermaid and the minotaur.* New York: Harper/Colophon.

Doherty, W. J., & Jacobson, N. S. (1982). Marriage and the family. In B. Wolman (Ed.), *Handbook of development psychology.* Englewood Cliffs, NJ: Prentice-Hall.

Donnberry, H., & Hoffman, S. (1988). What are the economic consequences of divorce? *Demography, 25,* 641–645.

Douglas, A. (1977). *The feminization of American culture.* New York: Knopf.

Duck, S. (1993). *Friends for life: The psychology of close relationships.* Brighton, Sussex: Harvester.

Duuall, E. M. (1971). Family development (5th ed.). Philadelphia: Lippincott.

Eccles, J. S. (1987)). Adolescence: Gateway to gender roles transcendence. In D. B. Carter (Ed.), *Current conceptions of sex roles and sex typing: Theory and research,* (pp. 225–241.) New York: Praeger.

Eccles, J. S. (1987). Gender roles and women's achievement related decisions. *Psychology of Women's Quarterly, 11,* 135–172.

Ehrenreich, B. (1983). *The hearts of men.* Garden City, NY: Doubleday.

Ehrenreich, B. (1990, Fall). Sorry, sisters, this is not the revolution. *Time* (Special Issue, *Women: The road ahead*), p 15.

Eichorn, D. H., Clausen, J. A., Naan, H., Honzik, M. P., & Mussen, P. H. (Eds.). (1981). *Past and present in middle life.* New York: Academic Press.

Eisler, S. (1987). *The chalice and the blade: our history, our future.* New York: Harper & Row.

Elder, G., & Caspi, A. (1990). Studying lives in a changing society: Sociological and personological explorations. In A. I. Rabin, Robert Zucker, R. Emmons, & S. Frank (Eds.), *Studying persons and lives.* New York: Springer.

Elder, G. H. (1974). *Children of the great depression.* Chicago: Chicago University Press.

Elshtain, J.B. (1982, Fall). Feminism, family and community. *Dissent.*

Engle, P. (1995). *Men in families: Report of a consultation on the role of men and fathers in achieving gender equality.* UNICEF Report. June 13–14.

Erikson, E. A. (1959). *Identity and the life cycle.*

Erikson, E. (1968). *Identity: Youth and crisis.* New York: Norton.

Erikson, E. H. (1975). *Life history and the historical movement.* New York: Norton.

Erikson, E. H. (1978). *Adulthood.* New York: Norton.

Evans, S. (1988, September 16). The gender gap revisited. *National Review,* p. 41.

Fagot, B., Leinbach, M., & O'Boyle, C. (1992). Gender labeling, gender stereo-typing, and parenting behaviors. *Developmental Psychology, 28,* 225–230.

Fallo, M., & Ryff, C. D. (1982). Preferred timing of female life events: Cohort differences. *Research on Aging. 4*(2), 249–267.

Faludi, S. (1991). *Backlash: The undeclared war against American women.* New York: Crown.

Farrell, M. P., & Rosenberg, S. D. (1981). *Men at midlife.* Boston: Auburn.

Fiebert, M. (1990, October.). Dimensions of the female role. *Psychological Reports,* p. 633.

Fischer, L. (1986). *Linked lives: Adult daughters and their mothers.* New York: Harper & Row

Fisher, E. (1979). *Woman's creation: Sexual evolution and the shaping of society.* Garden City, NY: Anchor/Doubleday.

Fountain, G. (1961). Adolescent into adult: An inquiry. *Journal of the American Psychoanalytical Association, 9,* 417–433.

Fraiberg, S. (1977). *Every child's birthright: In defense of mothering.* New York: Basic Books.

Freeman, J. (Ed.). (1979). *Women: A feminist perspective.* Palo Alto, CA: Mayfield.

French, M. (1985). *Beyond power: on women, men and morals.* New York: Ballantine.

French, M. (1992). *The war against women.* New York: Summit.

Freud, S. (1935). *A general introduction to psychoanalysis.* London: Liveright.

Freud, S. (1961). Some psychical consequences of the anatomical distinction between the sexes. In J. Strachek (Ed.), *The standard edition of the complete psychological works of Sigmund Freud,* (Vol. 19, pp. 248–258). London: Hogarth Press. (Original work published 1905.)

Freud, S. (1974). Femininity. In J. Strouse (Ed.). *Women and analysis.* New York: Dell Publishers. (Original work published in 1933.)

Frey, B.A., & Noller, R. B. (1983). Mentoring: a legacy of success. *Journal of creative behavior, 17*(1), 60–64.

Friday, N. (1977). *My mother, MySelf.* New York: Delacorte.

Friedan, B. (1993). *The fountain of age.* New York: Simon & Schuster.

Friedl, E. (1975). *Women and men: An anthropological view.* New York: Holt, Rinehart & Winston.

Friedman, M. (1990). Does Sommers like women? More on Liberalism, gender, hierarchy, and Scarlett D'ttara. *Journal of Social Philosophy, 21*(2).

Fromm, E. (1968). *The art of loving.* New York: Harper & Row.

Gallese, L. R. (1985). *Women like us.* New York: William Morrow.

Garner, D. J., & Mercer, S. O. (1989). *Women as they age: Challenge, opportunity, and triumph.* New York: Haworth.

Genevie, L., & Margolies, E. (1987). *The motherhood report.* New York: MacMillan.

George, L. K. (1980). *Role transitions in later life.* Monterey, CA: Brooks/Cole.

George, L. K., & Weiler, S. J. (1981). Sexuality in middle and late life. *Archives of*

General Psychiatry, 38, 919–923.

Gergen, M. M. (1992). Life stories: Pieces of a dream. In G. Rosenwalk & R. Ochberg (Eds.), *Storied lives.* New Haven, CT: Yale University Press.

Gerzon, M., (1982). *A choice of heroes. The changing face of american manhood.* Boston, MA: Houghton Mifflin.

Gilligan, C. (1982). *In a different voice.* Cambridge, MA: Harvard University Press.

Gilligan, C., & Attanucci, J. (1988). Two moral orientations: Gender differences and similarities. *Merrill Palmer Quarterly, 343,* 223–237.

Gilligan, C., & Brown, L. M. (1992). *Meeting at the crossroads: Women's psychology and girls' development.* Cambridge, MA: Harvard University Press.

Gilligan, C., Lyons, N. P., & Hammer, T. J. (1990). *Making connections: The relational worlds of adolescent girls at Emma Willard School.* Cambridge, MA: Harvard University Press.

Gilligan, C., Ward, J. V., & Taylor, J. M. (1988). *Mapping the moral domain.* Cambridge, MA: Harvard University Press.

Gilligan, C., Brown, L. M., & Rogers, A. (1990). Psyche embedded: A place for body, relationships, and culture in personality theory. In A.I. Rabin, R. Zucker, R. Emmons, & S. Frank (Eds.), *Studying persons and lives.* New York: Springer.

Gilligan, C., Rogers, A., & Brown, L. M. (1990). Epilogue. In C. Gilligan, N. Lyons, & Hammer, T. (Eds.), *Making connections* (pp. 315–328). Cambridge, MA: Harvard University Press.,

Glover, J. (1988). *I: The philosophy and psychology of personal identity.* London: Penguin.

Goldman-Rakic, P., Isseroff, A., Schwartz, M., & Bugbee, N. (1983). The neurobiology of cognitive development. In P. Mussen (Ed.), *Handbook of child psychology.* New York: Wiley.

Goode, W. J. (1982). Why men resist. In B. Thorne & M. Yalom (Eds.), *Rethinking the family.* New York: Longman.

Gottlieb, B. (1985). *Social support strategies: Guidelines for mental health practice.* Beverly Hills, CA: Sage.

Gould, R. (1978). *Transformations.* New York: Simon & Schuster.

Gould, R. L. (1988). *Transformations: Growth and change in adult life.* New York: Simon & Schuster.

Gradman, T. J. (1994). *Does work make the man: Masculine identity, and work identity during the transition to retirement* (Research report No. P-7626, University of California at Los Angeles). Santa Monica, CA: RAND.

Greenberg, J. R. (1991). Problems in the lives of adult children: Their impact on aging parents. *Journal of Gerontological Social Work, 16,* 148–161.

Greene, A. L., & Boxer, A. M. (1986). Daughters and sons as young adults: Restructuring the ties that bind. In N. Datan, A. L. Greene, & H. W. Reese (Eds.), *Life-span developmental psychology: Intergenerational relations* (pp. 125–149). San Diego, CA: Academic Press.

Greer, G. (1988, June 3). The proper study of womankind. *Times Literary Supplement.*

Greif, G. L. (1986). Mothers without custody and child support. *Family Relations, 35,*(1), 87–93.

Griffin, S. (1978). *Woman and nature: The roaring inside her.* New York: Harper & Row.

Gutmann, D. (1975). Parenthood: A key to the comparative study of the life cycle. In N. Datan & L. H. Ginsberg (Eds.), *Lifespan developmental psychology*. New York: Academic.

Gutmann, D. (1980). The clinical psychology of later life: Developmental paradigms. In N. Datan & L. H. Ginsberg (Eds.), *Transactions of aging*. New York: Academic.

Hall, C. M. (1990). *Women and identity*. New York: Hemisphere.

Hancock, E. (1989). *The girl within*. New York: Dutton.

Hanson, S. M. H., & Sporakowski, J. J. (1986). Single parent families. *Family Relations, 35*(1), 3–8.

Harding, M. E. (1990). *The way of all women*. Boston, MA: Shambhala.

Hare-Mustin, R. T., & Marecek, J. (Eds.) (1990). *Making a difference: Psychology and the psychology of gender*. New Haven, CT: Yale University Press.

Hareven, T. C. (1978). *Transitions: The family and the life course in historical perspective*. New York: Academic Press.

Harlow, M. F., & Harlow, M. K. (1965). The affectional systems. In A. M. Schrier, M. F. Harlow, & F. Stollwit (Eds.), *Behavior of non-human privaces* (Vol. 2). New York: Academic.

Harris, A. K. (1989). Women, work and the social order. In *Feminist frontiers: rethinking sex, gender, and society*. New York: Random House.

Hart, D. (1992). *Becoming men*. New York: Plenum.

Harter, S. (1983). Developmental perspectives on the self-system. In P. Mussen (Ed.), *Handbook*.

Hartstock, N. (1983). *Money, sex and power: Toward a feminist historical materialism*. New York: Longman.

Haveven, T. K., & Masoaka, K. (1988). Turning points and transitions: Perceptions of the life course. *Journal of Family History, 13,* 271–289.

Havighurst, R. J. (1982). The world of work. In B. B. Wolman & G. Stricker (Eds.), *Handbook of developmental psychology* (pp. 771–786). Englewood Cliffs, NJ: Prentice Hall.

Hazen, C., & Shaver, P. R. (1993). Attachment as an organizational framework for research on close relationships. *Psychology Inquiry, 3,* 127.

Heilbrun, C. G. (1979). *Reinventing womanhood*. New York: Norton.

Helson, R. (1967). Personality characteristics and developmental history of creative college women. *Genetic Psychology Monographs, 76,* 205–256.

Herzog, A. R., Bachman, J. G., & Johnston, L. D. (1983). Paid work, child care and house work. *Sex Roles, 9,* 109–135.

Hess, B. B., & Sussman, M. B. (Eds.). (1984). *Women and the family: Two decades of change*. New York: Haworth.

Hesse, K. A. & Camion, E. W. (1984). Attitudinal stumbling blocks to geriatric rehabilitation. *Journal of American Geriatrics Society, 32,* 745–750.

Hewlett, S. W. (1987). *The lesser life: The myth of women's liberation*. New York: Warner.

Hill, G. S. (1992). *Masculine and feminine: The natural flow of opposites in the psyche*. Boston, MA: Shambhala.

Hochschild, A. (1989). *The second shift*. New York: Viking.

Hudson, F. M. (1991). *Adult years: The art of self-renewal*. California: Jossey-Bass.

Hunt, J. G., & Hunt, L. L. (1982). The dualities of careers and families: New integrations or new polarizations. *Social Problems, 29,* 499–510.

Huyck, M. H. (1989). Midlife parental imperatives. In R. A. Kalish (Ed.), *Midlife loss: Coping strategies* (pp. 115–148). Newbury Park, CA: Sage.

Hymowitz, C., & Weissman, M. (1978). *A history of women in America.* New York: Bantam.

Jacklin, C. N. (1989). Female and male: Issues of gender. *American Psychologist, 44,* 127–133.

Jacob, E. (1987). Qualitative research traditions: A review. *Review of Educational Research, 57,* 1–50.

James, F. W. (1909). *The principles of psychology.* New York: Holt.

Janus, S., & Janus, C. (1993). *The Janus report on sexual behavior.* New York: Wiley.

Johnson, K., & Ferguson, T. (1990). *Trusting ourselves: The sourcebook on psychology for women.* New York: Atlantic Monthly Press.

Johnson, M. J. (1988). *Strong mothers, weak wives.* Berkeley, CA: University of California Press.

Johnson, R. A. (1986). *He: Understanding masculine psychology.* New York: Harper & Row.

Jordan, J. V., Kaplan, A. G., Miller, J. B., Stiver, I. P., & Surrey, J. L. (1991). *Women's growth in connection.* New York: Guilford Press.

Josephs, R. A., Markus, H. R., & Tafarodi, R. W. (1992). Gender and self-esteem. *The Journal of Personality and Social Psychology, 63,* 391–402.

Josselson, R. (1987). *Finding herself: Pathways to identity development in women.* San Francisco: Jossey-Bass.

Jung, C. G. (1957). *The undiscovered self.* New York: Mentor Books.

Kaschak, E. (1992). *Engendered lives: A new psychology of women's experience.* New York: BasicBooks.

Kaufman, S. (1986). *Ageless self: Sources of meaning in late life.* Madison: University of Wisconsin Press.

Keen, S. (1991). *Fire in the belly.* New York: Bantam.

Kegan, R. (1982). *The evolving self.* Cambridge, MA: Harvard University Press.

Kerber, M.S. (1996). Women and autonomy. *Journal of Human Development, 18,* 418–427.

Knowles, M. (1973). *The adult learner.* Houston: Gulf.

Kohlberg, L. (1973). Continuities in childhood and adult moral development revisited. In P. B. Baltes & K. W. Schaie (Eds.), *Lifespan developmental psychology: Personality and socialization.* New York: Academic Press.

Kolbenschlag, M. (1981). *Kiss sleeping beauty good-bye: Breaking the spell of feminine myths and models.* New York: Bantam.

Koller, A. (1983). *An unknown woman.* New York: Bantam.

Kolodny, A. (1988, May 4). Respectability is eroding the revolutionary potential of feminine criticism. *Chronicle of Higher Education,* pp. 52–64.

Kotre, J., & Hall, E. (1990). *Seasons of life: Our dramatic journey from birth to death.* New York: Little, Brown.

Krenz, C., & Sax, G. (1986). What quantitative research is and why it doesn't work. *American Behavioral Scientist, 30,* 58–69.

Kupers, T. (1993). *Revisioning men's lives: Gender, intimacy and power.* \ New York:

Guilford.

Labouvie-Vief, G. (1982a). Dynamic development and mature anatomy. *Human Development, 25,* 161–191.

Labouvie-Vief, G. (1982b). Growth and aging in life span perspectives. *Human Development, 25,* 65–78.

Labouvie-Vief, G. (1982c). Learning and memory in later life. In B. B. Wolsman (Ed.), *Handbook of developmental psychology.*

Laing, R. D. (1969). *The politics of the family.* Toronto: CBC Publications.

Lamb, M. E. (1981). *The role of the father in child development* (2nd ed.). New York: Wiley.

Lamb, M.E. (1987). *The father's role: Cross-cultural perspectives.* Hillsdale, NJ: Elbaum.

Larson, R. (1978). Thirty years of research on the subjective well-being of older Americans. *Journal of Gerontology, 33,* 109–125.

Larwood, L., & Gutek, B. A. (1989). *Women's career development.* Newbury Park, CA: Sage.

Laufer, M., & Laufer, M. E. (1984). *Adolescence and developmental breakdown.* New Haven: Yale University Press.

Lee, P. C. & Gropper, K. B. (1979). Sex-role culture and educational practice. *Award Educational Review, 42,* 369–410.

Lerner, H. G. (1989). *The dance of intimacy.* New York: Harper & Row.

Lessing, D. (1973). *The summer before the dark.* New York: ALfred Knopf.

Levinson, D. J. (1978). The seasons of a man's life. New York: Alfred A. Knopf.

Levinson, D. (1994). *Seasons of a woman's life.* New York: Knopf.

Levinson, D. J., Darrow, C. N., Klein, E. B., Levinson, N. H., & McGee, B. (1978). *The seasons of a man's life.* New York: Ballantine.

Lidz, T. (1976). The person: His and her development throughout the life cycle. New York: Basic Books.

Lifton, R. J. (1993). *The Protean self.* New York: BasicBooks.

Litwak, E. (1989). Forms of friendships among older people in an industrial society. In R. G. Adams & R. Blieszner (Eds.), *Older adult friendship* (pp. 65–88). Newbury Park, CA: Sage.

Loevinger, J. (1976). *Ego-development.* San Francisco: Jossey-Bass.

Loevinger, J., & Wessler, R. (1970). *Measuring ego development: Construction and use of a sentence completion test.* San Francisco, CA: Jossy-Bass.

Long, J., & Porter, K. (1994). Multiple roles of midlife women. In Baruch, G., & Brook-Gunn, J. (Eds.), *Women in midlife.* New York: Plenum.

Lourdes, B., & Stimpson, C. R. (1987). *Women, households, and the economy.* New Brunswick, NJ: Rutgers University Press.

Lowenthal, M., Chiriboga, D., & Thurnker, M. (1975). *Four stages of life.* San Francisco: Jossey-Bass.

Luria, J. S. (1986). Women and human development. *Journal of Sex Research, 27,* 527–551.

Maccoby, E., & Jacklin, C. (1974). *The psychology of sex differences.* Stanford, CA: Stanford University Press.

Magolda, M. B. (1989). Gender differences in cognitive development: An analysis of cognitive complexity and learning style. *Journal of College Student Development, 30,* 213–220.

Mahler, M. (1973). The experience of separation—individuation—through the course of life: Panel Reports, APA. *Journal of the American Psychoanalytic Association, 21,* 135, 633.

Mahler, M. S., & McDevittt, J. B. (1982). Thoughts on the emergence of the sense of self with emphasis on the body self. *Journal of the American Psychoanalytical Association, 30,* 827–848.

Mahoney, M. (1991). *Human change processes: The scientific foundations of psychotherapy.* New York: BasicBooks.

Mancini, J. A. (1980). Friend interaction, competence, and morale in old age. *Research on Aging, 2,* 416–431.

Marcia, J. E. (1976). Identity six years after: A follow-up study. *Journal of Youth and Adolescence, 5,* 145–160.

Marcia, J. E. (1980). Identity in adolescence. In J. Adelson (Ed.), *Handbook of adolescent psychology.* (pp. 159–187). New York: Wiley.

Marcus, I. M. (1973). The experience of separation-individuation in infancy and its reverberations throughout the life course. *Journal of the American Psychoanalytical Association, 21,* 155–67.

Marsiglio, W. (1988). Commitment to social fatherhood: Predicting adolescent males' intentions to live with their child and partner. *Journal of Marriage and the Family, 50,* 427–442.

Marsiglio, W., & Donnelly, D. (1991). Sexual relations in later life: A national study of married persons. *Journal of Gerontology, 46,* S338–S344.

Marsiglio, W., & Greer, D. (1994). Sexual relations in later life: A national study of married persons. *Journal of Gerontology, 46,* 5338–5344.

Marsiglio, W., & Greer, R. (1994). A gender analysis of older men's sexuality: social, psychological, and biological dimensions. In E. Thompson (Ed.), *Older men's lives).* Thousand Oaks, CA: Sage.

Maslow, A. (1987). *Motivation and personality.* (Re. ed.) New York: Harper & Row.

Maslow, A. H. (1956). Self-actualizing people: A study of psychological health. In C.E. Moustakas (Ed.), *The self.* New York: Harper Collins.

Matthews, K. A., & Rodin, J. (1989). Women's changing work roles: Impact on health, family and public policy. *American Psychologist, 44,* 1389–1393.

Matthews, S. H. (1986). *Friendships through the life course: Oral biographies of old age.* Beverly Hills, CA: Sage.

Matthews, S. H., & Sprey, J. (1989). Older family systems: Intra- and intergenerational relations. In J. A. Mancini (Ed.), *Aging parents and adult children* (pp. 63–77). Lexington, MA: Lexington.

McAdams, D. (1994). *Stories we live by.* New York: Morrow.

McBride, A. B. (1990). Mental health effects of women's multiple roles. *American Psychologist, 45,* 381–384.

McCrae, R., & Costa, P. T., Jr. (1984). *Emerging lives, eduring dispositions: Personality in adulthood.* Boston: Little, Brown.

McCreary, D. R. (1990). Self-perceptions of life-span gender role development. *International Journal of Aging and Human Development, 31*(2), 135–146.

McMillan, C. (1982). *Women, reason and nature.* Princeton, NJ: Princeton University Press.

Mead, M. (1974). On Freud's view of female psychology. In J. Strouse (Ed.), *Women and analysis*. New York: Grossman.

Medmick, M. (1989). On the politics of psychological constructs: Stop the bandwagon, I want to get off. *American Psychologist, 44*, 1118–1123.

Mercer, R. T., Nichols, E. G., & Doyle, G. C. (1989). *Transitions in a woman's life: Major life events in developmental context*. New York: Springer.

Merton, R. K. (1949). *Social theory and social structure: Toward the codification of theory and research*. Glencoe, IL: Free Press.

Miller, D. T., Taylor, B., & Buck, M. L. (1991). Gender gaps: Who needs to be explained? *Journal of Personality and Social Psychology, 61*, 5–12.

Miller, J. B. (1976). *Towards a new psychology of women*. Boston: Beacon.

Moore, K., Spain, D., & Bianchi, S. (1984). Working wives and mothers. In B. B. Hess & M. B. Sussman (Eds.), *Women and the family: Two decades of change*. New York: Haworth.

Moore, T. (1992). *Care of the soul*. New York: Harper Collins.

Morgan, E. (1972). *The descent of woman*. New York: Stein & Day.

Morgan, E. (1980). Toward a reformulation of the Eriksonian model of female-identity development. *Adolescence, 17*, 194–211.

Moyers, W., & Bly, R. (1990). *A gathering of men* [video]. New York: Nnational Educational Television.

Munnichs, J. M. A., (Eds.). (1985). *Lifespan and change in a gerontological perspective*. Orlando, FL: Academic Press.

Murray, J. (1982). *Strong minded women*. New York: Pantheon.

Nemiroff, R. A., & Colarusso, C. A. (Eds.) (1990). *New dimensions in adult development*. New York: BasicBooks.

Neugarten, B. L. (1968). Adult personality: Toward a psychology of the life cycle. In B. Neugarten (Ed.), *Middle age and aging*. Chicago, Ill: University of Chicago Press.

Neugarten, B. L. (1969). Continuities and discontinuities of psychological issues into adult life. *Human Development. 12*, 121–130.

Neugarten, B., & Datan, N. (1973). Sociological perspectives on the life cycle. In P. B. Baltes & K. W. Schaie (Eds.), *Life span development psychology*. (pp. 121–130). New York: Academic Press.

Newsletter (1992). *New York State Coalition Against Domestic Violence Newsletter. 10*(2).

New York State Children and Family Trust Fund. (1992). *Fact about family violence: The campaign to prevent family violence*. Albany, Author.

Noller, R. B. (1983). *Mentoring: An annotated bibliography*. Buffalo, NY: Bearly.

Nussbaum, J. F. (1985). Successful aging: A communicative model. *Communication Quarterly, 33*, 262–269.

Nussbaum, J. F. (1983a). Perceptions of communication content and life satisfaction among the elderly. *Communication Quarterly, 31*, 313–319.

Nussbaum, J. F. (1983b). Relational closeness of elderly interaction: Implications for life satisfaction. *Western Journal of Speech Communication, 47*, 229–243.

Nussbaum, J. F. (1994). Friendship in older adulthood. In *Interpersonal communication in older adulthood*. Thousand Oaks, CA: Sage.

Nussbaum, J. F., Thompson, T., & Robinson, J. D. (1989). *Communication and aging*.

New York: Harper & Row.

O'Brien, T. (1991). Sex differences in components of self-esteem. *Psychological Reports, 68,* 241.

Ochberg, R. L. (1987). *Middle-aged sons and the meaning of work.* Ann Arbor, MI: UMI Research Press.

Owens, U. (1985). *Fathers: Reflections by daughters.* New York: Pantheon.

Peck, T. (1986). Women's self-definition in adulthood: From a different model. *Psychology of Women Quarterly, 10,* 274–284.

Pelham, B. W., & Swann, W. B. (1989). From self-concepts to self-worth: On the sources and structure of global self-esteem. *Journal of Personality and Social Psychology, 57,* 672–680.

Piaget, J. (1926). *The language and thought of the child.* New York: Harcourt, Brace, Jovanovich.

Pifer, A., & Bronte, L. (Eds.) (1986). *Our aging society: Paradox and promise.* New York: Norton.

Pleck, J. (1980). Men's power with women, other men, and society. In E. Pleck & J. Pleck, (Eds.), *The American Man.* Englewood Cliffs, NJ: Prentice Hall.

Pleck, J. H. (1985). *Working wives/Working husbands.* Beverly Hills, CA: Sage.

Plutzeer, E. (1988, August). Work life, family life and women's support of feminism. *American Sociological Review,* p. 640.

Prager, K. (1982). Identity development and self-esteem in young women. *Journal of Genetic Psychology, 141,* 177–182.

Randour, M. (1992) *Women's psyche, women's spirit.* New York: Columbia University Press.

Rawlins, W. K. (1992). *Friendship matters: Communication, dialectics, and the life course.* New York: De Gruyter.

Rebecca, M., Hefner, R., & Olenshansky, B. A. (1976). A model of sex role transcendence. *Journal of Social Issues, 32,* 197–206.

Reinke, B., Ellicott, A., Harris, R., & Hancock, E. (1985). Timing of psychosocial change in women's lives. *Human Development, 28,* 259–280.

Richardson, L., & Taylor, V. (1986). *Feminist frontiers: Rethinking sex, gender and society.* New York: Random House.

Riegel, K. (1979). *Foundations of dialectical psychology.* New York: Academic Press.

Rivchun, S. B. (1980). Be a mentor and leave a lasting legacy. *Association Management, 32*(8), 71–74.

Robertiello, M.S. (1975). Cited in Friday, N. (1977). *My mother, my self* (p.68). New York: Delacorte.

Robertiello, R. C. (1975). *Hold them very close, then let them go.* New York: Dial.

Roberts, P., & Newton, P. M. (1987). Levinsonian studies of women's adult development. *Psychology and Aging, 2*(2), 154–163.

Robins, L., & Rutter, M. (1990). *Straight and devious pathways from childhood to adulthood.* Cambridge England: Cambridge University Press.

Rodgers, R. H. (1973). *Family interaction and transactions: The developmental approach!* Englewood Cliffs, NJ: Prentice Hall.

Rogers, D. (Ed.). (1980). *Issues in life span human development.* Monterey, CA: Brooks/Cole.

Rogoff, B. (1991). *Applenticeship in thinking: Cognitive development in social context.* New York: Oxford University Press.

Rosaldo, M., & Lamphere, L. (1974). *Women, culture and society.* Stanford, CA: Stanford University Press.

Rosenberg, M. (1979). *Conceiving the self.* New York: Basic.

Rossi, A. (1980). Life-span theories and women's lives. *Signs, 6*(1), 4-32.

Rossi, A. (1984). Gender and parenting. *American Sociological Review, 49,* 1-18.

Rossi, A.S. (Ed.). (1985). *Gender and the life course.* New York: De Gruyters.

Rubin, L. (1979). *Women of a certain age: The midlife search for self.* New York: Harper & Row.

Rutter, M. (1989). Pathways from childhood to adult life. *Journal of Child Psychology and Child Psychiatry, 30,* 23-50.

Sanford, L. T., & Donovan, M. E. (1985). *Women and self-esteem.* New York: Penguin.

Santrock, J., & Yussen, S. (1992). *Child Development.* Dubuque, IA: Brown.

Sartorn, M. (1973). *As we are now.* New York: Norton.

Sassen, G. (1980). Success anxiety in women: A constructivist's interpretation of its source and significance. *Harvard Education Review, 50,* 13-24.

Scarf, M. (1980). *Unfinished business.* New York: Ballantine.

Schroeder, T. (1992). *Lifespan development.* New York: Prentice Hall.

Schwalbe, M. L., & Staples, C. L. (1991). Gender differences in sources of self-esteem. *Social Psychology Quarterly, 54*(2), 158-168.

Sears, R. R., & Sears, P. S. (1982). Lives in Berkeley. *Contemporary Psychology, 27,* 925-927.

Segal, H. (1974). *Introduction to the work of Melanie Klein.* New York: BasicBooks.

Segal, L. (1990). *Slow motion: Changing masculinities, changing men.* New Brunswick, NJ: Rutgers University Press.

Serakan, U. (1989). Understanding the dynamics of self-concept of members in dual-career families. *Human Relations, 42*(2), 97-116.

Settlage, C. F., Curtis, J., Lozoff, M., & Milton, M. (1988). Conceptualizing adult development. *Journal of the American Psychoanalytical Association, 36,* 347-69.

Sheehy, G. (1976). *Passages: Predictable crisis of adult life.* New York: Dutton.

Shreve, A. (1989). *Women together, women alone: The legacy of the consciousness-raising movement.* New York: Fawcett Columbine.

Sidel, R. (1987). *Women and children last.* New York: Penguin.

Sidel, R. (1990). *On her own: Growing up in the shadow of the American dream.* New York: Viking.

Smelson, N. J., & Erikson, E. (Eds.). (1980). *Themes of work and love in adulthood.* Cambridge, MA: Harvard University Press.

Sommers, C. H. (1994). *Who stole feminism: How women have betrayed women.* New York: Touchstone.

Spence, J. J. (1985). Achievement American style: The rewards and costs of individualism. *American Psychologist, 40,* 1285-1295.

Spock, B. (1954). *The pocket book of baby and child care.* New York: Pocket Books.

Sroufe, L. A., & Cooper, R. (1992). Child development. New York: Knopf.

Stacey, J. M. (1991). Family dynamics and history. In *Lifespan development: Concepts, theories and intervention.* New York: Methuen.

Stafford, I. P. (1984). Relation of attitudes toward women's roles and occupational behavior to women's self-esteem. *Journal of Counseling Psychology, 31,* 332-338.

Stambler, S. (Ed.). (1970). *Women's liberation: Blueprint for the future.* New York: Ace Books.

Starr, B. D., & Weiner, M. B. (1981). *The Starr-Weiner report on sex and sexuality in the mature years.* New York: McGraw-Hill.

Steele, M. (1985). *Life in the round: A model of adult female development.* Doctoral dissertation. Wright Institute, Berkeley, CA.

Stein, J., Newcomb, M. D., & Bentler, P. M. (1992). The effect of agency and communality on self-esteem: Gender differences in longitudinal data. *Sex Roles,* Vol. 26, Nos. 11 and 12.

Stern, D. (1983). The early development of schemas of self, of others and of various experiences of self with others. In J. Lichtenberg and S. Kaplan, eds., Reflections on Self Psychology. Hillsdale, NJ: Analytic Press.

Stern, L. (1990). Disavowing the self in female adolescence. *Women and Therapy, 11*(3), 105-117.

Stevens-Long, J. (1979). Adult life: Developmental Process. Palo Alto, CA: Mayfield.

Stevens-Long, J. (1988). *Adult life.* (3rd ed.). Palo Alto, CA: Mayfield.

Stewart, W. A. (1976). *A psycho-social study of the formation of the early adult life structure in women.* Unpublished doctoral dissertation, Columbia University, New York.

Storr, A. (1988). *Solititude: A return to the self.* New York: Ballantine.

Stroufe, L. A., & Jacobvitz, D. (1989). Diverging pathways, developmental transformations, multiple etiologies and the problem of continuity in development. *Human Development, 32,* 196-203.

Sullivan, H. S. (1949). *The collected works of Harry Stack Sullivan* (Vols. 1 & 2). New York: Norton.

Summers, A. (1988, Dec.). 25 years that shook the world. *MS Magazine,* p. 50.

Super, D. E. (1957). *The psychology of careers.* New York: Harper & Row.

Super, D. E. (1983). Assessment in career guidance: Toward truly developmental counseling. *Personnel and Guidance Journal, 61,* 555-562.

Super, D. E., & Thompson, A. S. (1981). *The adult career concerns inventory.* New York: Columbia University Teachers College.

Surrey, J. (1985). *Self-in-relation: A theory of women's development* (Stone Center Working Papers, No. 13). Wellesley, MA: Wellesley College.

Tavris, C. (1992). The mismeasure of woman. New York: Simon & Schuster.

Tavris, C. (Ed.). (1986). *Everywoman's emotional well-being.* New York: Prentice Hall.

Taylor, V. (1989, October). Social movement continuity: The women's movement in abeyance. *American Sociological Review,* p. 761.

Teachman, J. D., & Polonko, K. A. (1985). Timing of the transition to parenthood: A multi-dimensional birth-interval approach. *Journal of Marriage and the Family, 47,* 867-879.

Terkel, S. (1977). *Working.* New York: Ballantine.

Terman, L. M. (1925). *Mental and physical traits of a thousand gifted children: Vol. 1, Genetic studies of genius.* Stanford, CA: Stanford.

Terman, L. M. (1925). *Genetic studies of geniuses.* Stamford, CA: Stamfor University Press.0

Tesch, S. A. (1983). Review of friendship development across the lifespan. *Human development, 26,* 266-276.

Thomas, J. L. (1994). Older men as fathers and grandfathers. In E. H. Thompson (Eds.), *Older men's lives.* Thousand Oaks, CA: Sage.

Thurer, S. (1994). *Myths of motherhood.* New York: Houghton-Mifflin Publishing.

Treas, J., & Bengston, V. L. (1987). The family in later years. In M. B. Sussman & S. K. Steinmetz (Eds.), *Handbook of marriage and the family* (pp. 625-648). New York: Plenum.

U.S. Department of Health and Human Services (1991). Premarital sexual intercourse among adolescent women: U.S., 1970-1988. *Morbidity and Mortality Weekly Report, 39*(51/52), 929-932.

Vaillant, G. (1977). *Adaptation to life.* Boston: Little Brown.

Vygotsky, L. (1986). *Thought and language.* Cambridge: Massachusetts Institute of Technology Press.

Wainrib, B. R. (1992). *Gender issues across the life cycle.* New York: Springer.

Walker, B. A., & Mehr, M. (1992). *The courage to achieve: Why america's brightest women struggle to fulfill their promise.* New York: Simon & Schuster.

Walker, L. E. (1979). *The battered women.* New York: Harper/Perennial.

Wallace, P. A. (1982). *Women in the workplace.* Boston: Auburn.

Wallace, R. (1989). *Feminism and sociological theory.* California: Sage.

Wallis, C. (1989, December). Onward women, the superwoman is weary. *Time Magazine* p. 80.

Walsh, A. (1991). Self-esteem and sexual behavior: Exploring gender differences. *Sex Roles, 25,* 7-8.

Walsh, A., & Balazs, G. (1990). Love, sex and self esteem. *Free Inquiry in Creative Sociology, 18,* 37-41.

Walsh, M. R. (Ed.) (1987). *The psychology of women: Ongoing debates.* New Haven, CT: Yale University Press.

Walters, M., Carter, B., Papp, P., & Silverstein, O. (1988). *The invisible web: Gender patterns in family relationships.* New York: Guilford.

Waterman, A. S. (1982). Identity development from adolescence to adulthood: An extension of theory and a review of research. *Developmental Psychology, 18,* 341-358.

Watson, D., & Clark, A. L. (1984). Negative affectivity: The disposition to experience aversive emotional states. *Psychological Bulletin, 96,* 465-490.

Weiss, R.S. (1990). *Staying the course.* New York: Free Press.

Weitzman, L. (1985). *The divorce revolution: The unexpected social and economic consequences for women and children in America.* New York: Free Press.

Wells, A. (1988). Variations in mother's self-esteem in daily life. *Journal of Personality and Social Psychology, 55,* 661-668.

West, C., & Zimmerman, D. H. (1987). Doing gender. *Gender and Society, 1,* 125-151.

White, L. (1992). The effect of parental divorce and remarriage on parental support for adult children. *Journal of Family Issues, 13,* 234-250.

White, M. S. (1985). Ego development in adult women. *Journal of Personality, 53,* 561-574.

White, R. W. (1959). Motivation reconsidered: The concept of competence. *Psychological Review, 66,* 297-333.

Williams, J. H. (1985). *Psychology of women: Selected readings.* New York: Norton.

Winnicott, D. W. (1965). *Maturational processes and facilitating environments.* International University Press.

Wolf, N. (1991). *The beauty myth: How images of beauty are used against women.* New York: Morrow.

Wolfson, M. (1989). *A review of the literature on feminist psychology.* Unpublished manuscript, Boston College, Chestnut Hill, MA.

Wolman, B. B. (Ed.). (1982). *Handbook of developmental psychology.* Englewood Cliffs, NJ: Prentice Hall.

Wood, V., & Robertson, J. F. (1978). Friendship and kinship interaction: Differential effect on the morale of the elderly. *Journal of Marriage and the Family, 40,* 367-375.

Woodward, B. (1991. *The commanders.* New York: Simon & Schuster.

Worell, J. (1988). Women's satisfaction in close relationships. *Clinical Psychology Review, 8,* 477-498.

Wright, P. H. (1982). Men's friendships, women's friendships and the alleged inferiority of the latter. *Sex roles, 8,* 1-20.

Wylie, R. C. (1974). *The self concept: A review of methodological considerations and measuring instruments* (Vol. 1, 2nd ed). Lincoln: University of Nebraska Press.

Young-Eisendrath, P., & Hall, J. A. (Eds.). (1987). *The book of the self: Person, pretext, and process.* New York: New York University Press.

Index

AAUW *see* American Association of University Women (AAUW)

Abortion legalization, 34

Adult children returning home
  family development patterns and, 29
  mother/daughter/grandmother transitions and, 48–50

Adult development
  female psychology approach to
    common ground of, 10–11
    friendship and, 140–141
    gender dichotomies reassessment and, 15–17
    identity stage outcomes concept and, 12
    "inner space" attachment and inclusion of, 4–5, 10
    knowledge stages concept and, 12–13
    midlife sex role turnover and, 16
    psychological models overview of, 11–13
    relational models of, 10, 11, 12, 13, 140–141, 175, 253–254, 261–262
    relational models fallacies and, 13–15, 175, 254–255
    self-in-relation model of, 13
  life-style options in, 1–2
  new conceptual view of
    life-ties theme of, xi–xiii, 24–25, 280–282
    NCWRR study of, 22–23
    ongoing process of, 23–24
  self-esteem research and
    critique of, 20–22
    traditional role views of, 17–20
  study of change in, x
  traditional research on
    age-stage approach critique and, 7–9
    age-stage approach to, 4–6
    childhood development theory and, 2–4
    life-span development theory and, 6–7

nuclear family concept and, 34
  see also Identity development; Self-esteem

Age demographic, of survey population, xvi

Age factors, in friendship, 139–140

Age-specific behaviors, 4

Age-stage development theory, 4–7
  critique of, 7–9
  of family, 27–29
  see also Adult development; Erikson, Erik; Family of origin; Identity development; Work identity

American Association of University Women (AAUW) report
  challenges to, 95, 108–110
  on female discrimination, 88, 94–96

Andragogical teaching model, 91–92

Attachment and Loss (Bowlby), 139

Attachment theory, of child development, 139, 173–174, 209, 225

Autonomous thought adult development concept, 6

Autonomy
  of men, 18, 20, 74–77, 113–114
  of women, 14, 140–141, 175, 253–255

Birth control, 34, 251

Bloom, Allan, 87

Blue-collar class, age stages of, 8

Caregiving role, mother/daughter relationship renegotiation and, 40–44

Childhood development theory, 2–4
  adult development and, 2–3

Children
  in adult life-cycle, 1
  fathers and
    of the 50s: control by, 227, 228, 229
    absent fathers and, 230–231, 237–239
    "father's rights movement" and, 231
    identity confusion of, 227–230
    NCWRR findings regarding, 210, 226, 230, 232

Identity development: of women
  AAUW report on, 94–96, 108–109
  adult daughter and father relationships
    and, 55, 56–58
    approval necessity and, 55
    chosen daughter tie and, 56–58
    phantom fathers and abusive
      replacements and, 59–61
    power to wound and, 58–59
    protective daughters tie and, 61–63
    warfare society vs. paternal child
      rearing and, 52–54
  adult daughter and mother relationships
    and
    good-enough daughter/mother tie
      and, 36, 50–52
    guilt-laden tie and, 44–48, 85
    identity development process example
      of, 37–40
    impact of, 36–37
    late-life triggering old behaviors and,
      40–44
    mother/daughter/grandmother
      transitions and, 48–50
    mothering task complexity and, 35–36
  context issue of, 10–11
  education tie and
    adolescence and identity and, 96–98
    decisions made by others and,
      106–108
    early education and, 94–96
    late-life learning and, 102–104
    returning to school and, 98–109
    sex-role development and, 92–94
    sexist bias against, 88–89, 93, 94–97,
      108–109
    as a tool of change for adults, 98–99
  Freud and, 18, 169, 171, 172, 175
  friendships and
    identity and validation by, 145–148,
      164–165
    in late-life, 137–138, 144–145
  intimate relationships and
    domestic violence and, 183–185, 203
    intimacy ties established too early and,
      178–181, 203
    late maturation and, 185–188, 204
    NCWRR study findings regarding,
      174–175, 283
    new women, new challenges and,
      176–178
    relational role development theory of,
      175–178

  self-definition before intimacy and,
    181–183, 203
  self-sacrifice, self-esteem of, 176–178
life process of, 37–40, 50–52, 56–58
mentor relationships and
  career challenges and, 153–154
  career vs. family and, 159–160
  NCWRR findings and, 154–156, 165,
    283
  older protégé/younger mentor and,
    157–159
midlife sex-role turnover and, 16–17
as mothers
  career preference and, 221–224, 242,
    243
  catalyst for growth of, 214–215
  low self-esteem and, 211–212,
    218–221, 242
  mother-blaming and, 219–221, 225
  mother's guilt and, 44–48, 85
  NCWRR findings regarding, 210, 218,
    224, 226, 283
  paradox of mothering and, 210–212,
    224–226, 242
  "perfect mother/children" concept
    and, 218–219
  positive life-ties of, 212–217
  problems in, 218–224
  single careers of, 215–217, 243
  summary regarding, 241–244
  working mothers issue and, 224–226
as protector, 61–63
relationship maintenance and, 10, 11,
  12, 13, 140–141, 175, 253–255
traditional concepts of, 4–5, 10–11
work and
  barriers to, 249–251
  historical perspective on, 249–251
  from labor of love to work, 255–257,
    277
  men threatened by, 17
  NCWRR findings on, 245–246,
    251–252, 254, 283
  new female psychology and, 253–255
  relational theory of, 253–255,
    261–262
  self-esteem and, 251–253, 283
  summary regarding, 276–279, 283
  tangible product need and, 258–260,
    277
  traditional career track and, 257–258,
    277
  volunteerism and, 260–262, 277–278